Israel's Messiah and the People of God

Israel's Messiah and the People of God

A Vision for Messianic Jewish Covenant Fidelity

MARK S. KINZER

JENNIFER M. ROSNER
EDITOR

CASCADE *Books* · Eugene, Oregon

ISRAEL'S MESSIAH AND THE PEOPLE OF GOD
A Vision for Messianic Jewish Covenant Fidelity

Copyright © 2011 Mark Kinzer. All rights reserved. Except for brief quotations in critical publications or reviews, no part of this book may be reproduced in any manner without prior written permission from the publisher. Write: Permissions, Wipf and Stock Publishers, 199 W. 8th Ave., Suite 3, Eugene, OR 97401.

Cascade Books
A Division of Wipf and Stock Publishers
199 W. 8th Ave., Suite 3
Eugene, OR 97401

www.wipfandstock.com

ISBN 13: 978-1-60608-883-8

Cataloging-in-Publication data:

Kinzer, Mark.

    Israel's messiah and the people of God : a vision for messianic Jewish covenant fidelity / Mark S. Kinzer. Edited with an introduction by Jennifer M. Rosner.

    xxviii + 222 p. ; 23 cm. Includes bibliographical references and index.

    ISBN 13: 978-1-60608-883-8

    1. Messianic Judaism. 2. Jewish messianic movements. 3. Israel (Christian theology)—Biblical teaching. 3. Judaism—Relations—Christianity. 4. Bible. N.T.—Criticism, interpretation, etc. I. Rosner, Jennifer M. II. Title.

BS2417.J4 K56 2011

Manufactured in the U.S.A.

All scripture quotations, unless otherwise indicated, are taken from the Holy Bible, New Revised Standard Version, NRSV, copyright 1989, Division of Christian Education of the National Council of the Churches of Christ in the United States of America. Used by permission. All rights reserved.

Contents

Acknowledgments vii
Introduction to the Thought and Theology of Mark Kinzer ix

PART I VISION FOR MESSIANIC JUDAISM

1 The Messianic Fulfillment of the Jewish Faith 3

2 Toward a Theology of "Messianic Judaism" 14

PART II JUDAISM FROM A MESSIANIC PERSPECTIVE

3 Messianic Judaism and Jewish Tradition in the Twenty-First Century: A Biblical Defense of Oral Torah 29

4 Prayer in Yeshua, Prayer in Israel: The Shema in Messianic Perspective 62

PART III YESHUA-FAITH FROM A JEWISH PERSPECTIVE

5 Beginning with the End: The Place of Eschatology in the Messianic Jewish Canonical Narrative 91

6 Final Destinies: Qualifications for Receiving an Eschatological Inheritance 126

7 *Lumen Gentium*, Through Messianic Jewish Eyes 156

Epilogue *Postmissionary Messianic Judaism*, Three Years Later: Reflections on a Conversation Just Begun 175

General Bibliography 197
Chronological Bibliography of Material Related to Postmissionary Messianic Judaism 202
Scripture Index 205
Subject/Name Index 214

Acknowledgments

WE WOULD LIKE TO gratefully acknowledge the Hashivenu Board and all who participate in the annual Hashivenu forums. You have provided a setting in which many of the ideas in this volume could be born and raised. Also, much gratitude is due the Roman Catholic—Messianic Jewish Dialogue Group, which may have begun a new chapter in the history of the relationship between the Christian church and the Jewish people. Thank you also to Howard Loewen for his visionary passion for people and ideas, and for arranging our initial meeting. Fuller Seminary continues to be a place that is not afraid to challenge old paradigms and venture into new territory, and we are grateful for the ways in which the seminary has supported each of us and the path of Messianic Judaism. Finally, thank you to the Handsel Press for permission to include *The Messianic Fulfillment of the Jewish Faith*. This book is a testimony to the collective dedication and perseverance of so many, and we hope that its fruits provide continued encouragement and nourishment to those whose friendship has nurtured us.

J. Rosner
M. Kinzer

Introduction to the Thought and Theology of Mark Kinzer

THE FIRST TIME I met Mark Kinzer, we sat at a coffee shop in Pasadena, CA and shared our stories. As a Jewish believer in Jesus living primarily in the Christian world, I sensed intuitively the existential angst inherent in self-identifying as a Messianic Jew. I had all but buried my Jewish identity, and I knew that this was in many ways the easy road. But recently, I had felt repeatedly allured to acknowledge and explore my Jewishness, and my meeting with Mark came at an opportune time. One of my Christian mentors had told me that bridges are useful, but no one lives on a bridge. With this in mind, I mused about how isolating it must be to live between two worlds, and I will never forget Mark's response: "Yeshua[1] never said that our way would be easy." The gravity of this statement penetrated deeply, and I have not stopped reflecting on—and experiencing—the truth of it since.

Messianic Judaism's path is anything but easy. Mark Kinzer continues to play a pioneering role in a movement fraught with trials on

---

1. Referring to Jesus by his Hebrew name, Yeshua, issues a reminder that Jesus was (and is) a Jew and that this fact carries with it certain implications that are all too often overlooked by the church. Kinzer feels strongly about this and related terminological specifications, for they serve to linguistically reinforce his theological position. In *Postmissionary Messianic Judaism*, Kinzer includes the following explanation of terms: "The one known in the church as Jesus Christ will here be referred to as *Yeshua the Messiah*. As a matter of historical record, all scholars today recognize that the first-century figure Yeshua of Nazareth was a Jew. However, very few of those who believe that he was raised from the dead acknowledge that he remains a Jew today and will do so forever, or consider the implications of this fact. By using an alien, Jewish-sounding name to refer to the one who is so familiar to the church, I hope to suggest that Yeshua is still at home with those who are literally his family, and that the church must reckon with the subtle ways it has lost touch with its own identity as a messianic, multinational extension of the Jewish people" (Kinzer, *Postmissionary Messianic Judaism*, 22).

Kinzer's early writings, including some of the sources printed and referenced in this volume, employ more typically Christian parlance. The changes in his terminology reflect his own process of theological and existential development.

all sides, and his negotiation of the numerous (and often conflicting) dynamics that characterize the movement is masterful. Kinzer is deeply committed to Jewish tradition and life while firmly holding on to belief in the messiahship of Yeshua. For Kinzer, Yeshua is not just someone who gets tacked on to a vibrant Jewish faith—Yeshua is at the heart of that faith, giving it its true texture and its deepest meaning. As a theologian, Kinzer holds a passionate conviction that we must do theology with Jewish religious tradition in one hand and Christian religious tradition in the other.

Judaism and Christianity[2] have historically, since the proverbial "parting of the ways," most often been construed in contradistinction from one another, holding mutually exclusive theological claims. In this schema, Yeshua becomes the dividing line. Jews often quip that the one thing all branches of Judaism agree upon is that Yeshua was not the Messiah. Against this traditional and ingrained paradigm, Kinzer proposes a radically new arrangement of the theological puzzle pieces, one in which Yeshua is the *essential link* between Judaism and Christianity rather than their fundamental distinguishing factor.

Kinzer is unwilling to accept Judaism and Christianity as two completely separate phenomena and argues convincingly that this is not the configuration we see in the New Testament. Rather, the two are fundamentally linked and inextricably bound together—to each other and to God's redemptive purposes for all of creation. Of course this argument cannot undo or deny the historical development by which the two have empirically become separate, distinct, and in many ways averse to one another. In Kinzer's paradigm, Messianic Judaism and Messianic Jews provide the link that binds these two realities together. Kinzer's ideas have relevance that reaches far beyond Messianic Judaism alone—his claims, if true, radically affect both the church and the people of Israel. According to Kinzer, each tradition holds a unique component of cre-

---

2. Kinzer understands the term "Christianity" to refer to the religious tradition of the Gentile wing of the Body of Messiah that developed to a large extent in distinction from and opposition to Judaism. In *Postmissionary Messianic Judaism*, Kinzer writes: "Because the terms themselves imply mutual exclusivity, in this book I will not use the words *Christianity*, *Christians*, and *church* in a conventional manner. I will employ them only to refer to the developed institutional reality that became overwhelmingly Gentile in composition and character. In speaking of realities that should be conceived of as integrally bound to Judaism and the Jewish people, or even as situated within those spheres, I will speak of Yeshua-*faith* (rather than Christianity), Yeshua-*believers* (rather than Christians), and the ekklesia (rather than the church)" (Ibid., 22).

ation's unfolding redemption, and the truth is only revealed when these two pieces are united.

Kinzer's method represents the cross-directional twin tasks of explaining the Jewish piece to Christians (who have historically perceived Judaism as either spiritually bankrupt because of its rejection of Yeshua or as a typologically significant precursor to Yeshua whose significance has since been superseded by the church) and the Christian piece to Jews (who have historically experienced and therefore justifiably perceived Christianity as a threat to the very lifeblood of Jewish existence). In the implementation of this dual representation, Messianic Judaism emerges as the critical link, and Kinzer's theology offers a call to Jewish Yeshua-believers to embody the bridge-building role to which they have been existentially assigned.

The radical nature of Kinzer's proposal has produced a host of critics,[3] yet Kinzer feels a prophetic call to speak the truth as he sees it. In a manner reminiscent of Martin Luther, the great reformer, Kinzer stands behind his controversial paradigm claiming, "I can do no other." The connection that Kinzer builds between Israel, Yeshua and the Yeshua-believing community (or *ekklesia*) creates a rich and nuanced interpretation of salvation history that opens new vistas for understanding God's redemptive work in the world. The relationship that Kinzer develops between each of these component parts lays the groundwork for his theological paradigm—a paradigm with far-reaching implications.

THE PEOPLE OF ISRAEL

Kinzer's understanding of Messianic Judaism is "postmissionary," and he emphasizes the significance of Messianic Judaism's primary identity lying fundamentally *within* the people of Israel. According to Kinzer, Messianic Jews do not stand apart from or over against the people of Israel but rather should identify deeply with Israel's complex history and ongoing journey. By living in solidarity with the people of Israel, Messianic Jews take upon themselves the many facets of Jewish covenantal life and build a bridge between Israel and the church. Kinzer offers three primary markers of a postmissionary stance:

---

3. See Kinzer, "Postmissionary Messianic Judaism, Three Years Later: Reflections on a Conversation Just Begun," 175–95.

> First, *postmissionary Messianic Judaism summons Messianic Jews to live an observant Jewish life as an act of covenant fidelity rather than missionary expediency* . . . Second, *postmissionary Messianic Judaism embraces the Jewish people and its religious tradition, and discovers God and Messiah in the midst of Israel* . . . Third, *postmissionary Messianic Judaism serves the (Gentile) Christian church by linking it to the physical descendants of Abraham, Isaac, and Jacob, thereby confirming its identity as a multinational extension of the people of Israel.*[4]

Each of these three markers provides an important foundational element for Kinzer's theology. Kinzer's first claim is twofold, asserting unequivocally that Messianic Jews are indeed "to live an observant Jewish life." This core tenet of Kinzer's theology, stated firmly throughout his writings, is a significant statement in its own right. This stance goes against the grain of much of Christian history and points toward a radical reconfiguration of the church's understanding of the Jews in its midst.[5] For Kinzer, the ecclesiological implications of this claim are grounded in its biblical precedent. "Contrary to what is usually assumed, I conclude that the New Testament—read canonically and theologically—teaches that all Jews (including Yeshua-believers) are not only permitted but are obligated to follow basic Jewish practice."[6]

The implications of this claim undergird Kinzer's entire theological system. Commenting on *Postmissionary Messianic Judaism,* Kinzer asserts that "while the message of *PMJ* goes far beyond the obligatory nature of Torah-based Jewish practice and identity for Jewish Yeshua-believers, one cannot underestimate the centrality of this proposition for the argument of the book as a whole. It is far more important as the basis for reaching other conclusions than as a conclusion in its own right."[7]

The second part of the first claim is equally important: Messianic Jewish covenant fidelity is not motivated by "missionary expediency." If Messianic Jews understand themselves as part of the larger people of

---

4. Kinzer, *Postmissionary Messianic Judaism*, 13–15.

5. Kinzer comments on the strange reversal perpetuated by the church with regard to Jews and Gentiles—"while the early Jewish Yeshua-movement decided that a Gentile did not need to become a Jew in order to be saved, the growing consensus among Christians was that in effect a Jew did need to become a Gentile to be saved!" (Ibid., 194).

6. Ibid., 23.

7. Kinzer, "Three Years Later," 184.

Israel, then their commitment to that people and their acceptance of Israel's covenant responsibilities are rooted in their identification with and participation in that covenant.[8] According to Michael Wyschogrod,

> To be a Jew means to labor under the yoke of the commandments... Now the point is that once someone is a Jew, he always remains a Jew. Once someone has come under the yoke of the commandments, there is no escaping this yoke. So baptism, from the Jewish point of view, does not make eating pork into a neutral act. In fact, nothing that a Jew can do enables him to escape from the yoke of the commandments.[9]

The implication is clear—belief in Yeshua as the Messiah does not cause a Jew to cease being a Jew, and thereby does not exempt them from Jewish covenant responsibilities. While Wyschogrod (an Orthodox Jew) does not agree with Kinzer's theological convictions regarding Yeshua, he does agree with Kinzer's position on how Messianic Jews ought to live.

> In fact, throughout the centuries, Jews who entered the Church very quickly lost their Jewish identity. Within several generations they intermarried and the Jewish traces disappeared... In short, if all Jews in past ages had followed the advice of the Church to become Christians, there would be no more Jews in the world today. The question we must ask is: Does the Church really want a world without Jews? Does the Church believe that such a world is in accordance with the will of God? Or does the Church believe that it is God's will, even after the coming of Yeshua, that there be a Jewish people in the world?... If, from the Christian point of view, Israel's election remains a contemporary reality, then the disappearance of the Jewish people from the world cannot be an acceptable development. Closely related to the survival of the Jewish people is the question of the Mosaic Law.[10]

Just as Wyschogrod offers this challenge to the church, Kinzer sees his theology as a clarion call for the church to reconsider its stance toward the Jewish people. "Christians who now affirm the irrevocable nature of the covenant between God and Israel must rethink their ap-

---

8. This of course raises questions about a Messianic Jewish stance toward Oral Torah, the necessary bridge between biblical commandments and their execution. Kinzer addresses this question in chapter 7 of *Postmissionary Messianic Judaism*, as well as in the essay "A Biblical Defense of Oral Torah," 29–61.

9. Wyschogrod, *Abraham's Promise*, 206.

10. Ibid., 207–8.

proach to Jewish practice as rooted in the Torah—for all Jews, including Jewish Yeshua-believers."[11]

The second marker of postmissionary Messianic Judaism highlights the solidarity between Messianic Jews and the larger Jewish world, pointing the way to a Christology rooted in God's covenant with Israel and positing significant continuity between the Hebrew Bible and the New Covenant Scriptures. The third marker lays the groundwork for understanding Messianic Judaism as an essential link between Israel and the church. Again, this configuration offers a new way of understanding Yeshua as a bridge rather than a wedge and puts forth a paradigm whereby Judaism and Christianity are joined while retaining their unique, complementary distinctions.[12] The *ekklesia* becomes an extension—rather than a replacement—of Israel.

While Kinzer makes the case for Messianic Jewish identification with the Jewish people as a whole, belief in Yeshua is not without significant implications.

> Messianic Judaism involves more than the subtle tweaking of an existing form of Jewish life and thought—adding a few elements required by faith in Yeshua and subtracting a few elements incompatible with that faith. Instead, the Judaism we have inherited—and continue to practice—is entirely bathed in the bright light of Yeshua's revelation. In a circular and dynamic interaction, our Judaism provides us with the framework required to interpret Yeshua's revelation even as it is reconfigured by that revelation. In this way our Judaism and our Yeshua-faith are organically and holistically "integrated."[13]

Kinzer's construal of the relationship between Messianic Jews and the larger people of Israel follows Pauline remnant theology, seen most clearly in Romans 9–11. The remnant is both *part of* and *distinct from* the people as a whole. "In Paul's view the remnant does not replace Israel but instead represents and sanctifies Israel. It serves a priestly function

---

11. Kinzer, *Postmissionary Messianic Judaism*, 210.

12. Following Paul in Galatians 3:28, Kinzer treats the union between Jew and Gentile as analogous to the union between man and woman in marriage. Kinzer claims that "the unity of Jew and Gentile does not imply the elimination of all distinction between the two, any more than the unity of husband and wife eliminates all gender differentiation" (Ibid., 170).

13. Kinzer, "Prayer in Yeshua, Prayer in Israel: The Shema in Messianic Perspective," 63.

on behalf of the entire nation."[14] The remnant is called to identify with the Jewish people as well as point this people toward their long-awaited Messiah who fully embodies the mission and identity of Israel.

If this is the role of the remnant of Israel that accepts Yeshua's messiahship, the reality remains that the vast majority of Israel denies this claim. While much of Christian history has condemned Israel for this fatal blunder, Kinzer views the Jewish people's rejection of Yeshua as part and parcel of God's plan for salvation. "Whereas a traditional reading of Romans 9–11 has seen the hardening of nonremnant Israel as exclusively punitive in nature, the texts we have been exploring point in another direction. They depict Israel's partial hardening as a form of suffering imposed by God so that God's redemptive purpose for the world might be realized."[15]

Here Kinzer joins with a number of scholars who have begun to read Israel's rejection of Yeshua in a new light. According to Paul van Buren,

> The Gospel met Gentiles as a demand to abandon their pagan ways and the service of the gods that are not God. The Gospel met Jews, as the church after Paul's time preached it, as the demand to abandon the express commands and covenant of the very God whom the church proclaimed! Here is a profound incoherence that has arisen because of the lack of a proper Christian theology of Israel. The theological reality which such a theology must address, then, is that Israel said No to Jesus Christ out of faithfulness to his Father, the God of Israel.[16]

In accordance with van Buren's assertion, Kinzer observes that "not only does Israel suffer despite its fidelity to the covenant—it actually suffers because of its fidelity to the covenant."[17] Richard Hays offers a similar assessment, noting that Israel's partial hardening comes as a result of God's action, not merely Israel's obduracy.

> Israel's temporary rejection has occurred for the sake of the Gentiles. It is *God* who has broken the Jewish branches off in order to allow the Gentile branches to be grafted on . . . Thus, in Paul's mind there is a definite—if mysterious—analogy between

---

14. Kinzer, *Postmissionary Messianic Judaism*, 125.
15. Ibid., 129.
16. Van Buren, *A Theology of the Jewish-Christian Reality*, vol. 2, 34, 276.
17. Kinzer, *Postmissionary Messianic Judaism*, 132.

the 'hardening' of Israel and the death of Jesus: God has ordained both of these terrible events for the salvation of the world. Thus, the fate of Israel is interpreted Christomorphically, including the hope of the Jews' ultimate 'life from the dead' ([Romans] 11:15). Any Christian community that reckoned seriously with this soteriological analogy between a rejected Israel and a Christ who became a curse for us (Gal. 3:13) would certainly find its treatment of the Jewish people transformed.[18]

According to the notion that Israel's suffering mysteriously participates in Yeshua's suffering, we see the full implication of Kinzer's Christology in continuity with Israel. Not only does Yeshua represent the one-man Israel (as we will explore below), but the people of Israel are likewise ontologically tied to their Messiah, even when they do not recognize him. Hence, Kinzer asks, "is it possible that Paul is hinting through these striking parallels between Romans 8 and Romans 9–11 that Israel's temporary unbelief in Yeshua is itself, paradoxically, a participation in Yeshua's vicarious, redemptive suffering?"[19]

Thomas Torrance notes a similar connection between Yeshua and Israel. "To be the bearer of divine revelation is to suffer, and not only to suffer but to be killed and made alive again, and not only to be made alive but to be continually renewed and refashioned under its creative impact. That is the pre-history of the crucifixion and resurrection of Jesus in Israel."[20] While Torrance references Israel's suffering as prefiguring that of Yeshua, Clemens Thoma asserts that Israel's role was more than merely precursory; the suffering of the Jewish people continues to mirror that of Yeshua.

> Auschwitz is the most monumental modern sign for the most intimate bonding and unity of Jewish martyrs—representing all Judaism—with the crucified Christ, although this could not have been conscious for the Jews concerned. The Holocaust is for believing Christians, therefore, an important sign of the unbreakable unity, grounded in the crucified Christ, of Judaism and Christianity despite all divisions, individual paths, and misunderstandings.[21]

Kinzer reaches a similar conclusion, offering a reading of Isaiah 53 that synthesizes the classic Jewish interpretation of the text with the classic Christian interpretation. "Since the Middle Ages, Jewish reading

---

18. Hays, *The Moral Vision of the New Testament*, 433.
19. Kinzer, *Postmissionary Messianic Judaism*, 133.
20. Torrance, *The Mediation of Christ*, 11.
21. Thoma, *Christian Theology of Judaism*, 159.

of this text has largely followed the classic commentary of Rashi, who views the suffering servant described in the chapter as the people of Israel. Traditional Christian commentators, on the other hand, see this figure as the Messiah and consider the suffering, death, and resurrection of Yeshua to be the fulfillment of the prophecy. In light of the Holocaust, some Yeshua-believing interpreters are suggesting that *the two readings should be combined*."[22] If Israel's corporate life is represented by and embodied in Yeshua, then Yeshua's suffering reverberates through his own flesh and blood family. According to Kinzer, "Israel's apparent no to Yeshua resulted in Israel's intimate participation in Yeshua's yes to God."[23]

THE PERSON OF YESHUA

As we have already noted, Kinzer's Christology highlights the continuity between God's work in Israel and the mission and identity of Israel's Messiah. Kinzer places Yeshua within the narrative framework of Israel, showing how he comes as the fulfillment of Israel's destiny. "While the enfleshment of the *Memra* (Word) is a new and unique event, it should nonetheless be viewed in continuity with what precedes it—as a concentrated and intensified form of the divine presence that accompanies Israel throughout its historical journey. Thus, contrary to the common Christian canonical narrative, the divinity of Yeshua can be seen not as a radical rupture and disjunction in the story but as a continuation and elevation of a process initiated long before."[24]

One of the ways in which we see Yeshua embodying "a concentrated and intensified form of the divine presence" is through the invasive quality of his holiness. While Israel was commanded to refrain from contact with ritually unclean objects and persons, lest Israel's holiness be defiled, Yeshua's holiness flows *outward* into the impure world. "Yeshua's contact with the impure does not defile him, but instead transmits purity, holiness, and life to the impure ones around him. Yeshua's life and mission

---

22. Kinzer, *Postmissionary Messianic Judaism*, 228. Italics added. Martin Hengel offers support for interpreting Isaiah 53 as referring to both the people of Israel as well as a future Messiah. "Under certain circumstances the two possibilities could be viewed simultaneously as different aspects of the text, because a Messianic figure is always at the same time a representative of the whole people" (Hengel, "The Effective History of Isaiah 53 in the Pre-Christian Period," 81).

23. Kinzer, *Postmissionary Messianic Judaism*, 230.

24. Kinzer, "Beginning with the End," 104.

thus display a new type of *kedushah*, a prophetic, invasive holiness that needs no protection, but reaches out to sanctify the profane."[25]

Here we see Yeshua enacting the fulfillment of Israel's destiny, as Israel's holiness was always intended to expand outward and sanctify the world. When Abraham is called by God in Genesis 12, this element of outward expansion is already present—"I will bless those who bless you, and whoever curses you I will curse; and *all peoples on earth will be blessed through you*"(12:3). The prophet Isaiah repeats this idea: "It is too small a thing for you to be my servant to restore the tribes of Jacob and bring back those of Israel I have kept. *I will also make you a light for the Gentiles, that you may bring my salvation to the ends of the earth*" (49:6). In this way, the presence of God that rests on Israel is mediated to the world through Yeshua.

Once again, Kinzer's ideas align with those of Michael Wyschogrod. Wyschogrod makes the claim that, along with the temple in Jerusalem, the Jewish people are God's actual dwelling place. "This is the utter seriousness of the election of Israel. God has decided to tie to himself a people, a people defined by a body, by the seed of Abraham and Sarah, Isaac and Jacob, and this people, who constitute a physical presence in the world, are at the same time the dwelling place for God in the world."[26] While Wyschogrod does not accept the idea of God's incarnation in the person of Yeshua, he sees this claim as a variation of a Jewish idea rather than something entirely novel. "My claim is that the Christian teaching of the incarnation of God in Jesus is the intensification of the teaching of the dwelling of God in Israel by concentrating that indwelling in one Jew rather than leaving it diffused in the people of Jesus as a whole."[27]

The intensification and concentration that Wyschogrod speaks of perfectly characterizes Kinzer's Christology. "In Yeshua the tent of the divine presence takes a new form. As the true Israelite, blameless and holy, Yeshua sums up all that Israel was intended to be. He becomes the perfect temple, priest, and sacrifice, offering himself to God on behalf of Israel, the nations, and the entire creation. Yeshua dies not only as a sacrifice but also as Israel's perfect martyr, who, like Isaac in the *Akedah*, embodies all

---

25. Ibid., 107.
26. Wyschogrod, "Incarnation," 212–13.
27. Wyschogrod, *Abraham's Promise*, 178.

of Israel's martyrs in himself, and whose blood is shed both to atone for sins and to prepare the way for the coming of *Olam Haba*."[28]

In fact, Kinzer's Christology posits that Yeshua is precisely the intensification of God's presence in Israel—for Kinzer, Yeshua is the one-man Israel. "The New Testament employs many biblical images in its attempt to explore the meaning and significance of Yeshua. One of those images has special relevance to our topic of study: Yeshua as representative and individual embodiment of the entire people of Israel."[29] Yeshua both sums up the story of Israel and points forward toward the prophetic fulfillment of Israel's ultimate destiny as a light to the nations and the sanctifying agent for the whole world. Along these lines, N.T. Wright observes that the gospels "tell the story of Jesus in such a way as to convey the belief that this story is the climax of Israel's story. They therefore have the *form* of the story of Israel, now reworked in terms of a single human life."[30]

As well as seeing the incarnation as an intensification of the reality of God in Israel, Kinzer views Yeshua's death in a similar manner.

> Just as the Apostolic Writings [New Testament] portray the divine enfleshment in the priestly imagery of the *Mishkan*-temple, so they portray the death of Yeshua in the priestly imagery of atoning sacrifice . . . If Yeshua is the perfect one-man Israel, then his death as a martyr under the Romans sums up all of Israel's righteous suffering through the ages, provides the ultimate expression of the commitment to God and self-giving love shown first in the *Akedah*, and effects definitive atonement . . . A Messianic Jewish version of the canonical narrative will see the death of Yeshua in continuity not only with Israel's temple system but also in continuity with Israel's ongoing life in this world. As with the incarnation, so with Yeshua's atoning death: the Messiah epitomizes and elevates Israel's story, rather than ending it and beginning something entirely new.[31]

Christology conceived in this manner implies a close *ongoing* connection between Yeshua and the life of Israel, as noted in the previous section. R. Kendall Soulen makes this connection explicit: "Jesus, the firstborn from the dead, is also the first fruits of God's eschatological

---

28. Kinzer, "Beginning with the End," 122–23. The *Akedah* is the binding of Isaac in Genesis 22; *Olam Haba* is the world to come.

29. Kinzer, *Postmissionary Messianic Judaism*, 217.

30. Wright, *The New Testament and the People of God*, 401–2.

31. Kinzer, "Beginning with the End," 108.

vindication of Israel's body. In light of Jesus' bodily resurrection, it is certain not only that God will intervene on behalf of the whole body of Israel at the close of covenant history but also that by this very act God will consummate the world."[32] Such an understanding also prevents the possibility of a high Christology leading to an over-realized eschatology. According to Kinzer, Yeshua not only embodies Israel's history but also points forward to the future consummation of that history.

> Israel's experience of the abiding presence of Hashem anticipates the consummation of the world, when "the land will be filled with the knowledge of God as the water covers the sea" (Isaiah 11:9). That anticipatory experience is brought to a new height in the coming of Yeshua, the one-man Israel, in whom the divine Word becomes flesh. The Apostolic Writings begin their story by narrating the birth of Yeshua, who is Immanuel, "God with us" (Matthew 1:23), and conclude by describing the New Jerusalem as "the dwelling of God" (Revelation 21:3) . . . The incarnation, like the building of the *Mishkan*, also needs to be viewed in terms of proleptic eschatology—it points forward to a reality that is not yet fully in our grasp.[33]

While Yeshua's life, death and resurrection are intimately intertwined with Israel's ongoing story, Yeshua inaugurates a future that Israel has not yet experienced. "Thus, certain features of Yeshua's identity and mission (his incarnation and his atoning death) are in continuity with Israel's past history, whereas other features (his resurrection and the founding of the twofold *ekklesia*) are pledges of Israel's promised future."[34]

THE BODY OF MESSIAH

Having explored Kinzer's theology with regard to Israel and Yeshua, we are now prepared to turn to the ecclesiological implications of his position. Kinzer's ecclesiology is in many ways the capstone of his entire theological system; it provides a blueprint for healing the rupture that currently characterizes the people of God. Kinzer's constructive ecclesiological proposal is what he terms "bilateral ecclesiology in solidarity with Israel."[35]

---

32. Soulen, *The God of Israel and Christian Theology*, 166.
33. Kinzer, "Beginning with the End," 104.
34. Ibid., 112.
35. See Kinzer, *Postmissionary Messianic Judaism*, chapter 4.

Bilateral ecclesiology is the practical outworking of Kinzer's constellation of theological claims. In *Postmissionary Messianic Judaism*, Kinzer argues against the supersessionist notion that the church replaces Israel, claiming instead that "the Jewish people as a whole retains its position as a community chosen and loved by God. While, in Pauline language, Israel has experienced a 'partial hardening' that temporarily prevents her from corporately embracing Yeshua-faith, she nevertheless remains a holy people, set apart for God and God's purposes." This claim, coupled with the assertion that the "remnant" of Israel within the *ekklesia* is called to be "a representative and priestly component of Israel that sanctifies Israel as a whole,"[36] necessarily requires a new ecclesiological configuration.

According to Kinzer, if the remnant is to fulfill its God-given role, "this portion of Israel must truly *live as Israel*—that is, it must be exemplary in observing those traditional Jewish practices that identify the Jewish people as a distinct community chosen and loved by God."[37] However, the New Testament also makes clear that the body of Messiah is to include Gentiles who are not required to live as Jews.[38] How is the *ekklesia* to accommodate both the calling of the remnant to live as Israel *and* the acknowledgment that Gentile believers need not adopt Jewish practice? "Only one structural arrangement would allow for distinctive Jewish communal life within the context of a transnational community of Jews and Gentiles: the one ekklesia must consist of two corporate subcommunities, each with its own formal or informal governmental and communal structures."[39] According to this arrangement, the Jewish branch of the *ekklesia* remains distinct from the Gentile branch, and thus serves as a link between the wider *ekklesia* and the wider Israel.

Bilateral ecclesiology "provides the Gentile branch of the ekklesia with a way of sharing in Israel's life and blessings without succumbing to supersessionism."[40] Theologians across the spectrum are increasingly acknowledging a deep and destructive supersessionism woven throughout the church's history.[41] According to Thomas Torrance,

36. Ibid., 151.
37. Ibid.
38. See, for example, the ruling of the Jerusalem council in Acts 15.
39. Kinzer, *Postmissionary Messianic Judaism*, 152.
40. Ibid.
41. For an excellent assessment of supersessionism throughout the history of the

> the deepest schism in the one People of God is the schism between the Christian and the Jewish Church, not that between East and West or Roman and Protestant Christianity. The bitter separation between the Catholic Church and the Synagogue that set in after the Bar Cochba revolt in the second century after Christ was one of the greatest tragedies in the whole of our history, not only for the People of God but for all western civilization . . . Only with the healing of that split in a deep-going reconciliation will all the other divisions with which we struggle in the ecumenical movement finally be overcome.[42]

Kinzer's proposed ecclesiological shift offers a promising step toward repairing and renouncing this corrosive shadow-side of church history. In Kinzer's assessment, "the rise of Christian supersessionism is correlated with schism between the Jewish and Gentile branches of the ekklesia, schism between the Jewish branch and the wider Jewish people, and the demise of Jewish Yeshua-faith as a viable corporate reality."[43] If these are the factors that led to supersessionism's triumph, each must be addressed in order to repair the church's derailment with regard to the Jewish people.

Kinzer believes that restoring the Jewish branch of the *ekklesia* is a key factor in righting history's wrongs and healing the schism between Jews and Christians. Thus, as Kinzer states, "while I *am* arguing for the legitimacy and importance of Messianic Judaism, my thesis is that the church's own identity—and not just the identity of Messianic Jews—is at stake in the discussion."[44] While church history has perpetuated supersessionism, the church nonetheless remains fundamental in God's plan for reconciliation and redemption.

> Supersessionism and the crumbling of the ecclesiological bridge, i.e., the Jewish ekklesia, damaged the church in a profound way. But we must avoid the temptation to see church history in purely negative terms. The Gentile ekklesia preserved the essential message entrusted to it. It continued to proclaim Israel's risen Messiah. It rejected Marcionism and accepted the Jewish Bible as inspired, authoritative, and canonical. It collected the books of the New Testament and arranged them in a manner that further

---

church, see Soulen, *The God of Israel and Christian Theology*.

42. Torrance, "The Divine Vocation and Destiny of Israel in World History," 92.
43. Kinzer, *Postmissionary Messianic Judaism*, 152.
44. Ibid., 13.

countered Marcionite anti-Judaism. The most virulent forms of anti-Jewish teaching in the second century did not carry the day but were moderated by Irenaeus and later by Augustine. *The church faithfully preserved and carried within it the truths that would allow it eventually to reexamine its history and recognize supersessionism as an error demanding correction.* At the same time, the triumph of supersessionism and the crumbling of the ecclesiological bridge produced a schism in the heart of the people of God.[45]

In other words, buried within the church's tradition and heritage lay the resources to repair the schism. However, these resources alone are not sufficient. Because the Jewish people remain a people elected by God and crafted according to his purposes, their role in salvation history is equally significant and necessary for the reunification of God's people. Just as Kinzer's method is cross-directional, so too is the healing of the schism in Kinzer's scheme. What piece does Israel contribute to the matrix of healing?

> If the obedience of Yeshua that led him to death on the cross is rightly interpreted as the perfect embodiment and realization of Israel's covenant fidelity, then Jewish rejection of the church's message in the second century and afterward can rightly be seen as a hidden participation in the obedience of Israel's Messiah . . . When Christians sought to compel Jews to become Christians, they were also seeking to compel them to deny Judaism and the Jewish people—and thus God himself! In this case, saying no to the Yeshua proclaimed by the church became a way of sharing in his perfect yes to God . . . Paradoxically, the Jewish no to Yeshua becomes a sign of his presence in Israel rather than of his absence.[46]

While Israel has apparently rejected God's redemptive work in the person of Yeshua, rabbinic Judaism[47] has safeguarded a key element of the very message the church proclaims. Kinzer argues that in order for God's consummative purposes to prevail, the church must acknowl-

45. Ibid., 211. Italics added.
46. Ibid., 225–26.
47. According to Peter Ochs, "there is, in one sense, no other Judaism for Jews than that which comes by way of Rabbinic Judaism, or the Judaism of the Mishnah, Talmud, synagogue, prayer book, and Torah study that emerged after, in spite of, and in response to the loss of the Second Temple. All of the new Judaisms that have appeared since have appeared from out of and in terms of this Rabbinic Judaism" (Ochs in Yoder, *Jewish-Christian Schism Revisited*, 3).

edge and embrace the contribution Jewish tradition has to make. This particular aspect of Kinzer's theology closely resembles that of Franz Rosenzweig.

In the final sections of Rosenzweig's magnum opus, *The Star of Redemption*, he employs the image of a celestial star to describe the relationship and mutual dependence between Judaism and Christianity. Judaism constitutes the inner burning core of the star, and its vocation is to preserve the truth *by preserving itself*. Christianity represents the rays that shine forth from the star, bringing its light and heat to the surrounding environment. For Rosenzweig, Christianity is necessarily missionary,[48] while Judaism is inherently inward-focused.[49] Even as each has its own prescribed vocation, they need one another to avoid the dangers that their respective trajectories entail.

According to Rosenzweig, without the balancing counterpart of Judaism, Christianity is susceptible to three related dangers: "spiritualization of the concept of God, apotheosizing of the concept of man, pantheisizing of the concept of the world."[50] In other words, Christianity is in danger of domesticating God, exalting humanity, and acting as though the world were already redeemed. Judaism's dangers represent a distortion of its calling to self-preservation, and entail forgetfulness of God's plan to redeem the *whole world*. Judaism is in danger of privatizing God, forsaking the world and isolating itself in its own existence.

The dangers of Judaism and Christianity stem from their separate but related tasks and foundations.

> Christianity, by radiating outwards, is in danger of evaporating into isolated rays far away from the divine core of truth. Judaism, by growing inwards, is in danger of gathering its heat into its own bosom far distant from the pagan world reality. If there the dangers were spiritualization of God, humanization of God, making

---

48. "Christianity as eternal way must always spread further. Simple preservation of its continuance would mean for it the renouncing of its eternity and hence death. Christianity must be missionary" (Rosenzweig, *The Star of Redemption*, 362).

49. "The heart of the fire must burn without ever stopping. Its flame must eternally nourish itself. It does not want nourishment from anywhere else. Time must roll past it without power. The fire must beget its own time. It must beget itself eternally. It must make its life eternal in the succession of generations, each of which begets the following one, as it itself again will bear witness to the preceding one. The bearing witness takes place in the begetting" (Ibid., 317).

50. Ibid., 424–25.

God into the world, then here it was denial of the world, disdain for the world, mortification of the world . . . All three of these dangers are the necessary consequences of the inwardness turned away from the world, as those dangers of Christianity are the consequences of self-renunciation turned toward the world.[51]

While the specifics of Kinzer's "dangers" are slightly different, the framework is the same. For Kinzer, the message of God in Yeshua is structurally flawed when it unhitches itself from Judaism, its source and counterpart. When the church required Jewish "converts" to renounce their former practices, Christianity lost contact with its rootedness in Judaism and thus lost a part of its very self. While it may seem as though this error only affects Jewish believers in Yeshua, according to Rosenzweig, Christianity's very existence withers if it loses sight of the soil from which it sprouted. In losing its historical rootedness in Judaism, Christianity loses its very God.

Similarly, Judaism needs Christianity's reminder that the whole world is God's beloved creation, destined for redemption. Judaism's delight in the Torah cannot obscure the fact that, through faith in Yeshua, "a righteousness from God, apart from law, has been made known, to which the Law and the Prophets testify"(Romans 3:21). Judaism must remember that the God of Israel is also the God of the Gentiles.

In Kinzer's thought, redemption and reconciliation can only be accomplished when Judaism and Christianity offer their unique treasures and receive the offerings of the other. The implications of this model require the church to rediscover a part of itself that has been lost. "We have argued that the Christian church and the Jewish people together constitute the one people of God and, in a sense, the one Body of Messiah. The schism in the heart of this people has damaged each side and resulted, among Christians, in a truncated vision of the church's own identity and the identity of its Messiah. To rediscover its own catholicity, the church must rediscover Israel and its relationship to Israel."[52]

Messianic Judaism plays a mediating role between the church and the wider Israel, and its calling is to represent and recommend each to the other. Messianic Jews are to play a precarious bridging role—living under the messiahship of Yeshua while fully identifying with the Jewish world. "Bilateral ecclesiology in solidarity with Israel summons the Messianic

51. Ibid., 429–30.
52. Kinzer, *Postmissionary Messianic Judaism*, 310.

Jewish congregational movement to take a step towards the Jewish world and a step away from its evangelical matrix. Only by being distinct from evangelicalism, and connected to Judaism, can such a Messianic Judaism fulfill its vocation as an ecclesiological bridge enabling the church to discover its identity in relationship to Israel and enabling the Jewish people to encounter its Messiah as it has never done before."[53]

The essays included in this volume, several of which have never before been published, offer the reader a unique window into the richness and development of Kinzer's theology. Each essay refracts Kinzer's thought from a slightly different angle, allowing the reader to enter his theological system from many different portals. The nature of this volume makes it more accessible than *Postmissionary Messianic Judaism*, for it does not include the same type of sustained intricacies as the central, and groundbreaking, argument put forth in Kinzer's first volume.

The twenty-seven year period of Kinzer's life represented by these essays reveals that though his journey has been complex, the trajectory of his thought has remained constant. In many ways, the vision that is cast in seed-form in "The Messianic Fulfillment of the Jewish Faith" (1982) finds its mature expression in Kinzer's recent work, as well as in the development of Messianic Jewish Theological Institute (MJTI), founded in 1998. Kinzer's leadership of this growing educational institution (as well as Congregation Zera Avraham in Ann Arbor, MI) demonstrates the way in which he wholeheartedly lives out his vision for Messianic Judaism. Theology for Kinzer is more than an intellectual exercise—it is way of life.

The essays in this volume provide a tangible manifestation of Kinzer's cross-directional method. The first two essays offer a sketch of Kinzer's theology of Messianic Judaism. The third and fourth essays approach the topic from Jewish starting points, interacting with Oral Torah and Jewish prayer, respectively. The fifth and sixth essays begin from the traditional Christian loci of eschatology and soteriology. The seventh essay represents Kinzer's involvement in the Roman Catholic–Messianic Jewish dialogue group, which met for the first time in the fall of 2000 at

---

53. Kinzer, "Three Years Later," 191.

the Camaldoli monastery in Italy.[54] Finally, the last essay reveals Kinzer's assessment of the responses *Postmissionary Messianic Judaism* elicited in the first three years of its reception.

It is my hope that this volume will generate conversations—among the Messianic Jewish, Christian, and larger Jewish worlds—about the person of Yeshua, God's redemptive purposes for creation, and the indelible link between Judaism and Christianity. Rabbi Joseph Soloveitchik ventures that "when God created the world, He provided an opportunity for the work of His hands—man—to participate in His creation. The Creator, as it were, impaired reality in order that mortal man could repair its flaws and perfect it."[55] May we be among those whose lives contribute to the mending of the world, not least by working to repair the schism between Judaism and Christianity. But let us remember, the road will not be easy.

J. Rosner

---

54. The group has met every year since then, alternating between Italy and Israel (with the exception of 2008, when the meetings were held in Vienna).

55. Soloveitchik, *Halakhic Man*, 101.

Part I

Vision for Messianic Judaism

1

The Messianic Fulfillment of the Jewish Faith

Mark Kinzer describes his own story of coming to faith in Yeshua, and thereby to a richer understanding of Judaism and a deeper commitment to Jewish life. Upon becoming a believer in Yeshua in 1971, Kinzer never questioned that his newfound faith would be lived out in the context of Judaism. This commitment came at a time when a path for Jewish expression of Yeshua-faith had yet to be fully forged, and this essay represents Kinzer's burgeoning vision to pioneer such a path. In many ways, the convictions that Kinzer held in the early years of his messianic faith would cast the trajectory for the rest of his life and his life's work. In the impassioned reflections of a young man, we see here the seed-form of Kinzer's mature theological commitments.[1]

THE JEWISH CHRISTIAN[2] IS for many people an anomaly and enigma. His identity often seems incomprehensible to both his non-Messianic Jewish brethren and his Messianic Gentile brethren. The Jewish form of incomprehension was passed on faithfully to me in my younger years. I recall being unable to distinguish between the words *goy* (Gentile) and Christian; in my mind both words referred to all of those

---

1. Originally published in Torrance (editor), *The Witness of the Jews to God*, 115–25.

2. As Kinzer's theology developed and he became increasingly committed to living a life within the Jewish world, his terminology shifted as well. The term "Jewish Christian" indicates that one's primary identity lies in the Christian world while the term "Messianic Jew" clearly connotes emphasis on one's identity as a Jew. The former reflects Kinzer's situation in 1982, when this essay was written. As Kinzer has worked toward the goal of Messianic Judaism embodying an authentic branch of Judaism, his terminological choices have been very deliberate. See "Introduction to the Thought and Theology of Mark Kinzer," (ix, n. 1), as well as "Toward a Theology of Messianic Judaism" (14–26) for further explanation on the significance of terminology.

who were not Jews. The Christian form of incomprehension is reflected in the questions many Gentile believers ask me: "So you are a convert from Judaism?" or "So you were formerly a Jew?" The man who insists that he is a Jewish Christian looks to all the world as one who is trying to walk along a fence with a leg on each side, or as one who answers yes and no to the same question.

There are obvious historical explanations for this inability to yoke together the words Jew and Christian. Nonetheless, one cannot dismiss Jewish Christianity on historical or logical grounds. Jesus was a Jew, the apostles were Jews, the New Testament is a patently Jewish book, and the early messianic congregation saw the unity of Jew and Gentile within its halls as the paramount sign of God's having reconciled the world to himself (Ephesians 2:11–22). Even the non-Messianic Jew cannot fault the logic: If Jesus was indeed the Messiah, then a Jew is obligated to follow him, and can only experience the fullness of Judaism as a result. One can argue with the premise, but not with the inevitability of the conclusion.

The fulfillment of Judaism in Jesus the Messiah is to me both a theological and an experiential reality, a truth I believe and a truth I live. I am a Jew, seeking to follow Torah (the Jewish law) and living today a more Jewish life than ever before; I am also a Christian, believing that Jesus fulfills the promises made to my ancestors, and experiencing the fruits that come from a relationship with him.

BACKGROUND

My immediate family memory goes back only two generations. Just before World War I my grandparents made the long ocean voyage from the eastern European *shtetl* (Jewish village) to the great American metropolis. My mother's father was a humble carpenter, a jovial and simple man. My paternal grandfather was a learned and pious talmudic scholar. The rabbis would sit at his side and seek his opinion on abstruse matters of Jewish law. Though both of these men lived far beyond their allotted time of three score and ten years, a gulf separated their universe from mine—a gulf of language, culture, age, and worldview. I lived in the same house with each of them for a time, but I never really knew them.

My father was a kind man with few spiritual inclinations but with a passionate attachment to the synagogue and to Zionism. Through most of my youth he would drive twice daily to the *shul* (synagogue) to attend the morning and evening services. As President or Vice President of the congregation he would devote several full evenings each week to committee meetings and practical management of the building. He would also contribute generously to the Jewish National Fund and other Zionist causes. Though usually mild and reasonable, he could be inflamed to a fever pitch at the mere mention of the state of Israel.

My mother's temperament had a more intuitive bent. She believed deeply in God and in prayer, yet she had little knowledge of the Scripture or of Jewish tradition. She concentrated her prayer and her energy rather on raising the three unruly youths to whom she had given birth.

My two older brothers and I responded to my parents' faith with undisguised condescension. We were living in a new age and a new culture, and the old ways were clearly unsuitable. We would sit together in the synagogue on the High Holy Days and joke about the operatic falsettos of the cantor or the spiritual apathy of the congregation. We were unimpressed with Judaism as we knew it—a ritualistic faith based on a language that few understood and a set of spiritual realities that few experienced. After celebrating our bar mitzvah's in our thirteenth years, we all scrupulously avoided religion in any form.

Of course, I did have other obsessions. In my early years my life gained meaning from one main source—sports. My brothers and I ate, drank, and slept sports. We played them in the streets and fields, read about them in the newspapers, watched them on television, attended them at the stadiums and arenas, and talked about them everywhere. As I grew older I discovered another source of joy and purpose—music. Again I dove in with gusto—playing, singing, and listening until even in sleep my head vibrated with Chopin and Brahms and B. B. King. Finally, I stumbled upon what was to become my greater passion—philosophy. It all began when I pulled from the shelf of our local library a volume of Plato's *Dialogues*. I read it quickly, and was immediately conquered. Spinoza and Aristotle soon followed. Philosophy led to psychology, and I rapidly digested morsels from Freud, Jung, Fromm, and R. D. Lang. I had already read Dostoyevsky and Tolstoy, and now I appreciated them even more. My mind had come alive with hunger for knowledge and truth, and the passion was not less strong for being intellectual rather than physical.

At this time I had an ambivalent attitude toward Jesus—a mixture of fascination, attraction, fear and hostility that is common to many Jewish people. On the one hand, the very name of Jesus could cause me to cringe with apprehension and animosity. There was something alien and threatening in that name; it was associated not so much with a person as with ideas, institutions, and an ancient enmity that I did not understand. My mother once told me how she came home crying after her first day in a Gentile primary school and asked her parents, "Who is Jesus? They said I killed Jesus!" Such incidents leave their mark. Even many Jews who have never personally experienced the hostility of Christians still react with irrational fear and anger at the mention of the name of Jesus.

On the other hand, the man Jesus fascinated me. Something about his teaching and life caught my imagination and impressed me deeply. One night I stayed up until 3:00 a.m. watching a movie on television based on the life of Christ. I was so affected that I asked a Gentile friend the next day if I could borrow her Bible. I wanted to read the firsthand accounts of the life of this remarkable man. Unfortunately the Bible was in King James English, and I began with the first chapter of Matthew—sixteen verses of "begats." My zeal quickly waned, and I returned the Bible to my friend in as unused a condition as it was when I received it.

REVERSAL

The most significant year of my life began as I left my parents' household and enrolled at the University of Michigan in Ann Arbor. I had been eagerly awaiting this transition for many years. I looked forward to being independent of my parents and their authority. Even more, I looked forward to the academic environment of intellectual and social ferment that awaited me in Ann Arbor. I wanted to meet other seekers who could aid me in my quest for knowledge and truth. Hidden in me beneath many layers of youthful pretense and egoism lay an intense desire for that which was right and true. I was a product of the late sixties, and the idealism of those years left an imprint on my mind.

The disillusionment of my first year at school hit me harder because of my high expectations. There were several reasons for this disillusionment. First, I found the huge university bureaucracy oppressive and stifling. Like most freshmen, I lived in a residence hall that housed close to a thousand students. I developed personal relationships with few of my classmates and none of my instructors. Secondly, I soon discovered that at the university, knowledge was fragmented into a multitude of discrete yet warring compartments. My quest for an integrated worldview was frustrated on every side. Each of my professors was eloquent, knowledgeable, and persuasive; unfortunately, they all disagreed with one another. Thirdly, I found few people who were actually concerned with life's meaning and purpose. For years the main philosophical question that troubled me was the question of death. I was not so much afraid of death as I was unwilling to ignore it. What was the meaning of my work, my morals, my body, my relationships of love and friendship if all were destined to end in dust? I quickly found that very few people were concerned about such things, even at the university. Finally, I began to grow more conscious of my own shortcomings. My ideals were high, but my ability to live up to these ideals was substantially lower. In particular, I began to see some of my closest relationships deteriorate, and I knew that I was largely to blame. Therefore, the university sent me home for the summer disheartened, disillusioned, and slightly confused.

For three years much of my life had revolved around three close friends. We were all agnostics, and we were proud of our unbelief. During these years we were never apart from one another. I now decided that it was time for me to make a break with my past stabilities—especially the camaraderie of my friends. I needed to make up my mind decisively about what I thought, what I believed, and where I was headed. As an initial step in this direction, I purchased a backpack and reserved a seat on a cheap chartered flight to Europe. This would allow me to be away from my friends and family, visit some places I always wanted to see, and make some fundamental decisions about the direction of my life.

The next seven weeks proved to be a turning point. Every book I picked up seemed to speak about the reality of God and of Jesus Christ. I visited the magnificent cathedrals of Europe and marveled at the centuries of energy, treasure, and genius that men devoted to the glory of their God. A man approached me as I was eating lunch behind a Viennese palace and started speaking in German; as I told him that I did not speak his language, he broke out into a broad Kansas smile and began to speak to me in my native tongue about Jesus the Messiah. I spent a weekend with a Christian couple in Worcester, England, who talked with me about the Lord at great length and refreshed me with loving hospitality. They gave me a book that spoke of God as a personal and powerful being who ruled the world yet wanted us to know him consciously and intimately. I had been seeking an ultimate source of meaning, a foundational principle that could organize and integrate the field of human knowledge, an ethical system that was lofty yet livable; but I was totally unprepared for this type of God, who was less concerned that we pursue him and more concerned that we let ourselves be found.

The straw that broke the camel's back awaited me as I returned home. In the seven weeks that I had been gone all three of my friends had become Christians. Their experiences and lines of thought paralleled my own. With this fact, I was finished. I could not resist and still maintain my integrity. I now began to pray, read Scripture, and meet occasionally with other believers. Every day I found new confirmations of my still slightly half-hearted faith. Prayer was answered; Scripture blazed like a torch before my eyes and enlightened my mind with unexpected truths; my life and character started to undergo a radical change. This was an entirely new world, full of powers and principalities beyond my imagining.

I had sought the truth, and it had seized me. I had longed for a comprehensive intellectual system, and instead found myself face to face with a person who was more than a person. This new faith had intellectual solidity, but it soared far beyond the realms of philosophy. The quest had ended where it had begun—with the God of Israel. He had summoned me, and there was no possible response other than the response of my fathers: "Here am I."

A MESSIANIC JUDAISM

How could I reconcile my new faith with my former aversion to Christianity, that cluster of ideas and institutions and historical events that I had once associated with the name of Jesus? My initial approach was simple: I was not becoming a Christian in *that* sense. I was not joining myself to some entity called Christendom, but was merely believing that Jesus was the Messiah and deciding to follow him. In many ways I still identified Christianity with the *goyim* (Gentiles), and I was determined not to subject myself to a process of gentilization. My attitude has mellowed over the years as I have learned to appreciate many aspects of the Gentile Christian heritage, but that early determination to live as a Jewish follower of Jesus—a Jewish Christian—has remained the same.

My first Christian teacher was a Jewish man who was raised in an Orthodox home. He had become a believer in Yeshua (Jesus) at the age of nineteen, and had been serving the Lord faithfully for over twenty years. His wife was also a Jewish believer in Yeshua. They lived their lives in a fully Jewish way—their children went to Hebrew school, and their son was bar mitzvahed in my father's synagogue. This man taught me a basic principle that I have never forgotten: accept your Gentile brethren as your family in the Lord, but never abandon your Jewish life or identity.

The application of this principle had a striking impact on my parents. As can be imagined, at first they were appalled at my new religious convictions. My mother responded with vehement objections. My father, seeing that I would not change my mind, and wanting to calm my mother's agitated emotions, followed his usual course of trying to make the best of a bad situation: "Look at it this way, Marion—at least now he believes in God." However, after several weeks they began to notice some things that surprised them both. First of all, I had clearly not forfeited my Judaism. In fact, I was more concerned about Jewish things than I had ever been before. I accompanied my father to synagogue and peppered him with questions about Jewish life. I insisted that I was not departing from my heritage, but instead was returning to it. Secondly, they noticed changes in my way of relating to them. I was less rebellious, more respectful, more eager to help around the house. Something significant had obviously happened in my life.

The outcome of this summer at home was more dramatic than I had expected. Four months after I had professed faith in Yeshua, my mother received a vision of the Lord and heard him call her name. She responded, and also became a follower of the Messiah. She has remained steadfast in her faith to this day.

In my first few years as a Christian I would at times grow fearful of losing my Jewish identity. Would my Judaism erode before the powerful assimilating forces of the Gentile world and the Gentile church? I no longer have such fears. Experience has confirmed what I already knew to be true theologically—faith in the Messiah is the fulfillment of Judaism.

I have experienced this fulfillment in many ways. First and most importantly, I have entered into and experienced personal relationship with the God of Abraham, Isaac, and Jacob. This is the God whom Jesus reveals in unique fashion (Matthew 22:32). He is not Marduk, Moloch, or Baal, but the God of my fathers. When my brothers and I were children, my father wrote a prayer that he taught us and recited with us every night before going to sleep. We irreverently rattled it off as quickly as we could and never really understood its contents, but I still have it memorized today:

> The Lord is my shepherd, I shall not want.
> He is my rock, my fortress, my shield, my guide, my guardian,
>   my deliverer, my protector, my redeemer, my savior.
> He is the great God of Abraham, Isaac, Jacob, and Moses.
> He is the creator of all living things, in heaven and on earth.
> He is the maker of miracles and wonders.
> He is the God in whom I trust. Amen.

This is the same God whom I now confess, know, love, and serve. He is the source of the Jewish people, the covenant with Abraham, the promise of the land, the holy Torah, and the messianic deliverance. He is the God of my fathers.

Secondly, faith in the Messiah has led me to a great love and reverence for the Hebrew Scriptures, the Tanakh (a Hebrew acronym for the Law-*Torah*, the Prophets-*Nevi'im*, and the Writings-*Ketuvim*). The Scriptures are the true foundation of Jewish life. In *Bereshit* (Genesis) we read of God's irrevocable promise to Abraham and his children. In the subsequent books of Moses we read of the deliverance from Egypt, the covenant on Sinai, and the giving of the Torah. In the *Tehillim* (Psalms) we have the ancient prayers of Israel that have expressed for millennia the Jewish people's worship of God and longing for redemption. In the *Nevi'im* (Prophets) we read about the promised consolation of Israel, the hope that has sustained this people through times of darkest night. As a son of Abraham by faith and by circumcision, I have realized that the Scriptures are my most precious heritage and possession. They tie me to the God of my fathers, but they also tie me indissolubly to the fathers themselves, those of my people among whom this book emerged and who have lived and died for this book and the way of life enshrined in it. Faith in the Messiah has brought me to a love and understanding of the Jewish Scriptures that has confirmed me unalterably in my identity as a son of Israel.

Thirdly, my faith in the Messiah has planted in me a great zeal for Torah. This is certainly a point of controversy among both Messianic Jews and Gentiles, but I can only express here my own opinion and experience. I believe that Messianic Jews can and should (when possible) observe the Law of Moses, ceremonial as well as moral. My conviction is based largely on the evidence for early Messianic Jewish practice found in the New Testament writings. For example, in Acts 21:20–24 we have the following description of James' address to Paul and his co-workers upon their arrival in Jerusalem:

> You see, brothers, how many thousands there are among the Jews of those who have believed; they are all zealous for the law, and they have been told about you that you teach all the Jews who are among the Gentiles to forsake Moses, telling them not to circumcise their children or observe the customs. What then is to be done? They will certainly hear that you have come. Do therefore what we tell you. We have four men who are under a vow; take these men and purify yourself along with them and pay their expenses, so that they may shave their heads. Thus all will know that there is nothing in what they have been told about you but that you yourself live in observance of the law.

Paul followed James' suggestion in order to demonstrate that these rumors were false. Paul observed the ceremonial law, as did the pious messianic congregation of Jerusalem.

Of course, many complex questions now arise. How does one interpret the law? Should a Jewish Christian follow the traditional rabbinic interpretation and embellishment of the law? How much freedom does the Jewish Christian have in regard to Mosaic ceremonial injunctions? This is only the beginning of the questions. Such complex issues are very important, but my main point here is simple and elementary: I love Torah, believe that it has implications for the lives of all Jews, and strive to follow it according to the teaching and example of Yeshua and his disciples. Faith in the Messiah has not alienated me from the way of life given by God to my forefathers any more than it alienated the apostle Paul from Torah.

Fourthly, my new knowledge of God has unlocked for me the immense treasury of Jewish worship. The *Siddur Avodat Israel*, the Jewish prayer book, abounds in the praise of God as do few books I have ever read. The core of the *Siddur* goes back to the time of Yeshua and reflects something of the way he must have prayed. As I pray daily from the *Siddur*, I experience communion with Yeshua and am able to join my voice with Jewish saints, past and present, who have offered acceptable sacrifices of praise and thanksgiving to God. These prayers, which were once so meaningless to me, now embody and express what I have come to know in personal experience.

In addition to the daily pattern of worship found in the *Siddur*, I have also come to appreciate *Shabbat* (Sabbath) and the Festivals. I can recall my first experience of the feast of *Sukkot* (Tabernacles) after coming to believe in the Messiah. As I worshipped in the synagogue and waved my *lulav* (palm branch) and sang the *Hallel* (Psalms 113–118) and the great *Hoshannah* (Hosanna), my mind was drawn to Yeshua's grand entry to Jerusalem at the beginning of the last week before his death. I also meditated on the promise of his coming again in royal splendor, and how it would fulfill both Palm Sunday and the prophetic significance of *Sukkot*. I have had other such experiences and insights as I have celebrated *Shabbat*, *Pesach* (Passover), *Shavuot* (Pentecost), *Chanukkah* (Dedication), *Rosh Hashanah* (New Year), and *Yom Kippur* (Day of Atonement). Regular synagogue attendance and familiarity with Jewish prayer has also deepened my capacity to observe these days adequately.

Fifthly, my new appreciation for the Hebrew Scriptures and Hebrew worship has given birth to a great love for the Hebrew language. I am not a Hebrew scholar, but I can pray and read with understanding. The more I use the language, the more it seems to me that it was fashioned with the worship and service of God in view. It is vivid, concrete, musical, and flowing with oriental richness. Ancient Hebrew is not a language like Greek that easily lends itself to metaphysical speculation. But it is a language that easily flows with the praises of God, and the richness of Hebrew worship is incomparable.

Sixthly, faith in the Messiah has given me a new love for the Jewish people. I once viewed the Jewish people as merely another ethnic grouping with its own customs, language, and history. I was not ashamed to call myself a Jew, but I was just as at home in modern American culture as I was in Jewish culture. Now I realize that I belong to a people that has a special call and destiny, not because of its great intrinsic worth or unique genius, but because of its election by God. I am humbled and ashamed at my people's consistent failings, but I am also grateful for God's continued faithfulness and love "for the sake of their forefathers" (Romans 11:28). I identify with Israel as my people, and like Paul, "my heart's desire and prayer to God for them is that they may be saved" (Romans 10:1).

Seventhly and finally, faith in the Messiah has brought me to a new love and appreciation for my own family. I am grateful for my parents and their faith, and for my grandparents and their faith. I am especially grateful for my grandfather and his life of devotion to God. I delight in hearing stories about him from my parents; he was a man full of wisdom, faith, zeal, and charity. My faith in the Messiah has made me eager to imitate him.

I have often heard an accusation made by non-Messianic Jewish leaders that is thoroughly contradicted in my own experience. According to these leaders, Jewish Christians only live a sham-Jewish way of life. They adopt Jewish customs, not out of genuine personal conviction, but only so that they may deceive unsuspecting Jews into accepting the messianic claims of Jesus. Perhaps some Jewish Christians have done this, but my experience has been entirely different. I am a Jew, and I want to live as a Jew, even if I am the only Jew in a city and have no hopes of persuading some of my brothers regarding the messiahship of Yeshua. The Scriptures, worship, language, and destiny of Israel, and above all the God and Messiah of Israel are all part of my inheritance as a son of Abraham, and I have laid claim to that inheritance, for the God of Israel has laid claim to me.

Yeshua the Nazarene is the fulfillment of Judaism. He is the Jew *par excellence*, the personal embodiment of the people of Israel. Like the patriarchs and kings, and yet in even greater fashion, the Messiah *is* Israel, he is the personal head and representative and source and ruler of this people. This is the key to interpreting the great Suffering Servant passage of Isaiah 53—the servant refers both to the people Israel (as the Jewish interpretation states) and to a personal Messiah (as the Christian interpretation states). If this is true, then how can one lose one's Judaism by following this Jew who embodies and personifies the entire Jewish people? In fact, how can one be fully a Jew without following him?

Indeed, faith in the Messiah has fulfilled my Judaism. To be more precise, it has brought me *back* to the God of Israel whom I abandoned in my youth. I was an assimilated Jew, independent, cynical, and unbelieving, yet hungry for knowledge and truth, and Yeshua revealed himself to me as the wisdom and the power of God. To be even more precise, faith in the Messiah has brought me *forward* to a new Judaism consummated in the death and resurrection of Yeshua and already bringing forth the first fruits of the life of the age to come.

2

Toward a Theology of "Messianic Judaism"

In the early 1970s, the Hebrew Christian movement underwent a name change and a fundamental shift in identity—Messianic Judaism was (re-)born. Mark Kinzer explains the theological significance of the term "Messianic Judaism," highlighting the intentional primary identification as a branch of Judaism. In claiming to be a Judaism, Kinzer argues that Messianic Judaism must acknowledge the role and importance of Oral Torah and rabbinic tradition as the means by which Judaism has been interpreted and applied. However, the modifier "Messianic" is crucial. For Messianic Jews, all of Torah and tradition is interpreted through the lens of Yeshua, whose messiahship affects the way Judaism in its entirety is understood and lived out.[1]

DEFINING MESSIANIC JUDAISM: A THEOLOGICAL TASK

AFTER A QUARTER CENTURY of existence, one might have hoped that our movement would have progressed beyond matters of fundamental self-definition. As the topic of this UMJC Theology Forum demonstrates, such is not the case. We still struggle with basic identity questions. However, this struggle demonstrates more than just our collective immaturity (though it also demonstrates that!). It reflects the complex, challenging, and disturbing questions raised by our very existence for two communities who, through almost two millennia, have defined themselves in opposition to one another. The precise nature of

---

1. Originally presented at the Union of Messianic Jewish Congregations (UMJC) Theology Forum in 1999. Founded in 1979, the UMJC is the oldest Messianic Jewish congregational association, and the congregation in Ann Arbor founded and led by Kinzer is a member of the UMJC. This essay was originally published in Kinzer, *The Nature of Messianic Judaism*.

our relationship to these two communities and their histories and traditions defies simple formulas.

The task of defining Messianic Judaism could be construed in varied ways. One could study the question descriptively, either from a historical perspective (e.g., looking at the communal identity of Jewish believers in Yeshua of the first century and after) or from a sociological perspective (e.g., examining the communal identity of Messianic Jews at the end of the twentieth century). Such studies can offer crucial insights that assist us in our quest, but they do not answer our *real* question, which is prescriptive rather than descriptive. When we ask, "What *is* Messianic Judaism?" we mean, "What *should* Messianic Judaism be?" We are asking a theological question—how does *Hashem* see our relationship to the churches and to the wider Jewish community and its tradition? What is his purpose for us?

The question is theological in another sense as well. "Is Yeshua the Messiah?" is also a theological question, but it is one that—for a Messianic Jew, who accepts the authority of the writings of *Brit Hadashah* (New Testament)—can be answered with little intellectual exertion. Elementary exegesis suffices. However, the question we are now asking is of a different order. It requires sophisticated biblical exegesis, and much more. How do we understand certain biblical texts, whose meanings are at times ambiguous, and which reflect a social reality drastically different from our own, and then apply them to our world? How do we relate to Jewish history after the destruction of the temple, and to the form of Judaism that crystallized around the Mishnah and the Talmud? How do we think about the churches and their checkered history, especially in their dealings with Judaism and the Jewish people? These questions, and many others like them, are implicit in the deceptively simple question, "What is Messianic Judaism?" To answer them, we must do far more than cite biblical proof texts. We must engage in the disciplined intellectual activity that we call theology.

A THEOLOGY OF "MESSIANIC JUDAISM"

To paint a theology of Messianic Judaism that addresses such questions would require a far broader canvas than the present paper allows. Since it is not possible to offer here a careful and comprehensive theology of Messianic Judaism as a divinely sanctioned social and religious reality, I will attempt something more modest—a theological study of "Messianic

Judaism" as a term of self-designation. Whenever we employ new terms to describe realities pointed to in Scripture—whenever we go beyond merely repeating what the Bible says in its own words—we are doing theology. New terms that gain near universal acceptance within a community of faith—terms such as Christianity and Judaism, Trinity, sacrament, biblical canon, *tikkun olam* (healing the world), *Shekhinah* (divine presence), and *Torah she-be-al peh* (Oral Torah)—represent major developments in theology and spirituality, and themselves open up fresh possibilities for interpreting the data of revelation.[2] The renaming of our movement in the 1970s was itself such a major theological development, the implications of which we have not yet thoroughly probed. What is the significance of the fact that our movement calls itself "Messianic Judaism"? I am not just asking what we originally intended when we coined the term. I am also asking what the term itself implies.

Nevertheless, it would be wise to begin with the original intention. The self-designation for our movement's antecedent, reflected in the name of its most important organization, was "Hebrew Christianity." The new name was given for at least three reasons. First, it reflected the fact that the word "Hebrew," used commonly among (Reform) Jews of the nineteenth and early twentieth centuries as a religious and cultural self-designation, had fallen out of currency and had been replaced by the word "Jewish." Second, by inverting the order of the two elements of the compound term, from "Hebrew/Jewish Christianity" to "Messianic Judaism," relationship to the Jewish people and Jewish religious tradition was given new emphasis. "Judaism" became the genus and "Messianic" the species, rather than the reverse. Third, the change from "Christianity" to "Messianic" served to avoid misunderstandings, especially among Jewish people, for whom "Christian" often was equivalent to "*goy*" (Gentile). It also expressed our desire to find new cultural and linguistic forms, comprehensible and familiar to Jewish people, in which to express our faith in Messiah.

These original intentions, embodied in the bold new self-designation, provided us with foundational principles that continue to shape our movement in constructive ways. Any directions that conflict with those principles are certain to lead us astray from our original purpose. At the same time, I would suggest that the significance of the new name

---

2. Kadushin, *The Rabbinic Mind*, 1–58.

takes us beyond these original intentions, into what (at least for some of us) may be uncharted terrain.

"JUDAISM" AS GENUS

What does the name "Messianic Judaism" *imply* about the movement to which it refers? The decision to use the term "Judaism" speaks volumes. As already noted, its role as the fundamental category or genus in our self-definition gives new emphasis to our connection to the Jewish people and the Jewish religious tradition. At first, as biblically-oriented people, most prominent in our minds was the fact that the first followers of Yeshua were all Jews and continued to live as Jews. Thus, the Judaism of the Second Temple period stood foremost in our thoughts. However, it is not possible for a vital religious movement at the beginning of the third millennium after Messiah's coming to employ a term common in everyday language in a way that is substantially different from that in common use. Historians and archaeologists may hear the word "Judaism" and immediately think of the world of antiquity, but the non-specialist considers Judaism to be the religious tradition of the Jewish people, in all its diversity, throughout its history. Thus, we are claiming a meaningful relationship to the entirety of the Jewish tradition, not just to a Jewish world that passed away with the destruction of the Jerusalem temple and is now accessible only through the speculative reconstruction of scholars.

The word "Judaism," though coined in antiquity, has only become ascendant in the Jewish world in modern times. Unlike the term "Christianity," it does not point directly to the faith-content of the Jewish religion. Unlike the term "Torah," which it supplanted, it also does not point directly to the way of life of those who live and believe it. Instead, "Judaism" turns attention first to *the Jewish people*, and designates the religious faith and way of life of those people by invoking *their name*. Therefore, when we call our movement a type of Judaism, we are affirming our relationship to the Jewish people as a whole, as well as our connection to the religious faith and way of life that that people has lived throughout its historical sojourn.

At the same time, "Judaism" does refer to Jewish religious tradition. We could have called ourselves "Messianic Jews" without calling our movement "Messianic Jud*aism*." The name "Messianic Jew" implies that the bearer sees his or her Jewish identity as fundamental. However, many Jewish people consider their Jewish identity important without finding anything of great value in Judaism. Just as the term "Jew" is meaningful apart from the word "Judaism" (though the converse is not true), so the term "Messianic Jew" is meaningful apart from "Messianic Judaism" (though, once again, the converse is not true). Though perhaps unrecognized at the time, the decision to employ the term "Messianic Judaism" and not just the term "Messianic Jew" was of great moment. It implied identification with the Jewish religious tradition as well as with the Jewish people.

Finally, the name "Messianic Judaism" implies that our movement is fundamentally among Jews and for Jews. It may include non-Jews, but it is oriented toward the Jewish people, and those non-Jews within it have a supportive role. This contrasts with the view that our movement has as a basic objective the *teshuvah* (repentance) of "paganized" Gentile Christians under the yoke of Torah. In this context, it may be significant that many today prefer the term "Messianic movement" to "Messianic Judaism." The former term can easily denote a Torah-revival among Gentile Christians. The latter term cannot. A Messianic Judaism without Jews is no Judaism at all.

A COMPOUND TERM WITH A DESCRIPTIVE MODIFIER

The "Judaism" in "Messianic Judaism" is thus of tremendous significance. The fact that we added a modifier—"Messianic"—is also significant. It implies that we see ourselves as a particular type of Judaism, and that we acknowledge the existence of other forms of Judaism that may justly bear the name. Some Orthodox Jews do not like the term "Orthodox Judaism" for this very reason—it implies that there is some other form of Judaism, a tenet that they find unacceptable. The fact that we embrace and identify with our compound name implies that our view of Judaism is broader and more inclusive; we may think our form of Judaism is the truest and best, yet our name implies recognition of alternatives. And, in fact, it would be difficult for us to do otherwise, unless we were ready to propose that Judaism ceased to exist with the extinction of the early Messianic Jewish communities, and only returned to the world with the emergence of the 1960s Jesus movement.

The type of modifier we chose is also important. Some modifiers used in compound religious designations convey a clear value message: we are the ones who have this religion right, and all others have veered from the true path. Thus, in the Christian world, the terms "*Catholic* Church" and "*Orthodox* Church" make claims that other Christians cannot allow—that this particular church is *the universal church* or the one that *believes rightly*. Similarly, in the Jewish world "*Orthodox* Judaism" is a term that implies that other forms of Judaism are *unorthodox*. They may be forms of Judaism, but they are distorted forms, twisted out of shape. Thus, Rabbi Moshe Dovid Tendler refers to "the non-Orthodox (*non-Jewish*) branches of Judaism."[3] In contrast, other modifiers used in compound religious designations function primarily in a descriptive mode, though a positive connotation is always intended. Thus, in the Christian world the "*Lutheran* Church" is the church that is rooted in the teachings of Martin Luther, and the "*Episcopal*," "*Presbyterian*" and "*Congregational*" churches are those that place special emphasis on particular forms of church polity. Similarly, in the Jewish world "*Conservative* Judaism," "*Reform* Judaism," and "*Reconstructionist* Judaism" express the approaches of these movements to Jewish tradition and change in the modern world. They are all primarily descriptive in nature, rather than implicit claims to exclusive legitimacy.

We could have chosen a polemical, value-charged modifier for our compound name. We could have opted for "Fulfilled Judaism" (with its apparent implication that other forms of Judaism have potentiality but no actuality) or "Completed Judaism" (with its apparent implication that other forms of Judaism are homes under construction and not yet fit to live in). We could have called our movement "Biblical Judaism," implying that all other forms of Judaism are "unbiblical" and thus invalid. Of course, these terms can be used among us without intending such denigrating implications. Still, it is significant that the term we selected was one that is primarily descriptive in nature, while also containing a strong claim to a unique position within the world of Judaism. Ours is the Judaism that believes that the Messiah has come, and that his name is Yeshua of Nazareth. Ours is also a Judaism in which the proclamation of the coming messianic era is central to the way Jewish teaching is construed. In this latter sense, ours is not the only expression of "Messianic Judaism" (Lubavitcher *Hasidim* and Israeli religious nationalists would also qualify). Understood in the former more restricted sense, however, we have no others in the Jewish world that would dispute our claim to

---

3. Tendler, "Harsh Words," 36. Italics added.

the modifier. Dispute arises not over the modifier, but over the noun modified—our claim to be a "Judaism."

Thus, while affirming clearly and distinctly who we are and what we believe, our name also speaks about our relationship to the wider Jewish world. We cannot deny the legitimacy of other forms of Judaism, for without them we would have no Judaism. The Jewish way of life we live derives from these other forms of Judaism, and we must be grateful to them for handing it on to us. At the same time, we believe that we have something crucial to pass on to them. We have a message about the Messiah whom many of them await, and who has come to give them access to unexpected treasures.

A PROBLEMATIC ALTERNATIVE: "BIBLICAL JUDAISM"

More can be learned about the theological significance of our name by probing further one of the alternative designations mentioned above—"Biblical Judaism." While not employed by any Messianic Jewish groups as a *replacement for* "Messianic Judaism," it is commonly used as a *description of* Messianic Judaism—"Messianic Judaism is Biblical Judaism." Is this true? Or, perhaps more to the point, what does it *mean*, and is that meaning appropriate to our reality?

"Biblical Judaism" could refer descriptively to the Judaism of biblical times. Most biblical scholars would refrain from using the term "Judaism" to describe pre-exilic Judahite or Israelite religion, and would contend that "Judaism" begins in the post-exilic period and finds its great champion in Ezra.[4] If this rule of nomenclature is followed, then "Biblical Judaism" understood as a historical and descriptive term would have a rather narrow application—to the Judaism of Ezra, Nehemiah, and the post-exilic prophets. This is probably not what those Messianic Jews mean that claim to practice "Biblical Judaism." Perhaps they understand the term "biblical" to include *Brit Hadashah*. If so, they would be speaking of the Judaism practiced by Yeshua and his emissaries. However, of what value is such a term? If "Bible" is defined in this way—as including the Apostolic Writings (New Testament)—then other Jews would have no problem in conceding the claim that "Messianic Judaism" is "biblical." However, those Jews would then argue that this is a *Christian* rather than a *Jewish* way of defining "Bible," and would thereby gain support

---

4. Moore, *Judaism*, 1.

for their contention that Messianic Judaism is no Judaism at all. Given these problems, it is unlikely that any thoughtful Messianic Jews would characterize their religious life as "Biblical Judaism" in this descriptive and historical sense.

"Biblical Judaism" could also refer descriptively to a form of Judaism that treated the Bible as its sole authority for teaching on matters of ultimate religious significance (the *sola scriptura* of the Protestant Reformers). Messianic Jews who used the term in this way would be contrasting their faith with that of rabbinic Judaism, which ascribes to rabbinic tradition (Oral Torah) binding authority as the necessary complement to Scripture. It is worth noting that, understood in this way, the name has already been taken—the Karaites (meaning "Scripture-ites") adopted the term, and used it for just this purpose: to oppose the binding authority of rabbinic tradition. However, there is another problem with Messianic Jewish appropriation of the term. Once again, the meaning of the word "Bible" is ambiguous. Are these Messianic Jews claiming—like the Karaites—to hold only Tanakh as ultimately authoritative? Or are they instead, like the Protestant Reformers, including the Apostolic Writings as part of the "Bible"? The latter seems more likely. If so, these Messianic Jews are elevating the writings of *Brit Hadashah* to a level analogous to that held in rabbinic Judaism by the Talmud. The contrast then between Messianic Judaism (so conceived) and rabbinic Judaism is not between those who hold the Bible to be the sole authority and those who do not, but between those who think the apostolic tradition essential in interpreting Tanakh and those who see rabbinic tradition as serving this function. The fact that followers of Yeshua use the same word—biblical—to refer to Tanakh and *Brit Hadashah*, whereas rabbinic tradition distinguishes carefully between Mikrah and Mishnah,[5] can obscure this correspondence in function between *Brit Hadashah* and Mishnah. Once equivocation is removed, and terms are defined in the same way, Messianic Judaism is no more "biblical" (in this second descriptive sense of the term) than is rabbinic Judaism.

Even if one looked past this equivocation, and assumed Messianic Jewish inclusion of the Apostolic Writings within the biblical canon, there would still be a problem with this notion of Messianic Judaism as "Biblical Judaism." It is the same problem that confronted the Karaites. Is it possible to construct a viable form of Judaism with only the Bible

5. Danby, *The Mishnah*, xiii.

as an authoritative sourcebook? Does the Bible provide sufficient practical detail to enable us to keep *kosher* (Jewish dietary laws), hold a *seder* (Passover meal), observe *Shabbat* (Sabbath), fashion *tzitzit* (fringes), and lay *tefillin* (phylacteries)? Is it possible to have a Judaism that is truly *Jewish* (i.e., in accord with the sensibilities of the Jewish people) without drawing upon the *Siddur* (Jewish prayer book), the *Machzor* (High Holy Day prayer book), or the *Haggadah* (Passover religious text)? Undoubtedly Messianic Judaism must give unique authority to Tanakh and *Brit Hadashah*, and subordinate all other authorities to their all-encompassing, overruling, and ultimate scrutiny, and in this sense Messianic Judaism could be called biblical Judaism. However, a strict construal of *sola scriptura* as denying rabbinic tradition any role in determining Jewish teaching and practice cannot succeed in the long-run (a truth recognized eventually even by the Karaites).[6]

These two descriptive uses of the term "Biblical Judaism"—the one using "biblical" in a historical sense, the other in reference to the source of religious authority—are probably not primary in the minds of those who embrace it as equivalent to "Messianic Judaism." Like "Catholic Church" and "Orthodox Judaism," "Biblical Judaism" appears to be employed by its advocates as a value-charged polemical claim rather than as an objective description usable outside the ranks of the already committed. It implies the assertion that Messianic Judaism is in accord with the Bible's true message, that it is the one form of Judaism that expresses the divine intention for the Jewish people found in the Bible. It also implies that other forms of Judaism are *un*biblical—they are merely human inventions, which have no foundation in the Word of God. Those familiar with the idiom of popular conservative evangelicalism know that in that world the adjectives "biblical" and "unbiblical" are equivalent to "good" and "bad." In fact, "unbiblical" is usually taken to mean "contrary to the Bible," with the underlying assumption that all propositions or behavior are either biblically sanctioned or biblically proscribed, with no middle ground. It is this world of popular conservative evangelicalism that provides the background essential to understanding the term "Biblical Judaism" as it is often used in the Messianic Jewish movement.

On the all-important matter of Yeshua's identity as Messiah of Israel, Messianic Jews can and should claim to be more "biblical" than their non-Messianic Jewish counterparts. We believe and affirm the

---

6. See Neusner, *An Introduction to Judaism*, 284.

message of *Brit Hadashah*, that the words of the Torah point to Yeshua (John 5:46), and that the good news concerning Yeshua was "promised beforehand through his prophets in the Holy Scriptures" (Romans 1:2). Along with Philip, we can say "We have found him of whom Moses in the Torah and also the prophets wrote, Yeshua of Nazareth, the son of Joseph" (John 1:45). This does not mean that in every case the traditional prooftexting apologetics of the missionaries bests the exegetical efforts of the anti-missionaries. It does mean that we see Tanakh as a whole speaking of Messiah Yeshua. As Alfred Edersheim put it,

> These remarks are not intended to deprecate the application of individual prophecies to Christ; only to correct a one-sided and mechanical literalism that exhausts itself in fruitless verbal controversies in which it is not infrequently worsted . . . We fully and gladly add that even in strict exegesis many special predictions can be only Messianically interpreted. But we believe still more that the Old Testament as a whole is Messianic, and full of Christ; and we wish this to be first properly apprehended, that so from this point of view the Messianic prophecies may be studied in detail. Then only shall we understand their real purport and meaning, and perceive, without word-cavilling, that they must refer to the Messiah.[7]

In this sense, we may boldly speak of our biblical Judaism, for we proclaim the One who is himself the fullness of Torah.

At the same time, we must acknowledge that in many ways other forms of Judaism are more "biblical" than we are. Do we observe *Shabbat* as well as other branches of Judaism? Do we transmit Jewish identity as well as other branches of Judaism? Do we practice *tzedakah* (charity) as well as other branches of Judaism? Do we show as much reverence in our worship and in our treatment of holy things (e.g., texts containing the divine name)? Are we as committed to social justice? Are we as zealous in avoiding *lashon hara* (gossip)? Are our families as healthy, stable, and loving? All of this is part of being truly "biblical," in the value-charged sense of living in accordance with the divine Word. Thus, as soon as one looks beyond the strictly Christological significance of the claim to represent the true "Biblical Judaism," this claim appears less and less compelling.

---

7. Edersheim, *Prophecy and History*, 112–13.

The above analysis leads to the conclusion that "Messianic Judaism" is far superior to "Biblical Judaism" as the fundamental designation for our movement, and that the latter term suffers such great liabilities as to render it largely useless even as a secondary self-description.

"MESSIANIC" AS SPECIES

To this point our examination of the theological implications of "Messianic Judaism" as a term has yielded the following conclusions: (1) We are primarily concerned with the Jewish people, rather than in establishing a movement of Gentile *ba'aley teshuvah* (returners to Torah); (2) We profess a positive relationship to the Jewish people and its course through history; (3) We affirm a positive relationship to the Jewish religious tradition as it has developed throughout history; (4) We acknowledge the legitimacy of other forms of Judaism, and seek to learn from them as well as teach. Our focus has been on the commonality with the wider world of Judaism asserted through the use of this particular word ("Judaism"), through its placement in the compound as the basic category or genus of our identity, and through the decision to employ a compound and to choose a mainly descriptive rather than value-charged modifier as the first term in the compound. However, our treatment of the name would be incomplete without further discussion of our specific difference, that which distinguishes us from the other members of the broader genus or category. Messianic Judaism is *Judaism*, but it is also *Messianic* Judaism.

The distinctive feature of our Judaism is Yeshua the Messiah. This does not mean that we merely add faith in Yeshua to a preexisting religious system, "*Generic* Judaism," in order to produce the sum, *Messianic* Judaism. There are Messianic Jews who do just this, but the result is not Messianic Judaism. It may be Messianic, and it may be Judaism, but the integrated whole implicit in the compound term, *Messianic Judaism*, is not in evidence. Instead, Messianic Judaism is Judaism, in all facets of its teaching, worship, and way of life, understood and practiced in the light of Messiah Yeshua. In Messianic Judaism the Torah is read with reverence, just as in all other form of Judaism, but it is heard by those who find the fullness of Torah in Yeshua. In Messianic Judaism one can pray the *Amidah* (central prayer of Jewish liturgy) in its traditional form, unamended, with the traditional understanding that one is thereby sharing in the fulfillment of Israel's communal obligation of worship expressed in temple times by the daily sacrificial offerings. However, he or she would also recognize that the supreme fulfillment of that worship is found in Yeshua's self-offering, and that Israel's gift of prayer is now acceptable to God in and through its high-priestly Messiah. In Messianic Judaism the Sabbath and the Festivals are observed, much as in other forms of Judaism, but their preliminary eschatological fulfillment in Messiah Yeshua is proclaimed and celebrated, and their final eschatological fulfillment in him is anticipated and sought. Traditional forms of Judaism provide the fundamental way of life and thought, but they are all given new depths of meaning through union with Messiah in the Spirit.

A parallel to this integrated re-interpretation of the entirety of the tradition may be found in the annals of Jewish mysticism. The *Zohar* consists of a mystical commentary on the Torah. The Torah is of highest authority, and talmudic personages and idioms are invoked, but all is seen in a new light—the light of the *sefirot* (emanations through which God reveals God's self). Isaac Luria and his contemporaries and heirs continued this process in sixteenth-century Tzefat, developing the new theological system and re-interpreting traditional practices in light of it. Now the fulfillment of the *mitzvot* (commandments) is not merely an expression of Israel's covenant love and duty, but also a means of bringing unity to the fragmented inner world of the divinity and healing (*tikkun*) to the cosmos. Judaism as a system of life and thought remains intact, but it is at the same time transformed by the new perspective from which it is considered.[8]

Something similar is required of Messianic Judaism if it is to live up to its name. What distinguishes Messianic Judaism from other forms of Judaism is not a particular doctrine or practice, but the way the entirety of the tradition is perceived and lived. This does not entail the destruction of traditional Judaism, any more than did kabbalistic theology. Instead, Messianic Judaism must digest the tradition and make it part of itself, while at the same time transforming it into something new.

INSPIRED TRADITION?

While still immature as a movement, we have now existed long enough to have something of our own tradition to draw upon. The sources that theology probes consist not only of canonical texts but also of the tra-

---

8. Scholem, *Major Trends in Jewish Mysticism*, 28–32.

ditions of the community in which the theologian lives, worships, and conducts his or her scholarly craft. Theology is always "earthed" in a particular communal context. The theologian scrutinizes the traditions of his or her community both in order to test them to see whether they are faithful to the fundamental truths that the community affirms, and also in order to find in them new insights into those fundamental truths. Sometimes traditions are mere customs (*minhagim*) of thought and life, with only passing or local significance. This is "tradition" with a small "t." But sometimes traditions emerge as an earthly response to a heavenly impulse (such as Oral Torah), and shed new light on a familiar landscape. This is "Tradition" with a capital "T."

I would like to suggest that our movement's name constitutes our clearest and most valuable Tradition (with a capital "T"). It tells us more than we have yet allowed ourselves to hear—about who we are, and about how we are related to the two rival communities whose heritage we share. More careful attention to the implications of what we have called ourselves—and, perhaps, of what we have been called by One far greater than we—will foster growth toward a secure and mature identity as Messianic Jews practicing an authentic and integrated Messianic Judaism.

Part II

Judaism from a Messianic Perspective

3

Messianic Judaism and Jewish Tradition in the Twenty-First Century: A Biblical Defense of Oral Torah

As Messianic Judaism seeks to gain independence from its evangelical Christian roots and establish itself as a branch of Judaism, the question of Oral Torah and rabbinic tradition becomes inevitable. Because the Written Torah is not always explicit about the practices and traditions it institutes, and because at times its directives stand in tension, *halakhah*[1] cannot be implemented without an authoritative interpretive tradition. In this essay, Kinzer explores the significance of and biblical warrant for Oral Torah and explains how Messianic Judaism cannot claim legitimacy as a Judaism without acknowledging the necessity of such an interpretive tradition. While the long journey of developing authentic Messianic Jewish *halakhah* is just beginning, Kinzer charts a course for Messianic Jews to thoughtfully assert their unique contribution while embracing rabbinic tradition as an essential and authoritative heritage without which Judaism would not exist.[2]

OUR CURRENT FORUM HAS taken up the topic of "Jewish tradition." This term is deliberately broad in scope, including in its domain

---

1. *Halakhah* refers to the communally authoritative applications of the Torah to the changing circumstances of daily life.

2. Originally presented at the Hashivenu Forum in 2003 and published (in modified form) as chapter seven of *Postmissionary Messianic Judaism*. The Hashivenu Forum is the outcome of a small gathering convened in 1997 by Stuart Dauermann, a Messianic Jewish leader who desired to discuss the possibility of common work with other like-minded leaders. The group consisted of Stuart Dauermann, Mark Kinzer, Bob Chenoweth, Michael Schiffman, and Paul Saal, and this initial discussion led to the founding of Hashivenu, which held its first annual forum in March 1999 in Pasadena, CA. The word *hashivenu* appears at the end of the Torah service liturgy and means "bring us back."

the entire way of life and thought transmitted to Jews of the present from Jews of the past. While some Messianic Jews dispute the value of Jewish tradition in this sense, most recognize that we cannot construct a viable Messianic Jewish way of life without drawing at least minimally on the heritage received from our ancestors. We would narrow our sights substantially if we defined our topic as "rabbinic tradition." This would focus our attention on the mishnaic, midrashic, and talmudic writings, and on the exegetical, *halakhic*, theological, liturgical, and ethical traditions that they spawned. This would take us into more adventurous terrain—for Messianic Jews disagree passionately about the value of all things rabbinic. However, even this way of defining our topic seems uncontroversial in comparison to the term I have chosen to work with: Oral Torah. Messianic Jews might question the merits of rabbinic tradition, but we all agree that it exists. But the term "Oral Torah" contains a claim of divine sanction that few Messianic Jews have been willing to accept. Thus, most Messianic Jews deny that there is such a thing as Oral Torah.

As the discussion that follows will demonstrate, I would not argue on behalf of all that rabbinic authorities have asserted about Oral Torah. For example, I would not advocate the view that the teaching now found in the vast rabbinic corpus was revealed to Moses at Sinai. Still, I would contend that the term is useful, for it rivets our attention on the central issues we must confront: Does the Written Torah require an ongoing tradition of interpretation and application in order to become a concrete reality in daily Jewish life? Does the tradition of interpretation and application of the Written Torah developed and transmitted by the sages have any kind of divine sanction?

The question of Oral Torah has particular importance in the realm of *halakhah*. Most Messianic Jews in the Diaspora accept the traditional view that Jewish identity and existence should be rooted in the Torah (i.e., the Pentateuch)—though, for us, as interpreted and embodied in Messiah Yeshua. Most Diaspora Messianic Jews likewise acknowledge that the Torah contains authoritative practical instruction for the people of Israel as it seeks to fulfill its covenantal vocation as a *goy kadosh* (a holy nation). But once we affirm these propositions, we face a challenge: how to understand the Torah and live according to it as Messianic Jews in the twenty-first century. This brings us immediately into the realm of the Oral Torah: "How to face the confrontation between the text and the actual life situation, how to resolve the problems arising of this confrontation, is the task of the *Torah she'baal'Peh*, the Oral Law."[3]

Why is the notion of Oral Torah so repugnant to Messianic Jews? Some of the suspicion derives from proper concern for the primacy and unique authority of the Written Torah. Thus, some argue that the Written Torah is sufficient, and neither requires nor permits any supplement. It is further argued that the rabbinic doctrine of the Oral Torah was invented not just to supplement the Written Torah but to supplant it. Some of the suspicion derives from the Apostolic Writings (New Testament) and their treatment of the Pharisees (rightfully assumed to be the Second Temple precursors to the post-70 rabbinic movement). Yeshua's apparent reservations about the Pharisaic "tradition of the elders" are read as a direct rejection of any notion of the Oral Torah. Yeshua's bestowal of *halakhic* authority on his *shelichim* (apostles) likewise seems to preclude Pharisaic-rabbinic claims to such authority. Finally, Messianic Jewish suspicion regarding the Oral Torah derives also from the Pharisaic-rabbinic rejection of the messianic claims for Yeshua made by his followers, and from their subsequent treatment of those followers. In order to uphold any notion of Oral Torah for Messianic Jews, these objections must be addressed.

In this paper I will attempt just this task. I will not have adequate opportunity to deal with all the objections in a manner that they deserve. However, I hope at least to point in the direction that such answers might go. If I am successful, the notion of Oral Torah will no longer be off limits for us as Messianic Jews.

ORAL TORAH IN THE PENTATEUCH

Is the Written Torah sufficient, without any supplementary instruction? In order to answer this question, we must first ask, "sufficient for what?" In evangelical discussions of the meaning of *sola scriptura*, the issue is always soteriological: sufficient for instruction in what we must believe in order to go to heaven after we die.[4] However, within a Jewish context, the Torah is not primarily a document containing truths that we must believe in order to attain the afterlife. Instead, it is primarily Israel's na-

---

3. Berkovits, *Not in Heaven*, 1.

4. This is not to detract from the importance of soteriological questions. It is simply to note that the Pentateuch, when read in a Jewish context, is not primarily seeking to answer such questions.

tional constitution, the foundational text shaping its practical communal life. Thus, the issue is not, "what shall we believe in order to be saved?" but "how shall we live if we are to be faithful?"

Is the Written Torah sufficient for instructing the Jewish people in how we should live as individuals, families, and local communities? While it is certainly foundational and indispensable, it is not sufficient. The Torah requires a living tradition of interpretation and application if it is to be practiced in daily life. This is due in part to the lack of detail in its legislation. As Michael Fishbane notes, "frequent lacunae or ambiguities in their legal formulation tend to render [biblical] . . . laws exceedingly problematic—if not functionally inoperative—*without interpretation.*"[5] Thus, the Torah forbids all work (*melachah*) on *Shabbat* (Sabbath), but it nowhere defines the meaning of *melachah*.[6] Similarly, it commands that we "afflict ourselves" on *Yom Kippur* (Day of Atonement), but it does not tell us what this means in practice.[7] When the Torah teaches about unclean birds, it does not provide any criteria for distinguishing the clean from unclean (as it does for mammals and for fish), but only lists examples.[8] Is this a complete list? What about birds of prey that are not listed?[9]

But lack of practical legislative detail is not the only problem. There are also numerous inconsistencies and even apparent contradictions. Numbers 18:21–32 commands that Israelites give their tithe to the Levites, who then offer a tithe of the tithe to the *Kohanim* (priests). However, Deuteronomy 12:22–29 instructs Israelites to eat their own tithe at the central sanctuary, and to give it to the poor every three years. Exodus 21:7 indicates that a female slave is not freed in her seventh year as is the male slave, whereas Deuteronomy 15:17 appears to treat the female and male slave alike.[10] Exodus 12:1–13 seems to presume that *Pesach* (Passover) will be observed in the home, whereas Deuteronomy 16:2

---

5. Fishbane, *Biblical Interpretation in Ancient Israel*, 92. Italics original.
6. Exodus 20:10; Deuteronomy 5:14. See Cardozo, *The Written and Oral Torah*, 66, and Hoenig, *The Essence of Talmudic Law and Thought*, 15.
7. Leviticus 16:31. See Cardozo, *The Written and Oral Torah*, 67.
8. Leviticus 11:13–19; Deuteronomy 14:11–18.
9. "The Sages, generalizing from this list of kosher fowl, established four criteria for a kosher fowl, including that it not be a bird of prey" (Lieber, *Etz Hayim: Torah and Commentary*, 1073).
10. Halivni, *Revelation Restored*, 24.

Messianic Judaism and Jewish Tradition in the Twenty-First Century

requires that it be observed in the central sanctuary.[11] Exodus 12:5 says that the *Pesach* offering can be a sheep or a goat, whereas Deuteronomy 16:2 permits it also to be a bull.[12]

If Jews of the Second Temple period were to keep these laws, they would need to have an interpretive tradition that would allow them to address the apparent discrepancies. We can see evidence of such a tradition in Chronicles. Exodus 12:9 indicates that the *Pesach* offering is to be roasted in fire, whereas Deuteronomy 16:7 says *"u-vi-shal-ta"* (which usually means "you shall boil"). The two passages are brought together in 2 Chronicles 35:13, which states that the *Pesach* offering is to be "cooked (*b-sh-l*) in fire." Thus, the word *b-sh-l* is understood to mean "cooked" rather than "boiled."[13]

David Weiss Halivni concludes from such tensions in the Pentateuch that an oral interpretive tradition must have existed, at least by the time when the people as a whole accepted the text in its current form as authoritative:

> Both modern and traditional scholarship have noted in their respective ways that the text of the Pentateuch contains apparent inconsistencies, gaps, and even contradictions, sometimes in the most essential matters of observance . . . The problem is not only that the laws of the festivals and Sabbaths are nowhere detailed enough that they might immediately be put into practice . . . without extensive guidance beyond the written word. Even more challenging than the frequent lack of detail is the fact that those details that are spelled out are not always congruous from one part of the Pentateuch to the other . . . *coherent observance at the time of canonization cannot have been based on the scriptures alone. Some oral guidance must have accompanied the text as soon as observance was instituted.*[14]

Michael Fishbane goes further, arguing that an oral legal tradition must have originated much earlier:

---

11. Halivni, *Revelation Restored*, 24; Fishbane, *Biblical Interpretation in Ancient Israel*, 137.

12. Halivni, *Revelation Restored*, 25–26; Fishbane, *Biblical Interpretation in Ancient Israel*, 136–37.

13. Halivni, *Revelation Restored*, 25; Fishbane, *Biblical Interpretation in Ancient Israel*, 135–36.

14. Halivni, *Revelation Restored*, 23–24; italics mine.

> There need be no reasonable doubt that the preserved written law of the Hebrew Bible is but an expression of a much more comprehensive oral law. Such an oral legal tradition would have both augmented the cases of our collections and clarified their formulations to the scope and precision necessary for viable juridical decisions. Accordingly, the biblical law collections may best be considered as prototypical compendia of legal and ethical norms rather than as comprehensive codes . . . The received legal codes are thus a literary expression of ancient Israelite legal wisdom: exemplifications of the "righteous" laws upon which the covenant was based.[15]

Neither Halivni nor Fishbane contend that this oral legal tradition was identical to what is later found in the rabbinic corpus. However, they both rightly recognize that the Written Torah not only permits supplemental instruction—it requires it.

Does the Torah establish or envision an institutional framework for providing such necessary supplemental instruction? There are good reasons for thinking that it does. In a text set at a key juncture in the narrative of Exodus—at "the mountain of God" just before the Sinai theophany—Jethro visits Moses and offers him important advice.[16] The people of Israel have been coming to Moses with their disputes, and he has been inquiring of God, deciding (*shafat*) the disputes, and making known the relevant statutes (*chukkim*) and laws (*torot*). However, this activity exhausts both Moses and the people. Therefore, Jethro recommends that Moses establish tribal judges to handle the day-to-day disputes of the people. Only the major cases, too difficult for them to decide, should be brought to Moses. Moses accepts the advice of his father-in-law, and a new institution of subordinate and higher courts is born.

The significance of this incident is underlined by the position it occupies in the Deuteronomic retelling of the Exodus-Sinai-Wilderness narrative. It is the first event reported by Moses.[17] There the subordinate leaders are called "officials (*shotrim*) for your tribes" and "magistrates" (*shoftim*).[18] The wilderness judicial system serves as key background for the section of the Deuteronomic code that establishes the fundamental

---

15. Fishbane, *Biblical Interpretation in Ancient Israel*, 95.
16. Exodus 18:5, 13–27.
17. Deuteronomy 1:9–18.
18. Deuteronomy 1:15–16.

institutions of Israel's future government.[19] This section begins with the command to appoint "magistrates (*shoftim*) and officials (*shotrim*)" in every town, who shall "judge the people with righteous judgment."[20] Thus, the local judges of the future are identified with the tribal magistrates of the desert past. Deuteronomy then proceeds to institute a central judiciary in "the place that Hashem your God will have chosen" that is to hear every case too difficult for the local courts.[21] In light of the prominent placement of Deuteronomy 1:9–18, and its verbal resemblance to Deuteronomy 16:18–20, it is evident that the central judiciary carries on Moses' function just as the local courts carry on the function of the tribal courts of the wilderness period.

The importance of this central judiciary and its role as the latter day expression of the Mosaic office becomes clearer with a careful study of the pericope. The passage begins by directing that certain types of cases should be brought from the local courts to the central court. These are cases that are "too difficult for you (*yipalay mi-mecha*)," and that involve homicide (*beyn dam le-dam*), personal injury (*nega*), or disputes over the appropriate law (*din*) to apply.[22] The meaning of this last type of case (*beyn din le-din*) will become clear in a moment. The central court shall hear the case and render a decision. The persons involved are not free to disregard this decision, but "must carefully observe all that they instruct you to do" (*ve-shamarta la'asot ke-chol asher yorucha*).[23] The words "carefully observe" (*shamarta la'asot*) appear frequently in various forms in Deuteronomy, always enjoining obedience to the words of the Torah itself. Here they enjoin obedience to the high court. The verb used to characterize the decision of the judges is also significant: *yoru* ("they will instruct") shares the same consonantal root as *Torah*. This is no accident, as becomes evident in the subsequent verse commanding the concerned parties to "act according to the word of *Torah* that they teach you (*yorucha*)."[24] As if these exhortations to obedience were not enough, the passage proceeds to urge that the parties "not turn aside from the decision that they declare to you, neither to the right nor to the left," and warns that those who arrogantly disobey the central court shall

19. Deuteronomy 16:18—18:22.
20. Deuteronomy 16:18–20.
21. Deuteronomy 17:8–13.
22. Deuteronomy 17:8.
23. Deuteronomy 17:10.
24. Deuteronomy 17:11.

be put to death, so that evil might be purged from Israel, and so that all the people might hear and fear and not act in a similar manner.[25] Once again, such warnings appear frequently in Deuteronomy, but usually as a way of urging compliance with the Torah itself (rather than with those who administer it).[26]

Thus, the judgment of the central court is described in a manner that implies a scope beyond that of merely rendering verdicts in particular cases. In addressing difficult cases they are *teaching Torah*. They are functioning in the role that Moses occupied during the wilderness wandering, and their words have an authority analogous to that of the Mosaic Torah itself. Frank Crüsemann makes this point without equivocation:

> *The conclusion we must draw from this is absolutely clear: The decisions of the court have the same significance and the same rank as the things that Moses himself said—which means Deuteronomy itself.* The Jerusalem high court rendered decisions with the authority of Moses and it had his jurisdiction. It spoke in the name of Moses and extrapolated forward the will of YHWH.
>
> The development and structure of deuteronomic law cannot be separated from the institution of the Jerusalem central court ... According to Deut 17:8f. this court speaks with the same authority as Deuteronomy itself—the authority of Moses.[27]

Perhaps Crüsemann overstates his conclusion. Nevertheless, his essential thesis remains valid. Deuteronomy establishes an institution that carries on the Mosaic role of interpreting and applying the Torah in new and unforeseen circumstances.

According to 2 Chronicles 19, such an institution actually existed in ancient Israel. This chapter describes how King Jehoshafat appointed "magistrates" (*shoftim*) in all the fortified cities of Judah, and then established a high court in Jerusalem.[28] The high court would hear cases sent to them "from your brothers living in their cities."[29] As in Deuteronomy 17:8, prominent among these would be cases of homicide (*beyn dam le-dam*). The identical wording demonstrates that the author of 2

---

25. Deuteronomy 17:11–13.
26. Deuteronomy 13:6; 17:7; 19:19; 21:21; 22:21; 24:7.
27. Crüsemann, *The Torah*, 97, 269. Italics original.
28. 2 Chronicles 19:5, 8.
29. 2 Chronicles 19:10.

Chronicles 19 sees the action of King Jehoshafat as the realization of the intent of Deuteronomy 17. In addition to difficult cases of homicide, the high court should render judgment in disputes *beyn Torah le-mitzvah le-chukim ul-mishpatim* ("between Torah and commandment, statutes and ordinances"). This phrase corresponds to *beyn din le-din* in Deuteronomy 17:8, and helps to explain that enigmatic formulation. Crüsemann interprets the expanded version of 2 Chronicles 19:10 as referring to "cases that involve a 'collision of norms' and thus automatically involve something like precedents."[30] Sometimes compliance with one law may lead one to disobey another. In such cases one encounters a "collision of norms"—and an authorized interpretive agency is required in order to clarify what is permissible and what is required. Such clarification involves more than just rendering a verdict in a particular dispute. Such precedent-setting cases also provide new instruction on how the Torah is to be lived out. Thus, the high court teaches, interprets, and establishes Torah.

The role of the central judiciary, patterned on the role of Moses during the wilderness wandering, may be illustrated by the five instances in the Torah where new laws are given in response to unforeseen legal questions posed by the people.[31] These laws are unusual in the Torah. Normally, the Torah's narrative presents legal material as rooted solely in the divine initiative. God summons Moses, and gives him laws. No human circumstances on the ground provide a context to which God responds. However, in these five instances the initiative comes from the people, and the result is not merely the resolution of particular cases but the promulgation of new legislation.[32] These five narratives thus provide the Mosaic paradigm for the interpretive work of the central court in Jerusalem.[33] The central court will not derive its rulings in oracular

---

30. Crüsemann, *The Torah*, 94.

31. Leviticus 24:10–23—blasphemy by the son of an Egyptian man and an Israelite woman; Numbers 9:6–14—Pesach Sheni; Numbers 15:32–36—gathering wood on Shabbat; Numbers 27 & 36—the daughters of Zelophehad and the inheritance rights of women.

32. See Crüsemann, *The Torah*, 100–101, and Fishbane, *Biblical Interpretation*, 99. Fishbane notes that "in all cases but that of the wood-gatherer, the oracular *responsum* is formulated in the precise casuistic style of the Pentateuchal priestly ordinances ('if a man') and presents a law *more comprehensive than* the situation called for by the original oracular situation" (103).

33. "The preceding five legal pericopae explicitly acknowledge instances when

fashion (as does Moses), and this distinction preserves the primary and unique status of the Mosaic legislation. However, apart from this fact the central court will function as did Moses, and its authority to clarify and interpret the Torah derives from Moses himself.

The relationship between the future high court and Moses may also be implicit in Numbers 11. In this chapter, as in Exodus 18 and Deuteronomy 1, Moses is burdened by his task of leading the people of Israel, and, as in those other chapters, his burden is relieved by the appointment of other leaders to assist him.[34] However, there are also differences between the Exodus/Deuteronomy helpers and those described in Numbers 11. First, the leaders of Numbers 11 are not explicitly assigned responsibility for subordinate groupings (thousands, hundreds, fifties, tens), nor is their role restricted to local judgment. Second, their number is given, and that number is "seventy." They are thus identified with the seventy elders who ascended Sinai with Moses and "saw the God of Israel."[35] In this way they are more closely associated with Moses than are the subordinate judges of Exodus 18 and Deuteronomy 1. Third, just as they ascended Sinai with Moses, so their appointment occurs at the Tent of Meeting (*ohel moed*), corresponding to the future temple in Jerusalem.[36] Fourth and finally, they receive a measure of the prophetic spirit that Moses possesses.[37] This also associates the seventy elders closely with Moses himself. Just as Elisha will receive the spirit that is upon Elijah, so the seventy receive the spirit of Moses.[38]

All of these factors indicate that the seventy elders of Numbers 11 prefigure the central court of Deuteronomy 17 and 2 Chronicles 19, rather than the subordinate courts of the cities of Judah. The connection with Elijah and Elisha offers especially strong support for this thesis. Just as Elisha received Elijah's spirit and succeeded him in his role of prophet, so the seventy elders receive Moses' spirit and prefigure the institution that will succeed Moses in his role as teacher of the Torah. When the Sanhedrin of seventy elders was established in post-exilic Jerusalem as

---

the covenantal law required supplementary clarifications or amendments" (Fishbane, *Biblical Interpretation*, 106).

34. Numbers 11:11–15, 16–17, 24–25.
35. Exodus 24:9–11.
36. Numbers 11:16, 24.
37. Numbers 11:17, 25–30.
38. 2 Kings 2:9–10, 15.

the high court of the Jewish people, it was claiming to be the divinely sanctioned successor to Moses, extending the Mosaic office of interpreting and applying the Torah just as the seventy elders did in Numbers 11, and just as Jehoshapat's high court did in 2 Chronicles 19.

Numbers 11 also points to the basis of authority for the Jerusalem high court. The seventy are empowered by God to act in the role of Moses, but before their official appointment and empowerment they were already "elders (*z'kenim*) and officials (*shotrim*) of the people."[39] As we have seen, a group of seventy elders represented the people earlier at Sinai.[40] Thus, in a sense, authority is vested in the people of Israel as a whole. This view draws further support from the Deuteronomic instructions regarding Israel's governmental institutions.[41] Deuteronomy 16:18 begins this section with the foundational law of government: "You shall appoint magistrates (*shoftim*) and officials (*shotrim*)." Who is the singular "you" of this verse? It evidently stands for the hearers of Deuteronomy— the people as a whole. Similarly, the hearers of Deuteronomy are also told that they are permitted to have a king, if they so decide (17:14–15). That king must fit certain criteria (including a conviction among the people that God himself has chosen the man), but it is the people themselves who decide whether to have a king and who that king should be.[42]

The authority vested in the people of Israel as a whole to act as Moses' successor can also be seen in the book of Esther. After the Jewish people escape the destruction plotted by Haman, Mordechai and Esther urge them to celebrate an annual feast (*Purim*) to commemorate the event. The book—which never mentions the name of God—then describes the people's response: "The Jews established (*kiyyemu*) and accepted as a custom (*kibbelu*) for themselves and their descendants and all who joined them, that without fail they would continue to observe these two days every year, as it was written and at the time appointed."[43]

One talmudic interpretation of *kiyyemu ve-kibbelu* understands it to mean, "they [i.e., the heavenly court] upheld above what they [i.e., the Jewish people] had accepted below."[44] Or, in David Novak's paraphrase,

---

39. Numbers 11:16, 24.
40. Exodus 24:9–11.
41. Deuteronomy 16:18—18:22.
42. Crüsemann, *The Torah*, 238, 247.
43. Esther 9:27.
44. B. Megillah 7a.

"God confirmed what the Jewish authorities on earth had themselves decreed for the people."[45] This is probably not so far removed from the intent of the author. Just as the book of Esther depicts the providential power of God at work in the world through human action, without ever mentioning the divine Name, so it presents a divinely ordained institution established apparently by human authority. And that authority is not merely invested in the leaders, as Novak's paraphrase might suggest. Instead, it is the people as a whole who "established and accepted as a custom for themselves and their descendants and all who joined them" the celebration of *Purim*. And, by incorporating the book of Esther into the biblical canon, the Jewish people made clear their determination that in fact God had confirmed in heaven what the Jewish people had decreed and accepted on earth.

We thus may conclude that (1) because of its lack of legal detail and its abundance of apparent legal inconsistency, the Torah requires supplemental legal instruction; (2) the Torah itself recognizes this fact, and envisions a Mosaic teaching office whose role is to interpret and apply the Torah's regulations to new circumstances; and (3) this Mosaic teaching office, while having its ultimate authority from God, receives its immediate sanction from the affirmation of the Jewish people as a whole. While the Torah itself nowhere uses the term, there is no reason why the tradition of supplemental instruction in the Mosaic succession should not be called "Oral Torah." It is thereby both distinguished from the Written Torah, and identified with it—just as the high court of Deuteronomy 17 and the seventy elders of Numbers 11 are both distinguished from Moses and identified with him.

ORAL TORAH IN RABBINIC TRADITION

We have seen that it is possible to find in the Written Torah a justification for a certain kind of Oral Torah. How does this biblically-rooted doctrine compare with the traditional rabbinic understanding? What, in fact, is the rabbinic doctrine of the Oral Torah?

The naïve version of the doctrine has little grounding in the tradition itself. According to this way of construing the Oral Torah, God gave to Moses on Sinai two separate and complementary Torahs—one to be conveyed in written form, the other to be transmitted orally. The Written

---

45. Novak, *The Election of Israel*, 169–70.

Torah is the Pentateuch; the Oral Torah was passed on by word of mouth from one generation to the next, and was ultimately written down in the Talmud. Thus, the Talmud, like the Pentateuch, consists of words of God spoken to Moses on Sinai. The only differences between the Pentateuch and the Talmud are that the latter contains additional explanatory material required for understanding and keeping the former, and that the two were transmitted through different media.

While the Talmud does refer to a few non-Pentateuchal rules as *halakhot le-Moshe mi-Sinai* (oral laws of Moses received on Sinai), this term is never applied to the Mishnah as a whole or to the legal decisions of the Talmud in general. Anyone who has ever read the Talmud recognizes the absurdity of the notion that in its totality it embodies the words of God to Moses on Sinai. The Talmud consists primarily of rabbinic discussions and arguments. Did God argue with himself on Sinai, and then assign various sides of his inner debate to future rabbis, who were not truly arguing but merely acting out an oral script passed down from the time of Moses? We may safely reject such a doctrine as ridiculous. However, when we do so, we are not rejecting the rabbinic understanding of the Oral Torah.

A second way of construing the rabbinic doctrine of the Oral Torah has firmer grounds in the tradition. According to this view, not only the Pentateuch, but also the words of all the prophets and sages were revealed to Moses on Sinai. However, they were not then transmitted orally by Moses to the future generations of prophets and sages, but were received by the prophets through fresh inspiration, and developed by the sages as their own creative interpretation. This view is put forward by a contemporary Orthodox scholar: "Were the visions of the prophets and the praises of the psalmists really no more than a reiteration of what had already been said? Are the thousands of pages of Talmudic discussions only a re-recording of what God taught Moshe? In *Tiferet Israel*, Maharal (R. Judah Loew b. Bezalel, 1525–1609) explains that though the entire Torah—from the Chumash to the debates in the Talmud—was taught to Moshe, God concealed many parts of it from the nation as a whole. Each generation was allowed to reproduce the exegesis so as to strengthen its bond with the Torah."[46] Thus, the Oral Torah was both given to Moses on Sinai and discovered anew in every generation. It is both entirely divine,

---

46. Cardozo, *The Written and Oral Torah*, 8–9.

and at the same time something that requires active human participation (beyond merely repeating what has been heard).

While such a view of the Oral Torah can be found in the Talmud, it is not the dominant perspective. David Weiss Halivni argues that the doctrine of the Oral Torah "is hardly mentioned at all in Tannaitic litertaure."[47] Halivni contends that it likewise exercised little influence among the Babylonian *amoraim*, but that it first gained prominence among the *amoraim* of the land of Israel. Even when the notion of *halakhot le-Moshe mi-Sinai* was introduced in the Talmud, it was not always understood to imply that the *halakhah* in question had literally been taught to Moses. This is evident in the famous story of how Moses is transported to the future in order to hear Rabbi Akiba's exposition of the Torah, and is unable to comprehend a single word of Akiba's teaching.[48] Nevertheless, Moses is comforted (and we are entertained) when, in response to the question, "Master, how do you know this?" Rabbi Akiba answers, "It is a *halakhah le-Moshe mi-Sinai*." Here it is evident that Akiba's teaching is based on creative exegesis of the Written Torah, rather than on a *halakhic* tradition received from previous generations, and that the claim to Mosaic authority did not necessarily entail a literal assertion of Mosaic foreknowledge.

However, matters changed in the post-talmudic period. The view that the entire tradition had been revealed to Moses at Sinai attained general acceptance. Halivni regrets this development, and sees it as a reflection of a medieval "obsession with divine perfection": "The religious sensibilities of the Middle Ages required a belief in eternal and unchanging laws, not tainted by the human involvement that inheres in exegesis . . . The very notion that human beings had been required to mine and quarry for God's law . . . became religiously intolerable. Religiosity, in the Middle Ages, was an obsession with divine perfection . . . the notion of a Torah requiring human involvement was precluded on principle alone."[49] Though the medieval doctrine goes beyond the general talmudic sobriety over the nature of rabbinic authority, it should still be distinguished from the naïve fantasy of a tradition mechanically transmitted by rote repetition from Moses to the present day.

---

47. Halivni, *Revelation Restored*, 54.
48. B. Menahot 29b.
49. Halivni, *Revelation Restored*, 78.

The dominant view in the Talmud is quite different from both of these versions of the Oral Torah. The sages think less in terms of two Torahs given to Moses at Sinai, and more in terms of two types of law—which they call *d'oraita* (Written Torah law) and *d'rabbanan* (oral rabbinic law). The latter is also divinely authorized, so that rabbinic commandments can be treated as commandments of God. Why is this the case? Not because the rabbis are simply repeating laws received through a chain of tradents, but because the Written Torah in Deuteronomy 17 gives them the authority to act on behalf of God. This is clearly stated in the midst of a discussion concerning the lighting of *Chanukkah* candles—a custom commemorating a victory that occurred more than a thousand years after the giving of the Torah at Sinai: "What blessing is recited? 'Who sanctified us by His *mitzvot* and commanded us to kindle the light of Chanukkah.' And where [in the Torah] did He so command us? Rav Avi'a said: [It follows] from, 'You shall not turn aside [from the ruling that they declare to you, to the right or to the left]' (Deuteronomy 17:11)."[50] Thus, the fundamental talmudic claim for the authority of its teaching is not based on a myth of origins but on a text in the Pentateuch that, as we have already seen, had as its purpose the sanctioning of an ongoing Mosaic office of interpretation and application of the Torah.

However, some contend that the sages saw their own authority as far greater than any reading of Deuteronomy 17 would allow. Daniel Gruber has argued that the *tannaim* and *amoraim* explicitly placed their own authority over that of Scripture, so that their decrees took precedence over those of the Written Torah.[51] Lawrence Schiffman is more cautious, recognizing that the *tannaim* prohibited the writing down of their teaching "in order to highlight the greater authority of the written word."[52] But Schiffman then states that "by the amoraic period, the rabbis were openly asserting the superiority of the oral law," and that "when the amoraic commentary in the form of the Talmuds became available, this material became the new scripture of Judaism . . . Scripture had been displaced by Talmud."[53]

It must be acknowledged that certain *amoraic* sayings could be read in a way that supports Schiffman's thesis. It should be further acknowledged that post-talmudic Judaism often did give primacy to the Talmud,

50. B. Shabbat 23a.
51. Gruber, *Rabbi Akiba's Messiah*, 80–84.
52. Schiffman, *From Text to Tradition*, 266.
53. Ibid., 287.

functionally if not theoretically. However, a careful study of the talmudic approach to the Written Torah and rabbinic law does not sustain Gruber's claims, nor even the more moderate views of Schiffman. The Talmud consistently distinguishes between obligations that are *d'oraita* and those that are *d'rabbanan*, and treats the former as taking precedence over the latter. As Halivni notes, "There are differences with respect to severity of observance between a law which is biblically commanded and a law which is rabbinically ordained."[54] Thus, a *kal va-chomer* (from the greater to the lesser) argument is employed to demonstrate that one may interrupt one's recitation of the *Hallel* (Psalms 113-118) in order to greet someone in authority—for if one may interrupt one's recital of the Shema, which is *d'oraita*, one may surely interrupt the *Hallel*, which is merely *d'rabbanan*.[55] It is likewise decreed that in order to show respect for those in authority it is generally permitted to set aside rabbinic decrees—but not commandments that are *d'oraita*.[56] These are not exceptions to the talmudic approach, but typical.[57]

This talmudic principle of subordinating rabbinic law to biblical law is pointed out by David Novak, who sees it as fundamental to Judaism:

> And by reading *davar* in Deuteronomy 17:11 as a general term rather than a specific term, one is mandated by the Torah not only to heed rabbinic adjudication of individual cases, but to heed rabbinic legislation in general [b. Berachot 19b] . . . The only proviso is that the formal distinction between Scriptural law (*d'oraita*) and rabbinic law (*de-rabbanan*) be kept in view, and that the normative priority of Scriptural law over rabbinic law be consistently maintained [b. Betsah 3b].
>
> Of course, this power given to the Rabbis is not unqualified. First and foremost, it must function for the sake of the covenant. Their law stems from a covenant made between the people and their leaders before God. This means that rabbinic law is designed either to protect specific Scriptural laws that comprise the basic substance of the covenant [*gezerot*] or to enhance the covenant by the inclusion of new celebrations in it [*taqqanot*].[58]

---

54. Halivni, *Peshat and Derash*, 14.

55. B. Berachot 14a.

56. B. Berachot 19b.

57. See b. Berachot 15a, 16b, 20b, 21a; b. Nidah 4b; b. Sukkah 44a; b. Bava Kama 114b. See also Rashi's commentary on b. Berachot 17b and 20b.

58. Novak, *The Election of Israel*, 172-73.

Michael Wyschogrod likewise underlines the importance of this principle: "The Oral Torah is dependent on and is inconceivable without the Written Torah. It is the Written Torah that is the primary document of revelation. Only in the case of the Written Torah is there an authorized text, which, when written as specified, brings into being a physical object—the Torah scroll—that is holy."[59] Thus, the view that the sages placed their authority over that of the Written Torah should be discarded.

But what about those instances where the rabbis devised a way around biblical law, such as Hillel's prosbul, or those cases where a sage claims the authority to "uproot" a biblical commandment? As it turns out, such cases do not involve an arbitrary assertion of power over the Torah, but instead address situations where there is a "collision" of biblical norms, as enunciated in Deuteronomy 17:8 (*beyn din le-din*) and 2 Chronicles 19:10 (*beyn Torah le-mitzvah le-chukim ul-mishpatim*). Thus, Eliezer Berkovits shows how the Talmud deals with what was considered a biblical law stipulating a husband's right to invalidate a divorce document (*get*), when rigid adherence to that law damaged a fellow human being: "However, if we look at it carefully, we shall find that the legal philosophy behind the principle may reveal that the word 'uprooting' is not to be taken too literally . . . One is not really 'uprooting' a law of the Torah but is limiting its application with the authority of the Torah itself. The more comprehensive biblical command—in this case we refer to 'thou shalt love thy neighbor as thyself'—teaches how and when to use the specific law regarding the husband's right to invalidate a *get*."[60] This approach to the Torah resembles that of Yeshua, who used the love-commandment to shed light on Sabbath and purity laws. As Berkovits notes, such resolution of conflicts among biblical norms does not really involve an "uprooting" of a biblical command. "Our discussion brings to mind a saying of Resh Lakish: 'At times, the abolition of the Torah is its founding.'"[61]

In what sense, then, are the rabbinic decisions, authorized by the Written Torah in Deuteronomy 17, themselves based on oral instruction given to Moses at Sinai? According to the fifteenth-century scholar Joseph Albo, only a very general connection exists between the two: "Therefore Moses was given orally certain general principles, only briefly alluded to in the Torah, by means of which the Sages may work out the

59. Wyschogrod, *The Body of Faith*, xxxii.
60. Berkovits, *Not in Heaven*, 77.
61. Ibid., 69.

newly emerging particulars in every generation."[62] Many modern Jewish theologians pass over even such a minimal link, and stress instead the practical, concrete, and contingent quality of the Oral Torah. The Written Torah stands as an unchanging norm, but the Oral Torah is dynamic, flexible, reflecting the infinite diversity of circumstances that face the Jewish people in the course of their journey through history. According to Eliezer Berkovits (as already quoted above), this is the heart of the Oral Torah's job description.[63]

In fact, both Berkovits and Wyschogrod stress the essential *oral* dimension of the Oral Torah. Berkovits mourns over the fact that the Oral Torah was ever consigned to written form, calling this development "the exile of the *Torah she'baal Peh* into literature." "The main body of the Oral Torah, which was never meant to become a text, had thus been transformed into another kind of *Torah she'be'Ketav*. This result was not due to developments from within the oral tradition, but—contrary to its essential nature—was forced upon it by the power of the extrinsic circumstances of an inimical reality."[64] The appearance of the Oral Torah in written form could easily lead to a misunderstanding of its essential nature as the flexible, contingent application of the Written Torah to new situations. Wyschogrod goes so far as to describe the Oral Torah as the Torah's power to enter into Jewish life and shape it from the inside—so that Israel becomes "the incarnation of the Torah":

> In spite of the writing down of the oral law, it would be a grave mistake to erase the distinction between the written and oral law. Theologically speaking, the oral law can never be written down. The oral law is that part of the law carried in the Jewish people. The law does not only remain a normative domain that hovers over the people of Israel and judges this people. It does that, too, of course. But the Torah enters the being of the people of Israel. It is absorbed into their existence and they therefore become the carriers or the incarnation of the Torah. The oral law reflects this fact.[65]

---

62. Cited in Zemer, *Evolving Halakhah*, 43.

63. "How to face the confrontation between the text and the actual life situation, how to resolve the problems arising of this confrontation, is the task of the *Torah she'baal'Peh*, the Oral Law" (Berkovits, *Not in Heaven*, 1).

64. Ibid., 88.

65. Wyschogrod, *The Body of Faith*, 210.

Such a description of the Oral Torah approximates what we as Messianic Jews might say of the *Ruach Hakodesh* (Holy Spirit), the aspect of the Torah that acts upon the people of God from the inside out.

This view of the Oral Torah does not see it as a solidified code, given once for all to Moses on Sinai, and differing from the Written Torah only in its mode of transmission.[66] Instead, it sees the Oral Torah as the divinely guided process by which the Jewish people seeks to make the Written Torah a living reality, in continuity with the accumulated wisdom of generations past and in creative encounter with the challenges and opportunities of the present. It thus presumes that the covenantal promises of Sinai—both God's promise to Israel and Israel's promise in return—remain eternally valid, and that the God of the covenant will ever protect that covenant by guiding his people in its historical journey through the wilderness.

Thinkers who adopt such a perspective on the Oral Torah often emphasize the traditional role played by the Jewish people as a whole in the *halakhic* process. Thus, David Novak argues that the Jewish people have a more active part to play in the development of Oral Torah ("rabbinic law") than in the development of the Written Torah ("Scriptural law"):

> Finally, there is the factor of popular consent. In the area of Scriptural law, this factor does not seem to be at work. Although it is assumed that the law of God is for the good of man, nevertheless, its authority is assumed whether one sees the good the law is intending or not ... With rabbinic law, on the other hand, popular consent is indeed a major factor *ab initio*. Thus the Talmud assumes that 'a decree (*gezerah*) cannot be decreed unless it is obvious that the majority of the community will abide by it' (b. Avodah Zarah 36a). In other words, not only the Rabbis but the ordinary people too have more power in the area of man-made law than they do in the area of God-made law. Nevertheless, the fact that this power is not construed to be for the sake of autonomy *from* the covenant but to be more like autonomy *for* the covenant enables one to look to the Jewish people themselves as a source of revelation ... In cases of doubt about what the actual law is, where there are good theoretical arguments by Rabbis on

---

66. For those who see the writing down of the Oral Torah as a necessary evil that threatens the very nature of Oral Torah, the codification of the Oral Torah is seen as posing an even greater danger: "The very idea of codification violates the essence of the *Torah she'baal'Peh*" (Berkovits, *Not in Heaven*, 88–89). See also Dorff in Leiber (editor), *Etz Hayim*, 1474–75.

both sides of the issue, one is to "go out and look at what the people are doing" [b. Berachot 45a].[67]

This brings us back to what we saw earlier in the book of Deuteronomy. Biblical law is rooted in divine revelation, but it must be administered, interpreted, and applied by human authorities, and those authorities gain their legitimacy through being chosen by the covenant people. Thus, once again, we find that the view of the Oral Torah seen in at least one important strand of rabbinic tradition has much in common with the basic premises inherent in the Written Torah.

Just as Scripture has more to say than we might expect in support of an ongoing *halakhic* process and its necessary institutional form, so we also find that Jewish tradition has a more nuanced view of the Oral Torah and its relationship to the Written Torah than is commonly represented in the Messianic Jewish movement. It remains for us to examine the Apostolic Writings, to see if they can possibly be read in a way that permits us as Messianic Jews to adopt some version of the traditional doctrine of the Oral Torah as our own.

ORAL TORAH IN THE APOSTOLIC WRITINGS

It is generally recognized that rabbinic Judaism after 70 C.E. owes a great deal to the Pharisaic movement of the Second Temple period. Therefore, if we are to draw any conclusions from the Apostolic Writings in regards to what will become rabbinic tradition, we must pay close attention to the way those writings treat the Pharisees and their teaching.

The authors of the *Besorot* (Gospels), like Josephus, note that the Pharisees possessed a distinctive *halakhic* tradition (*paradosis*): "For the present I wish merely to explain that the Pharisees had passed on to the people certain regulations handed down by former generations and not recorded in the Laws of Moses, for which reason they are rejected by the Sadducaean group, who hold that only those regulations should be considered valid which were written down (in Scripture), and that those which had been handed down by former generations need not be observed."[68] It is important to note that neither Josephus nor the *Besorot* imply that the Pharisees saw their traditions as Mosaic in origin. Instead, they are "the tradition of the elders."[69] The mature doctrine of the Oral

---

67. Novak, *The Election of Israel*, 174–75.
68. Josephus, *Jewish Antiquities*, 13:297.
69. Matthew 15:2. See also Galatians 1:14.

Torah emerges much later in Jewish history. Nevertheless, the Pharisaic traditions lay the groundwork for the later rabbinic emphasis on the oral transmission of *halakhic* precedent.

What is the attitude of the Apostolic Writings in regards to the Pharisaic *paradosis*? We should begin with the discussion between Yeshua and the Pharisees on the topic of hand washing.[70] The practice of washing hands before eating became a standard practice in rabbinic Judaism, and is treated in Mark 7 and Matthew 15 as a characteristic Pharisaic custom.[71] According to Mark, it was observed also outside Pharisaic circles, but most scholars consider Mark's comment that it was done by "all the Jews" as a simplified generalization for the sake of his non-Jewish readers, and not to be taken literally. Matthew 15 and Mark 7 describe how a group of Pharisees criticizes some of Yeshua's disciples because they do not wash their hands before eating. Before proceeding further, three observations are noteworthy. First, these Pharisees do not criticize Yeshua himself. Why do they criticize the students and not the teacher? Perhaps they seek to show him respect as an esteemed holy man, miracle worker, and sage, and thus they criticize his personal practice indirectly rather than directly. More likely, in this instance the author wants us to assume that Yeshua did wash his hands, but some of his followers did not. This would mean that Yeshua honors this particular tradition, but does not see it as mandatory.[72] Second, the criticism is leveled only at "*some* of his students" (Mark 7:2). This seems to imply that the offending behavior was not universal even among his followers. Third, why find fault with Yeshua in regard to a custom that was distinctively Pharisaic, and not universally accepted and practiced by his Jewish contemporaries?[73] The most reasonable explanation would be that Yeshua's message and way of life led these Pharisees to consider him as one of their own; only so would the failure of his students to conform to normal Pharisaic custom in this matter of hand washing evoke surprise and rebuke. One cannot imagine

---

70. Matthew 15:1–20; Mark 7:1–23.

71. Many scholars argue that hand washing was not even universal among Pharisees. See Sanders, *Jewish Law from Jesus to the Mishnah*, 39–40, 228–31, and Harrington, *The Gospel of Matthew*, 232.

72. Luke 11:38 speaks of Yeshua's not "washing" before eating. This is usually understood to refer to the washing of hands. However, the verb is *baptizo* (immerse), and the text may actually be speaking about a full body immersion. See Mason, "Chief Priests, Sadducees, Pharisees and Sanhedrin in Acts," 137.

73. This question would not arise for the Gentile reader of Mark; but it would arise for the educated first-century Jewish reader of Matthew.

a Pharisee saying to a Sadducean teacher, "Why do your students not observe the tradition of the elders?"

Yeshua's response to the question demonstrates the two features of the Pharisaic tradition that he considers potentially problematic. First, Yeshua sees the Pharisaic preoccupation with the fine detail of ritual practice as at times obscuring the Torah's central concern for love and righteousness in human relationships. Thus, he both cites a case in which a man devotes property to sacred use and thereby evades or neglects his obligation to care for his parents, and also states the general principle that true defilement comes from what exits the mouth, not what enters it. This prophetic emphasis pervades Yeshua's teaching on observance of the Torah, and is summed up effectively by the verse he quotes from Hosea, "I desire mercy and not sacrifice" (meaning, for both Hosea and Yeshua, "Mercy is more important than sacrifice").[74] Second, Yeshua sees the Pharisaic preoccupation with "the tradition of the elders" as at times obscuring the primary authority of the biblical text. "Why do you transgress the commandment of God for the sake of your tradition?" Whatever value "the tradition of the elders" may have, it must always be ordered properly in relation to the biblical commands. The tradition must serve those commands, rather than undermine or replace them.

These concerns attributed to Yeshua by Mark and Matthew do not necessarily constitute a frontal assault on the Pharisaic tradition as a whole. They can be construed as prophetic correctives, issued by one who shares many of the same commitments and convictions as those being admonished. The rabbinic tradition that emerges in the post-70 period demonstrates some of the same concerns, even if it also at times succumbs to the excesses of which Yeshua warned.

The attitude of Yeshua towards Pharisaic tradition, according to the synoptic *Besorot*, is clarified greatly by Matthew 23:23–24 (Luke 11:42): "Woe to you, Pharisaic scribes, hypocrites! For you tithe mint and dill and cummin, and have neglected the weightier matters of the Torah, justice and mercy and faithfulness; these you ought to have done, without neglecting the others. You blind guides, straining out a gnat and swallowing a camel!" Once again, we see Yeshua's prophetic emphasis on love and righteousness in human relationships ("justice and mercy and faithfulness") as the central thrust of the Torah, over against fine details of ritual observance (in this case, tithing). Yet, what often goes unnoticed is his un-

---

74. Hosea 6:6; Matthew 9:13; 12:7.

equivocal affirmation of even these fine details ("these you ought to have done, without neglecting the others").⁷⁵ In other words, Yeshua provides guidance in dealing with situations in which norms collide, as alluded to in Deuteronomy 17 and similarly addressed in later rabbinic *halakhah*. He does not show contempt for detailed ritual norms, but he does subordinate them to what he considers "weightier matters of the Torah."

Even less often noticed is the fact that the ritual norms that Yeshua upholds in this text are not found in the Written Torah, but instead derive from *Pharisaic tradition*!⁷⁶ The tithing of small herbs such as mint, dill, and cummin was a Pharisaic extension of the Written Torah. Yet, according to Matthew, Yeshua not only urges compliance with this practice—he treats it as *a matter of the Torah* (though of lesser weight than the injunctions to love, justice, and faithfulness). This supports our earlier inference that Yeshua's teaching and practice encourage the Pharisees to think of him as one of their own. His criticism of the Pharisees (or, to be more precise, of some of the Pharisees) is a prophetic critique offered by one whose commitments and convictions position him as an insider rather than an outsider.

This perspective is reinforced by the verses that follow: "Woe to you, Pharisaic scribes, hypocrites! For you purify the outside of the cup and of the plate, but inside are full of extortion and rapacity. You blind Pharisees! First purify the inside of the cup and of the plate, that the outside also may be clean."⁷⁷ According to some scholars, Yeshua's prophetic critique here demonstrates a knowledge of inner Pharisaic disputes between the Shammaites and Hillelites over the purity status of the outside and inside of vessels, and also reveals an affinity for the Hillelite position.⁷⁸ Most likely the Shammaite party was dominant among the Pharisees of Yeshua's time, though the Hillelite party gained the upper hand in the post-70 period in which the rabbinic movement was born.⁷⁹ Thus, it is possible that Yeshua's criticism was especially focused on the leading wing of the Pharisaic movement, and should not be universal-

---

75. A scholar who does note this affirmation of the "less weighty" commandments is Sim, *The Gospel of Matthew and Christian Judaism*, 131–32.

76. See Davies and Allison, *The Gospel According to Saint Matthew, vol. 3*, 295.

77. Matthew 23:25–26.

78. Saldarini, *Matthew's Christian-Jewish Community*, 139–40.

79. Moore, *Judaism, vol. 1*, 81; Saldarini, *Pharisees, Scribes and Sadducees in Palestinian Society*, 205.

ized to the Pharisees as a whole (though we need not go so far as Harvey Falk in claiming that Yeshua was a Hillelite Pharisee himself).[80]

It thus appears that according to the *Besorot*, Yeshua's attitude toward the Pharisaic tradition is more complex than an initial reading of Mark 7 and Matthew 15 might suggest. He had his concerns about some of the tendencies he saw among the Pharisees, but he did not reject their tradition in itself as much as he rejected a particular way in which their tradition was being interpreted and applied. We must be even more careful when attempting to assess the implications of Yeshua's perspective on Pharisaic tradition for our evaluation of later *rabbinic* tradition. As already noted, Yeshua was probably responding to a Shammaite dominated movement, whereas the Hillelites shaped rabbinic Judaism. Still more important is the fact that the Pharisaic *paradosis* represented only one stream of Jewish interpretive tradition in Yeshua's day. It was very influential, and it was in all likelihood the stream with which Yeshua most identified. However, it was not acknowledged as authoritative by the Jewish people as a whole. In keeping with the later rabbinic valuation of the authority of universal Jewish opinion and practice, Yeshua seems to have embraced post-biblical traditions without qualification when those traditions were undisputed. Thus, he customarily attended synagogue for the Shabbat service, used reverent circumlocutions to speak of the action of God, and (according to John) portrayed his own identity in terms drawn from the water and light ceremonies of *Sukkot*.[81] Therefore, we cannot presume that Yeshua would treat the later rabbinic tradition (which was acknowledged as authoritative by the Jewish people as a whole) in exactly the same way as he treated the Pharisaic tradition, even though the one grew out of the other.

To this point we have been looking at Yeshua's view of Pharisaic tradition. But another question must also be raised that is just as significant for our purposes: according to Yeshua, who now had authority to interpret the Torah's provisions for Israel's national life? Yeshua could have been positively disposed to the Pharisaic *halakhic* tradition in part or as a whole, and still have determined that the Pharisaic opposition to his mission and message meant that they had no continuing legitimacy

---

80. See Falk, *Jesus the Pharisee*.

81. Luke 4:16; John 7:37–39, 8:12. On Yeshua's use of circumlocutions, see Jeremias, *New Testament Theology*, 9–14.

as *halakhic* authorities. What does Yeshua's teaching state or imply about the ongoing *halakhic* institutions of Jewish life?

To answer this question, we will begin by examining Yeshua's parable of the vineyard.[82] In all three synoptics, this parable follows Yeshua's prophetic action of ejecting merchants from the temple and confrontation in the temple with the "chief priests, scribes, and elders" over the question of authority.[83] This latter group represents the Jerusalem Sanhedrin, the official council governing the temple and Jerusalem under Roman oversight. As is clear from the book of Acts, the high priest and his Sadducean allies controlled the Sanhedrin.[84] There were prominent Pharisees (such as Gamaliel) on the council, but they were a minority and often a dissenting voice.[85] In all of the accounts of Yeshua's arrest and execution, and of the Jerusalem persecution of his followers, it is the Sanhedrin that bears responsibility for the actions.

The parable of the vineyard functions as a prophetic rebuke of the temple authorities, who are the wicked tenants of whom Yeshua speaks.[86] They have persecuted the prophets, and now they are about to arrest the Messiah and send him to his death. Therefore, God—the owner of the vineyard (which symbolizes at the same time the temple, the city of Jerusalem, the land of Israel, and their inhabitants)—will punish those tenants and give the vineyard to others. This is a prophetic announcement of the coming judgment on the temple, the city, and the land that will be realized four decades later. In Mark and Luke, one would presume that the "others" to whom the vineyard will be given are the Romans, who will execute the divine anger by overthrowing the city. However, in Matthew's

---

82. Mark 12:1–12; Luke 20:9–19; Matthew 21:33–46.

83. Yeshua's prophetic action in the temple: Mark 11:15–19; Luke 19:45–48; Matthew 21:10–17. Confrontation with the temple authorities: Mark 11:27–33; Luke 20:1–8; Matthew 21:23–27.

84. Acts 4:1–6; 5:17–18, 21, 27–28.

85. On Gamaliel, see Acts 5:33–39. Pharisees again exercise a restraining influence in the Sanhedrin in Acts 23:6–10. In describing Yeshua's conflict with the Jerusalem authorities, only Matthew (among the synoptics) depicts the Sanhedrin as "chief priests and Pharisees" (Matthew 21:45). His highlighting of the role of Pharisees on the council reflects his general polemic against the Pharisees. We will speak of this later.

86. Yeshua's parable is an expanded and modified version of Isaiah's "Song of the Vineyard" (Isaiah 5:1–7). Davies and Allison (*The Gospel According to St. Matthew*, 3:180) cite early parallels from Jewish literature showing a similar application of Isaiah 5 to the Jerusalem temple.

version the "others" are understood to be a newly constituted Sanhedrin, which will give the owner of the vineyard "the fruits in their seasons."[87]

We may conclude that Yeshua does pronounce judgment on the priestly Sanhedrin of his day. They have forfeited their legitimate right to govern, and their authority will be taken from them. However, this does not say anything about the Pharisees as a distinct organized movement. In fact, an adherent of rabbinic Judaism today might agree with the parable—even in its Matthean form. Where he or she would differ from Matthew's ecclesiastical interpreters (and probably Matthew himself) would be in proceeding to assert that the "others" to whom the vineyard is given are the sages of the rabbinic movement!

Matthew's own approach to this question of legitimate authority—especially in the *halakhic* sphere—is complex. On the one hand, Matthew provides us with two accounts in which Yeshua gives his students the authority to "bind and loose."[88] In accord with later rabbinic usage, these terms probably refer to the authority to render *halakhic* decisions.[89] Thus, it is reasonable to conclude that Matthew sees the leaders of the messianic community as the newly constituted Sanhedrin that replaces the wicked tenants.

On the other hand, we must deal with Matthew 23:1-3: "Then Yeshua said to the crowds and to his students: 'The Pharisaic scribes sit on Moses' seat; so carefully observe (*poiesate kai tereite*) all that they say to you (*panta hosa ean eiposin humin*).'" Samuel Lachs is one of the few exegetes who has recognized the biblical allusion that is central to the meaning and importance of this text: "This is based on Deut. 17:10, which is the biblical basis for rabbinic authority replacing that of the priests."[90] Whatever synagogue architecture was like in Yeshua's day, the "seat of Moses" in this verse refers primarily to the correspondence be-

---

87. Matthew 21:41, 43. Matthew 21:43 states that "the Kingdom of God will be taken away from you and given to an *ethnos* producing the fruits of it." This use of *ethnos* (usually translated "nation") has commonly been understood in a supersessionist manner as referring to a "New Israel." However, Saldarini (*Matthew*, 59-61) has argued persuasively that "the ordinary meaning of *ethnos* that fits Matthew's usage is of a voluntary organization or small social group . . . The vineyard, Israel, remains the same; subgroups within Israel are blamed or praised. The *ethnos* thus is a group of leaders, with their devoted followers, that can lead Israel well."

88. Matthew 16:19; 18:18.

89. Davies and Allison, *The Gospel according to Saint Matthew*, 2:787; Sim, *The Gospel of Matthew and Christian Judaism*, 197; Saldarini, *Matthew*, 119.

90. Lachs, *A Rabbinic Commentary on the New Testament*, 366.

tween the high court of Deuteronomy 17 and the role of Moses during Israel's time in the wilderness.[91] Thus, Yeshua is stating that the Pharisaic teachers occupy the position of the judges in Deuteronomy 17—they are the legitimate heirs of Moses, and have authority to interpret and apply the Torah for their generation as Moses did in his. This way of reading Matthew 23:1–3 is confirmed by what Yeshua says about how their words are to be received: "carefully observe all that they say to you." This is a paraphrase of Deuteronomy 17:10: "carefully observe all that they instruct you to do" (*ve-shamarta la'asot ke-chol asher yorucha*).

This text is crucial for our purpose. Yeshua here employs the same verse to justify the *halakhic* legitimacy of the Pharisaic teachers as is later used in rabbinic tradition to justify the *halakhic* legitimacy of the rabbis. As we have seen, such a reading of Deuteronomy 17:10 suits well its original function within the Pentateuch. Though Matthew 23 proceeds to castigate those very same Pharisees for their unworthy conduct, this fact only throws the initial verses into bolder relief. In effect, the Pharisaic teachers have authority to bind and loose—even as the students of Yeshua have authority to bind and loose. The book of Matthew does not tell us how these two authorities coexist or interrelate.

This picture of Pharisaic leadership as possessing some kind of divine sanction finds further support in the Lukan writings (Luke and Acts). Luke's *Besorah* depicts the Pharisees in a more careful and moderate manner than does Matthew. Thus, many Pharisees invite Yeshua to their homes—even though he regularly uses such occasions to admonish them.[92] Some Pharisees warn Yeshua that Herod Antipas wants to arrest him and have him executed; thus, they evidently seek to protect him from harm.[93] Yeshua tells some Pharisees that "the reign of God is among you"—and this may imply that God is especially among them *because*

---

91. "We must remember here to see the people's representatives and especially the elders as we find them in the exilic/postexilic variants of the story from Ex 18 in Deut 1 and Num 11 as functioning in the line of Moses, as established and imbued with his spirit. The pronouncement and interpretation (or application) of law made by them is thus a part of a comprehensively interpreted Mosaic office. *When, in Matt 23:2, the Pharisees and the Scribes sit on the seat of Moses, this goes far beyond the question of the existence of a seat of Moses in the synagogue—an actual piece of furniture—and it refers to the same phenomenon*" (Crüsemann, *The Torah*, 103; italics mine).

92. Luke 7:36–50; 11:37–52; 14:1–24. "Jesus will criticise the Pharisees at every opportunity, but they nonetheless continue to treat him as a respected colleague" (Mason, "Chief Priests, Sadducees, Pharisees and Sanhedrin in Acts," 135).

93. Luke 13:31–33.

they are Pharisees.[94] Luke's account of the early messianic community in Acts depicts the Pharisees in an even more favorable light. Gamaliel speaks in the Sanhedrin on their behalf, and succeeds in winning the release of the imprisoned *shelichim*.[95] Many Pharisees become members of the messianic community in Jerusalem.[96] Luke's Paul proudly identifies himself as a Pharisee, and does so in the present rather than the past tense.[97] When Paul appears before the Sanhedrin, the Pharisaic members of the council come to his defense, even as Gamaliel earlier defended the *shelichim*.[98] Thus, the Pharisees are not, as in Matthew, the enemies of Yeshua, of his followers, or of the good news. Instead, Luke presents them as the group most open and sympathetic to the new movement.[99]

Why does Matthew treat the Pharisees more harshly than Luke does? The answer to this question is simple yet paradoxical: Matthew is the most *polemically anti*-Pharisaic book in the Apostolic Writings because it is also the most *substantively Pharisaic* book in the Apostolic Writings. The polemic intensity derives not from distance but from proximity. David Sim has noted this aspect of Matthew: "It is now well recognized that polemical and stereotypical language such as we find in Matthew does not reflect the distance between the two parties. On the contrary, it indicates both physical and ideological proximity between the disputing groups, since its very purpose is to distance one party from the other. A general sociological rule of thumb is that the closer the relationship between dissenting groups, the more intense the conflict and the sharper the resultant polemic."[100]

---

94. Luke 17:20-22. "Jesus' most compassionate statement to the Pharisees comes when they inquire of him, still the respected teacher, 'when the kingdom of God comes' (17:20). In responding that 'the kingdom of God is *within you*' (17:22), Jesus is declaring that the Pharisees have the kingdom in themselves, as the 'older brother' [Luke 15: 25–32] with heaven's resources at their disposal, as the righteous and healthy of society; but as we have seen time and again, they squander their potential" (Mason, "Chief Priests, Sadducees, Pharisees and Sanhedrin in Acts," 142).

95. Acts 5:34–40.

96. Acts 15:5.

97. Acts 23:6. See also Acts 26:4–8.

98. Acts 23:9.

99. Though he uses anachronistic and misleading terminology, Robert Brawley nonetheless accurately perceives Luke's attitude toward the Pharisees: "Luke ushers the Pharisees right up to the portals of the Christian faith . . . Paul himself then becomes the example of a Pharisee most faithful to the hopes of Israel" (Brawley, *Luke-Acts and the Jews*, 158).

100. Sim, *The Gospel of Matthew and Christian Judaism*, 121.

In fact, Matthew shares many features characteristic of the later rabbinic movement and its literature. First, the leadership of his community is scribal—its legitimacy is not only charismatic but also derives from the authenticity and erudition of its teaching on the Torah.[101] Second, its leadership is *halakhic*. It claims the authority to bind and loose, offers *halakhic* principles for resolving apparent conflicts between *mitzvot* (commandments), and even seems to be aware of inner Pharisaic *halakhic* controversies.[102] Third, it shows religious sensibilities characteristic of the later rabbinic movement, such as the use of circumlocutions (such as "heaven") in place of the word "God." Fourth, it follows a topical method of organization (like that in the Mishnah) rather than the more dramatic narrative form found in Mark and Luke. Fifth, it shows a fondness for numerical patterning (five discourses, ten mighty deeds, seven petitions, seven parables, seven woes), *gematriya*[103] (fourteen generations and the name "David"), and mnemonic devices. Sixth, in its version of the Lord's Prayer it resembles later synagogue liturgy ("on earth as in heaven" and the *Kedushah*[104]). Seventh, as we have already seen, Matthew cites words from Yeshua that uphold Pharisaic *halakhic* authority, alluding to the same verses in Deuteronomy later employed by the rabbis to undergird their right to issue binding *halakhic* decrees. He also presents Yeshua as referring to distinctive Pharisaic traditions of tithing as "matters of Torah."[105] All of these elements point to a close relationship between Matthew and the Pharisees. It is the closeness of this relationship that explains the bitter polemic that characterizes this book.

This perspective on Matthew has significant implications for us as twenty-first century Messianic Jews. Just as Matthew develops a first-century form of messianic faith that builds upon the distinctive traditions of the Pharisaic movement, and even (though perhaps grudgingly) acknowledges their ongoing role as *halakhic* authorities, so we can develop a twenty-first century form of messianic faith that builds upon the distinctive traditions of the rabbinic movement that emerged out of

---

101. Matthew 13:51–52; 23:34.

102. Matthew 16:19, 18:18; 9:13, 12:7, 7:12, 22:40, 15:18–20; 19:3, 9.

103. *Gematriya* is a system of assigning numerical value to a word or phrase in the belief that words or phrases with identical numerical values bear some relation to each other and reveal insight into the interrelation of concepts and ideas.

104. The *Kedushah* is a unit in the Jewish liturgy that contains as its centerpiece the threefold angelic sanctification of God found in Isaiah 6.

105. Matthew 23:23.

Pharisaism, and acknowledge its ongoing role in *halakhic* development. However, in a new pluralistic religious world, where Jews and Christians are for the first time formally seeking to build a relationship of mutual understanding and friendship, and where Judaism permits a greater breadth of expression, we need not imitate Matthew's polemical orientation. Instead, Luke's irenic attitude suits our circumstances better.

In conclusion, it appears that many common assumptions regarding the Pharisees in the Apostolic Writings are unfounded. According to those Writings, Yeshua and his followers do not reject the Pharisaic tradition or movement as a whole. In fact, the Yeshua of the *Besorot* offers a qualified endorsement of the Pharisees. Texts that reflect this fact are even found in Matthew, a book that simultaneously castigates the Pharisees and adopts many of their distinctive positions. Thus, the Apostolic Writings need not prevent us as Messianic Jews from accepting some version of the doctrine of the Oral Torah.

ORAL TORAH IN THEOLOGICAL-HISTORICAL PERSPECTIVE

Before proceeding further, we should summarize what we have learned to this point. If the Pentateuch is to serve as the basis for the Jewish way of life, then it must be accompanied by a tradition of interpretation and application. The Pentateuch itself takes account of this fact, and establishes a central court that is authorized to develop such a tradition of interpretation and application. This court carries on the work of Moses and functions in the ongoing life of the Jewish people in a manner analogous to the way Moses himself functioned as he governed the people in the wilderness. The central court derives its legitimacy through the consent of the covenant people that it governs.

Upon this biblical foundation, rabbinic tradition builds a doctrine of Oral Torah. In its talmudic form, this doctrine presents the sages of Yavneh and their rabbinic successors as the true Sanhedrin, the central court authorized to act in the spirit and power of Moses. They transmit a tradition of interpretation that fills in biblical lacunae, reconciles apparently incompatible legal texts, and provides *halakhic* precedents for the future by addressing new and unforeseen situations. Their decrees are carefully distinguished from biblical law, and subordinated to it. However, as the leaders of their generation they are at times called upon to "uproot" a biblical law for the sake of upholding a more fundamental biblical principle. Their authority must be (and is) confirmed by the people as a whole, and the legitimacy of any rabbinic decree depends upon its acceptance by the community.

The Apostolic Writings present Yeshua as standing in an ambivalent relation to the Pharisaic predecessors of the rabbinic tradition. On the one hand, he offers prophetic criticism of Pharisaic practice, finding fault with what he saw as their privileging of ritual minutiae over relational obligation, and their preoccupation with their tradition at the expense of the biblical witness. Close reading of the relevant texts shows this criticism to be a correction of emphasis rather than a rejection of basic convictions. But it nonetheless demonstrates a tension between Yeshua and his followers and the Pharisaic movement. On the other hand, Matthew and Luke-Acts present a picture of Yeshua and his followers that implicitly and at times explicitly expresses their affinity for the Pharisees.

The true opponents of the earliest messianic movement were the priestly rulers of the Jerusalem temple. They were the ones who had Yeshua arrested, and who persecuted the *shelichim*. In the parable of the vineyard, Yeshua denounces them and prophesies their destruction. This was realized when Jerusalem was destroyed by the Romans in 70 C.E. While foretelling the imminent end of the priestly Sanhedrin, Yeshua also (according to Matthew) affirmed that the Pharisaic scribes "sit on Moses' seat," and thus their position as heirs of Moses is reinforced. At the same time, Yeshua exercises his unique authority as the Messiah and grants *halakhic* authority to his closest followers. Thus, the old Sanhedrin loses its power, to be replaced by two institutions in tension with one another.

What do we, as twenty-first century Messianic Jews, make of all this? In order to form theological judgments based on this biblical analysis, we must go beyond mere biblical analysis and examine the historical developments of the past two millennia. Is it really possible for us to acknowledge the authority of a tradition that has emphatically denied the messiahship of Yeshua? Can we see this tradition as embodying "Oral Torah," carrying on the work of Moses from one generation to the next?

The *halakhic* authority given to Yeshua's followers encourages us in our efforts to develop a distinctively Messianic Jewish way of life. However, it is not sufficient to enable us to accomplish that task. This is the case for three important reasons. First, according to Matthew, the *halakhic* authority of the messianic community operates within the context of the *halakhic* authority of the Pharisaic scribes. Each is apparently incomplete without the other. Second, because the Torah-observant Jewish Yeshua movement faded away in the early centuries of the Common Era, no continuous tradition of Messianic Jewish *halakhah* exists. We do not know in any detail how the early Jewish Yeshua-movement kept *Shabbat*, *kashrut*, or the laws of family purity. However, even if we did, we would still not have the living memory of an ongoing community's attempt to live out the Torah and pass it on to their children through the changing circumstances of the past twenty centuries. Such a living memory is essential to the Jewish people's observance of the Torah. Third, the Jewish community as a whole decided to accept the *halakhic* authority of the rabbinic movement. Given the divinely appointed role of the community in establishing and confirming the legitimate successors to Moses, we cannot ignore rabbinic tradition, even if we believe that we also have a crucial contribution to make to the *halakhic* process.

The emergence of rabbinic Judaism is remarkable, especially in light of the Apostolic Writings. While the Jewish world as a whole did not accept Yeshua as the Messiah, it did accept as the successors to Moses those who Yeshua said "sit in Moses' seat." Other movements could have won the day—but they did not. Furthermore, the Shammaite school of Pharisaism, dominant during Yeshua's era and probably the object of most of his ire, lost control of nascent rabbinism to the Hillelites—who seem closer in spirit to Yeshua. While from our perspective the failure of the Jewish people to accept Yeshua as Messiah adds a tragic dimension to Jewish history, it is nonetheless true that our people could not have chosen better, given this failure, than to recognize the *halakhic* authority of the rabbinic movement.[106] The wisdom of this choice was confirmed by the success of rabbinic Judaism in preserving the Jewish people, the Torah, and the Jewish way of life for two millennia.

If, with Michael Wyschogrod, we understand the Oral Torah to be "that part of the law carried in the Jewish people," then we are compelled to see the rabbis of the Talmud and their successors as its official custodians.[107] In their role as *halakhic* authorities, interpreting and applying the Torah to ever-changing circumstances, they continued the work of

---

106. I have argued elsewhere that our people's culpability for its failure to accept Yeshua is mitigated by a variety of important factors. See *The Nature of Messianic Judaism*, 21–25, and "On the Nature of Messianic Judaism: Replying to My Respondents," *Kesher*, 56–61.

107. Wyschogrod, *The Body of Faith*, 210.

Moses in Israel. These conclusions are justified by the biblical sources and by a biblically informed theological assessment of the history of the Jewish people. Therefore, as Messianic Jews we should not hesitate to say, "Blessed are You, LORD our God, King of the Universe, who has sanctified us with His commandments, and commanded us to . . . " before lighting *Shabbat* and *Chanukkah* candles, chanting *Hallel*, waving the *lulav* (palm branch), or laying *tefillin* (phylacteries).

It is not inconsistent for us to respect the authority of the rabbinic tradition while rejecting its judgment concerning Yeshua. This is the case for two reasons. First, we should be open to the possibility that *halakhic* prohibitions of acts of faith in Yeshua might have been appropriate in certain situations in the past. For example, if a public act of faith in Yeshua necessarily includes renunciation of the Torah and the people of Israel, then *halakhic* disincentives to such action would be essential to the preservation of the covenant. Second, any Messianic Jewish version of the Oral Torah must recognize two legitimate *halakhic* authorities in tension— those recognized by the Jewish community as a whole, and those presiding over its messianic sub-community. Our *halakhic* authority to bind and loose is prophetic in nature, just as Yeshua's own authority derived not from institutional office but from messianic empowerment. When the requirements inherent in the faith of Yeshua conflict with the norms of rabbinic tradition and the institutions of the wider Jewish community, then we must find a way to be true to Yeshua while maintaining respect for the community and its tradition. This is often an excruciatingly difficult task; but Yeshua never said that our way would be easy.

I have devoted much time and effort to argue for a conclusion that would be the starting point for other forms of Judaism. I am not here advocating any particular perspective on what the Oral Torah says to us today. Taking my conclusion as a premise, one could develop an Orthodox, Conservative, Reform, or Reconstructionist Messianic approach to Jewish tradition. This further discussion is essential, but we cannot expect to engage in such a discussion fruitfully if we do not begin where all other modern Judaisms begin—with explicit acknowledgement of the validity of rabbinic tradition, the Oral Torah, as providing the necessary context for all practical interpretation and application of the Written Torah to contemporary Jewish life.

4

Prayer in Yeshua, Prayer in Israel: The Shema in Messianic Perspective

The recitation of the Shema and its blessings occupies the very heart of Israel's worship. As Jews across the world pray the Shema day after day, they re-enact the covenant at Sinai and recommit themselves to the *mitzvot* (commandments). They declare that even in death, their devotion to the One True God will not waver. Kinzer's exposition of this centerpiece of Jewish prayer reveals that Yeshua, though not explicitly mentioned, imbues this holy liturgy and is the one to whom the prayers and blessings ultimately point. He is the one whose sacrifice makes holy the people of Israel, and he is the one on whom was laid the punishments spoken of for Israel's disobedience. According to Kinzer, to pray "in Israel" is to pray "in Yeshua." Even though the majority of the Jewish people do not acknowledge Yeshua's intermediary role, Kinzer claims that their prayers are nonetheless acceptable by means of his obedience and their covenantal bond with God is grounded in the sonship of Yeshua.[1]

MESSIANIC JUDAISM AND THE CENTRALITY-MARGINALITY PARADOX

With the cry "Hashivenu" the Torah service concludes, imploring God to bring us back to himself. It is our conviction that Hashem brings Messianic Jews to a richer knowledge of himself through a modern day rediscovery of the paths of our ancestors—Avodah (liturgical worship), Torah (study of sacred texts), and Gemilut Chasadim (deeds of lovingkindness).

---

1. Presented at the Hashivenu Forum in 2008. See p. 29, n. 2.

THESE ARE THE OPENING words of the Hashivenu Mission Statement. In accordance with this conviction, the Hashivenu Forum follows the rhythm of the Jewish daily prayer cycle, and employs the liturgical forms of the *Siddur* (Jewish prayer book). Such temporal rhythms and liturgical forms have shaped and expressed the spiritual life of the Jewish people through the centuries. By making them our own, we demonstrate that the Jewish people are our people and that Jewish life is our life.

At the same time, we differ from other Jews in our conviction that God has raised Yeshua from the dead and in our acknowledgement of him as our Master and Messiah. We have encountered the Rabbi from Nazareth, and nothing can ever be the same for us again. This includes "the paths of our ancestors." We "rediscover" them as followers of Yeshua, and consequently understand and experience them in a new way.

The Hashivenu Mission Statement conveys this aspect of our calling in its second paragraph:

> However, Messianic Judaism is energized by the belief that Yeshua of Nazareth is the promised Messiah, the fullness of Torah. Mature Messianic Judaism is not simply Judaism plus Yeshua, but is instead an integrated following of Yeshua through traditional Jewish forms, and the modern day practice of Judaism in and through Yeshua.

From its inception, Hashivenu has rejected the formula of "Judaism plus Yeshua." Messianic Judaism involves more than the subtle tweaking of an existing form of Jewish life and thought—adding a few elements required by faith in Yeshua and subtracting a few elements incompatible with that faith. Instead, the Judaism we have inherited—and continue to practice—is entirely bathed in the bright light of Yeshua's revelation. In a circular and dynamic interaction, our Judaism provides us with the framework required to interpret Yeshua's revelation even as it is reconfigured by that revelation. In this way our Judaism and our Yeshua-faith are organically and holistically "integrated."

Is this really possible? Almost all Jews outside our ranks would say no, and perhaps most Christians would agree with them. This brings us to the theme of our forum. To say that Yeshua has been "marginal" to traditional Jewish life is an irenic understatement. Just as Christianity has historically positioned itself as "non-Judaism," so Judaism has defined itself largely as "non-Yeshua-faith." In the past this put us beyond the margins of both communities.

Despite this undeniable fact, we make the radical and scandalous claim that Yeshua constitutes the true center of Jewish life, just as Israel constitutes the true center of Yeshua's *ekklesia*.[2] The One who goes unmentioned in the *Siddur* is present on every page. He is present not simply through references to *Mashiach ben David*—such messianic references are few. He is present not simply through prayers for future redemption and the messianic age, though indeed such prayers pervade the Jewish liturgy. How is he present? He is there as the "fullness of Torah," the human embodiment of God's eternal Name and Word. He is there as the "fullness of Israel," the anointed King who sums up in himself Israel's true identity and destiny. He is there as the heavenly High Priest and *Shaliach Tzibbur* (emissary of the congregation), offering himself to God as Israel's liturgical representative. This is the message we proclaim and incarnate: the One pushed to the margins stands veiled at the center.

In the present paper I will attempt to concretize such an "integrated" Messianic Judaism through exposition of the core unit of Jewish daily liturgy, the Shema and its accompanying blessings. If successful, this exposition could serve as a model for how we encounter Yeshua through Jewish life and practice, and how our Yeshua-faith reconfigures our Judaism.

But first, we must look more closely at the meaning and basis of Jewish and Messianic prayer.

JEWISH PRAYER, MESSIANIC PRAYER

What is Jewish prayer? A text from the preliminary service to *Shachrit* (morning prayers) answers this question by first reflecting on the problematic nature of all prayer:

> Master of all worlds! Not upon our merit do we rely in our supplication, but upon your limitless love. What are we? What is our life? What is our piety? What is our righteousness? What is our attainment, our power, our might? What can we say, Lord our God and God of our ancestors? Compared to You, all the mighty are nothing, the famous nonexistent, the wise lacks wisdom, the clever lacks reason.[3]

---

2. The *ekklesia* refers to the Yeshua-believing community. See "Introduction to the Thought and Theology of Mark Kinzer," (x, n. 2) for further explanation of this terminology.

3. All quotations from the *Siddur*, unless otherwise noted, are from Harlow (editor),

On what grounds do we, finite, frail, and wayward human beings, approach the infinite and holy Creator of the universe? Prayer seems impossible—unless God makes it possible. According to this text, God does so by establishing a covenantal bond with a particular people—a bond expressed twice daily by the people of the covenant in its recitation of the Shema:

> But we are Your people, partners to Your covenant, descendants of Your beloved Abraham to whom You made a pledge on Mount Moriah.
> We are the heirs of Isaac, his son bound upon the altar.
> We are Your firstborn people, the congregation of Isaac's son Jacob whom You named Israel and Jeshurun, because of Your love for him and Your delight in him.
> Therefore it is our duty to thank You and praise You, to glorify and sanctify Your name . . . How blessed are we that twice each day, morning and evening, we are privileged to declare: Hear O Israel: The Lord our God, the Lord is One.

As Reuven Hammer explains, "according to this prayer, it is our membership in the people of Israel that makes prayer possible."[4] Jewish prayer is offered by God's covenant people, in response to God's gracious invitation and summons.

This is why the *Siddur* is so integral to Jewish prayer. It reflects the corporate Jewish encounter with God throughout Jewish history, and provides a common language of prayer for Jews at all times and places. It makes it possible for Jews to pray as a people. Hayim Donin puts it this way: "A Jew may choose his own words when praying to God; but when he uses the words of the siddur, he becomes part of a people. He identifies with Jews everywhere who use the same words and express the same thoughts. He affirms the principal of mutual responsibility and concern. He takes his place at the dawn of history as he binds himself to Abraham, Isaac, and Jacob. He asserts his rights to a Jewish future in this world and to personal redemption in the world-to-come."[5] To pray as a Jew is to pray "in Israel," as a member of the community with whom God has established an eternal covenant. The *Siddur* makes prayer "in Israel" a practical reality.

Siddur Sim Shalom.

4. Hammer, *Entering Jewish Prayer*, 10–11.

5. Donin, *To Pray as a Jew*, 7.

This provides the context necessary for understanding what it means to pray "in Yeshua." To explore the connection between prayer "in Israel" and prayer "in Yeshua," we turn to the thinking of Will Herberg. This Jewish theologian of the mid-twentieth century understood well the corporate and covenantal nature of Jewish prayer: "The central category of biblical thinking is covenant... In the biblical view, man has, so to speak, standing with God, and a direct personal relation to him, only by virtue of his membership in the people of God, the redeemed and redeeming community."[6] According to Herberg, the Apostolic Writings (New Testament) present Yeshua as a "one-man Israel," an individual who sums up in himself Israel's corporate covenantal identity. When a Gentile becomes united to Yeshua through faith, that person enters into God's covenant with Israel, and may approach God in prayer as part of the covenant people. Prayer "in Yeshua" is therefore an expression of prayer "in Israel," and Christianity involves the extension of Israel's covenant to the nations:

> In both Judaism and Christianity, as I have pointed out, there is no such thing as a direct and unmediated relation to God; this relation must in some way be mediated through one's covenant status. In Judaism, however, it is by virtue of his being a member of the People Israel that the believer approaches God and has standing before him; in Christianity, it is by virtue of his being a member of Christ. This is clearly brought out in the structure of prayer of the two faiths... *To be a Jew means to meet God and receive his grace in and through Israel; to be a Christian means to meet God and receive his grace in and through Christ.*[7]

Being "a member of Christ" is not merely an individual relationship with the Messiah, but participation in a community that is itself united through Yeshua to the original people of the covenant.

While Herberg helps us see the integral connection between prayer "in Israel" and prayer "in Yeshua," he does not go far enough. As the definitive "one-man Israel," Yeshua enables those from the nations to share in the riches of Israel; but he also comes to usher Israel into the fullness of its own inheritance. Herberg implies that praying "in Yeshua" has significance because it is a form of praying "in Israel"; we have begun to recognize that praying "in Israel" is also a form of praying "in Yeshua."

---

6. Herberg, *Faith Enacted as History*, 48.
7. Ibid., 52. Emphasis added.

Yeshua can become the "one-man Israel" because he was already God's eternal Beloved in whom Israel was chosen before the foundation of the world (Ephesians 1:4). God adopts Israel as his "firstborn son" (Exodus 4:22–23) by attaching Israel to the Son whom God knew and loved before anything was made (Ephesians 1:5–6). Yeshua becomes the servant of the people who have their being through him. Israel did not know this before his incarnation, and has not acknowledged it since. But such non-recognition cannot nullify Israel's ineradicable dependence on Yeshua, and Yeshua's unwavering commitment to Israel.

To pray "in Israel" is to participate in the relationship that God established with Abraham, Isaac, and Jacob, Sarah, Rebecca, Rachel, and Leah. What God was and is to them, God is now to us, their children. Similarly, to pray "in Yeshua" is to participate in his intimate filial relationship with God.[8] What God was and is to Yeshua, God is now to us, his disciples filled with his Spirit. Prayer "in Yeshua" is an expression of prayer "in Israel," since Yeshua is the elect Seed of Abraham whose relationship with God sums up all that God intended for the covenantal bond with the patriarchs and matriarchs. Even more, prayer "in Israel" ultimately depends upon and derives from prayer "in Yeshua," the incarnate Son in whom Israel has its adoption.

To pray "in Israel," we must embrace the temporal rhythms and liturgical forms concretized in the *Siddur*. To pray "in Israel" and "in Yeshua," we must discover how these rhythms and forms reveal something of Yeshua's own relationship with God, so that we may participate intelligently and passionately in that relationship as those who belong to him. We believe that this is a *discovery* rather than a forced and artificial reinterpretation, since we believe that the One whom "the builders rejected" and cast beyond the margins of Jewish life has never relinquished his hidden place at its center.

---

8. Jeremias, *New Testament Theology*, 180–81; Barth, *Prayer*, 22–23.

THE SHEMA: ISRAEL'S WITNESS IN YESHUA, YESHUA'S WITNESS IN ISRAEL

Sinai and Martyrdom

The Shema constitutes the core unit of the daily liturgy. It consists of three biblical texts[9] that are recited every morning and evening in literal fulfillment of the words, "when you lie down and when you rise" (Deuteronomy 6:7 and 11:19).

In its earliest form, the Shema began with the reading of the Decalogue.[10] David Hartman rightly infers from this practice that "the recital of the Shema was meant to be a reliving of the covenantal moment at Sinai."[11] The Mishnah confirms this interpretation by referring to the statutory recitation of Deuteronomy 6:4–9 as acceptance of the "the yoke of the Kingship of Heaven."[12] Thus, each morning and evening a Jew re-enacts and re-appropriates the encounter with God at Sinai, receiving anew God's self-revelation and reaffirming Israel's pledge to live in covenant fidelity. In reading the words, "You shall love Hashem your God with all your heart, soul, and strength," a Jew willingly accepts the obligation to give such love.

But how is such love expressed concretely? Its most extreme embodiment involves the laying down of one's life.[13] The Mishnah explains "with all your soul" as meaning "even if God takes away your soul."[14] An early midrash reiterates and elaborates this tradition:

> *And with all thy soul.* Even if God takes away your soul, as it is said, *For Thy sake are we killed all the day; we are accounted as sheep for the slaughter* (Psalm 44:23) . . . Simeon ben Azzai says: *With all thy soul:* love Him until the last drop of life is wrung out

---

9. Deuteronomy 6:4–9; 11:13–21; Numbers 15:37–41.

10. M. Tamid 5:1.

11. Hartman, *A Living Covenant*, 164.

12. M. Berachot 2:2. See Hammer, *Entering Jewish Prayer*, 131–32.

13. The unusual calligraphy in the traditional way of writing Deuteronomy 6:4 points to this interpretation of the Shema. In Torah scrolls, the third consonant of the first word "Shema" (*'ayin*) and the third consonant of the last word "echad" (*dalet*) are written in an enlarged script, so that one might mentally put the two letters together to form the word "*'ed*" (witness). The Greek word for "witness" is "martyr." Israel bears witness to God through living out the Shema to the point of shedding its blood.

14. M. Berachot 9:5.

of you ... R. Meir says: Scripture says, *Thou shalt love the Lord, thy God ... with all thy soul*, as did Isaac, who bound himself upon the altar, as it is said, *and Abraham stretched forth his hand, and took the knife to slay his son* (Gen 22:10).[15]

The *Akedah* represents the ultimate fulfillment of the first paragraph of the Shema, and Jews re-enact the *Akedah* whenever they face persecution for the sake of their faith.

The most famous example of this understanding of the Shema is the story of Rabbi Akiva's martyrdom:

> When Rabbi Akiva was taken out for execution, it was the hour for the recital of the Shema, and while they combed his flesh with iron combs, he was accepting upon himself the kingship of heaven. His disciples said to him: Our teacher, even to this point? He said to them: All my days I have been troubled by this verse, *"with all thy soul"*—"even if He takes thy soul." I said: When shall I have the opportunity of fulfilling this? Now that I have the opportunity, shall I not fulfill it? He prolonged the word *echad* until he expired while saying it.[16]

Jewish history has sealed this bond between the Shema and martyrdom and made Deuteronomy 6:4 not only a daily renewal of Sinai but also a pre-death confession offering covenantal exegesis on the meaning of one's individual life: "When reciting the Shema as part of worship, no sensitive person can help but be aware that he or she is saying words uttered by millions of Jews who were slain because of their faith. From Akiva to Auschwitz, believing Jews have proclaimed this verse as they faced the knowledge that because they were Jews they were about to be killed. It has also become the practice for any Jew to recite these words on his or her deathbed, departing this world with the words of Jewish belief on one's lips."[17] In this way the Shema constitutes the definitive statement of the meaning of the life of the Jewish people as a whole. Its ritual recitation, daily and at the end of life, bears witness to the same reality that is supposed to be reflected in every aspect of the individual and

---

15. *Sifre* Deuteronomy 6:5 (Piska 32). The translation is from Hammer, *Sifre on Deuteronomy*, 59, 62.

16. B. Berachot 61b. The translation is from Simon, *Hebrew-English Edition of the Babylonian Talmud: Berakoth*.

17. Hammer, *Entering Jewish Prayer*, 134.

communal existence of the people of the covenant: Hashem as Israel's only God, loved more than life itself.

Yeshua's Covenant Fidelity

Deuteronomy 6:4–9 plays a prominent role in the life and teaching of Yeshua. He views it as the first and greatest commandment, and links it to the commandment in the Torah to love one's neighbor (Leviticus 19:18).[18] This linkage does not add to the Shema but interprets it: all attempts at loving God that compromise love of neighbor are proven fraudulent.[19]

In John, Yeshua applies God's command to love one's neighbor to the mutual love required of his disciples, and presents "laying down one's life" as the ultimate expression of such love.[20] This is what Yeshua himself does for his own in willing fulfillment of his Father's commandment, and thus the disciples' love for one another participates in their Master's sacrificial self-giving.[21] Yeshua's obedience to his Father in laying down his life bears witness to his wholehearted love of God: "The ruler of this world is coming. He has no claim on me; rather, this is happening so that the world may know that I love the Father and that I do as the Father has commanded me" (John 14:30–31).[22] Yeshua's suffering and death thus embodies perfectly the love of God and neighbor required by the Shema.

In his sacrificial martyrdom, Yeshua actualizes the fullness of Israel's covenantal pledge at Sinai, recapitulates the *Akedah* at a higher level (i.e., God is now the Father whose son yields himself to sacrifice), and consummates the authentic demonstrations of covenant fidelity enacted throughout Israel's history. The unique and definitive character of Yeshua's loving martyrdom does not detract from the nobility of

---

18. Mark 12:28–34; Matthew 22:34–40; Luke 10:25–28.

19. "The commandment to love one's neighbor gives decisive guidance for understanding the commandment to love God" (Cosgrove, *Elusive Israel*, 44).

20. John 13:34; 1 John 2:7–11; John 15:13. The love commandment is "new" because of its eschatological realization in Yeshua's death and resurrection—not because it is absent from or marginal to Israel's revealed covenantal responsibilities. As the Shema (linked with Leviticus 19) demonstrates, the love commandment is at the heart of Israel's covenant.

21. John 10:11, 15, 17; John 10:18; 1 John 3:16.

22. All biblical citations are based on the NRSV, with modifications by the author.

those other witnesses to the covenant, but empowers them to attain their intended purpose. This is the import of Hebrews 11—12, which offers a capsule chronicle of the faithful men and women of Jewish history—described in 12:1 as a "great cloud of witnesses" (*martyrs*). It brings the chronicle to a climax by presenting Yeshua as "the pioneer and perfecter of our faith" who perfects not only "our" faith but also that of the heroes listed in Hebrews 11.[23]

This vision of Yeshua as the epitome of Jewish covenant fidelity should shape our recitation of the Shema as Messianic Jews. Just as the "faith" of Israel's greatest heroes cannot attain its purpose apart from Yeshua, so the covenantal summons to wholehearted love and obedience can only be realized in and through Yeshua. For us, the recitation of the Shema serves as more than just a renewal and reenactment of Sinai: it is a memorial of Yeshua's loving obedience unto death, which completes the covenantal encounter at Sinai and raises it to a higher level (Hebrews 12:18–24). Our recitation of the Shema involves grateful acknowledgement of Yeshua's covenant fidelity, and commitment to participate in his loving self-offering to the Father. It also involves the recognition that all Jews who have lived faithful but imperfect lives before God and who have recited the Shema daily and at the hour of their deaths can only attain the consummation of their aspirations through union with Yeshua, the one-man Israel.

Reward & Punishment

The second paragraph of the Shema (Deuteronomy 11:13–21) repeats many of the characteristic ideas and phrases of the first paragraph.[24] What distinctive material does it add that justifies its inclusion in Israel's most sacred confession of faith and loyalty?

The distinctive contribution of the second paragraph is found in verses 13–17:

---

23. Hebrews 12:2; 11:39–40.

24. "Loving the Lord your God . . . with all your heart and soul" (11:13; see 6:5); "You shall put these words of mine in your heart and soul, and you shall bind them as a sign on your hand, and fix them as an emblem on your forehead. Teach them to your children, talking about them when you are at home and when you are away, when you lie down and when you rise. Write them on the doorposts of your house and on your gates" (11:18–20; see 6:6–9).

> If you will only heed his every commandment that I am commanding you today . . . —loving Hashem your God, and serving him with all your heart and with all your soul—then he will give the rain for your land in its season, the early rain and the later rain, and you will gather in your grain, your wine, and your oil; and he will give grass in your fields for your livestock, and you will eat your fill. Take care, or you will be seduced into turning away, serving other gods and worshiping them, for then the anger of Hashem will be kindled against you and he will shut up the heavens, so that there will be no rain and the land will yield no fruit; then you will perish quickly off the good land that Hashem is giving you.

This teaches the principle of divine reward and punishment.[25] If Israel remains faithful to the covenant, Hashem will provide generously for its communal needs. If Israel renounces the covenant and worships other divinities, Hashem will withhold heavenly blessing. According to verse 17, the ultimate punishment consists of perishing "off the good land that the Lord is giving you"—i.e., exile.[26]

The Jewish commentary tradition also notes a difference in the formulation of the material that is common to the first and second paragraphs of the Shema: the commandments of Deuteronomy 6:4-9 employ second person singular verbs and pronouns, whereas the same commandments in Deuteronomy 11 are stated in plural form.[27] Based on this grammatical distinction, Donin concludes, "In the first paragraph, Moses addresses the individual Jew. In the second paragraph, he addresses the collective body of Israel."[28]

The promises of reward and punishment are thus directed here to the community as a whole. This makes good sense if, with Rashi, we take Deuteronomy 11:17 to be a reference to exile. Exile affects the nation in its entirety. Rashi sees the order of the various elements of the second paragraph of the Shema as reflecting a chronological sequence, so that the commandments of the first paragraph that are repeated in the plural form at the end of the second paragraph concern observance of the Torah *even in exile*: "Even after you will go into exile, be distinguished through performance of commandments; for example, put on *tefillin*

---

25. Donin, *To Pray as a Jew*, 152-54; Hammer, *Entering Jewish Prayer*, 125-27.
26. See Rashi on Deuteronomy 11:17.
27. See Rashi on Deuteronomy 11:13.
28. Donin, *To Pray as a Jew*, 151.

[phylacteries, Deuteronomy 11:18] and make *mezuzot* [Deuteronomy 11:20] so that they should not be new to you when you will return."[29]

The singular-plural distinction between paragraphs one and two of the Shema provides us with a key for reading the second paragraph as Messianic Jews. The singular forms of the first paragraph express our conviction that only one Jew has ever fulfilled the commandments perfectly, and that all other Jews are summoned to participate in his whole-hearted love of God. The plural forms of the second paragraph take account of our wayward disposition, and anticipate national infidelity and punishment. Nevertheless, the preeminent recitation of even this second paragraph belongs to Yeshua rather than to us. His recitation of the second paragraph explains the concrete form that his recitation of the first paragraph must take: he identifies with Israel in its covenantal infidelity and willingly bears the punishment that rightly belongs to Israel, so that Israel might receive the reward that rightly belongs to him. Thus, his whole-hearted love for God, which fulfills the first paragraph of the Shema, must take the concrete form of suffering and death on Israel's behalf.[30]

Israel does go into exile, despite Yeshua's atoning martyrdom. Yet, as Rashi recognized, exile from the land does not mean inevitable exile from Hashem or from the Torah. After Deuteronomy 11:17 mentions the punishment of exile, the following verses reiterate, in plural form, the commandments of Deuteronomy 6:4–9. We may be in physical exile, waiting for the day of redemption, but we need not remain in spiritual exile. Messiah Yeshua has taken our sins upon himself that we might be liberated from their weight, and he offers us his Spirit that we might share in his loving self-offering to God the Father. When Israel corporately appropriates his atonement and enters into his self-offering, then it will receive the blessing promised in Deuteronomy 11:21: "so that your

---

29. Rashi on Deuteronomy 11:18. A *mezuzah* (pl. *mezuzot*) is an encased piece of parchment inscribed with Deuteronomy 6:4–9 and Deuteronomy 11:13–21. *Mezuzot* are affixed to the doorframes of Jewish homes in fulfillment of the command in Deuteronomy 6:9 to write these words on "the doorframes of your homes and on your gates."

30. This is the meaning of Yeshua's immersion at the hands of John. John was appalled that Yeshua would be immersed, as he had no need for repentance and forgiveness (Matthew 3:13–15). Yet, Yeshua realized that his mission required that he identify completely with Israel and suffer the judgment that Israel deserved—figuratively in his immersion, literally in his atoning death (see Luke 12:50).

days and the days of your children may be multiplied in the land that Hashem swore to your ancestors to give them, as long as the heavens are above the earth."

In the first paragraph of the Shema we focus on Yeshua's wholehearted love of God, which fulfills the covenant. In the second paragraph we focus on Yeshua's love for his people Israel that leads him to suffer and die on our behalf. Yeshua's obedience to the second great commandment demonstrates the authenticity of his obedience to the first great commandment.

Messianic Redemption

The third paragraph of the Shema (Numbers 15:37–41) derives from the book of Numbers rather than Deuteronomy, and so its terminology and idiom differ from the first two paragraphs. Nevertheless, it shares much in common with the two preceding Deuteronomic texts. Like them, it focuses on the commandments and their faithful observance.[31] Like them, it charges Israel to honor the commandments through visual and tactile symbols.[32] Like Deuteronomy 11, it warns against turning away from Hashem.[33] These commonalities make Numbers 15 an appropriate conclusion to the Shema.

What distinctive content does this third paragraph bring to the Shema? Earliest rabbinic tradition found its special contribution in its final verse: "I am Hashem your God, who brought you out of the land of Egypt, to be your God: I am Hashem your God."[34] The Mishnah identifies this paragraph by the phrase *yetz'iat Mitzrayim* (the exodus from Egypt), and affirms the importance of remembering the exodus in the evening as well as in the morning through the recitation of the third paragraph of the Shema.[35] As Hammer notes, "The mention of the Exodus from Egypt adds the idea of redemption, another critical assertion which may be said to complete the fundamental ideas the Sages wanted us to affirm twice daily: God is one, the only one; He rewards and punishes; and He

---

31. Numbers 15:39–40; see Deuteronomy 6:6; 11:13.
32. *Tzitzit* (fringes) in Numbers 15, *tefillin* and *mezuzot* in Deuteronomy 6 and 11.
33. Numbers 15:39b; see Deuteronomy 11:16–17.
34. Numbers 15:41.
35. M. Berachot 1:5.

redeems."³⁶ As Hammer implies, the remembrance of the exodus from Egypt is intended to inspire hope for future redemption.

This final verse of the Shema also echoes its all-important first verse: "Hear O Israel, Hashem is our God, Hashem alone" (Deuteronomy 6:4). The three paragraphs of the Shema consist of an expanded explanation of the meaning and implications of this first verse. The final verse makes clear that the identity of Hashem is bound up with Hashem's redemptive action on Israel's behalf. In effect, the phrase "who brought you out of the land of Egypt" becomes an expanded form of the divine Name. The God who makes a covenant with Israel at Sinai and who asks for Israel's exclusive loyalty and love is the One who has acted redemptively in Israel's past, and who promises to act redemptively in Israel's eschatological future.

In the mouth of Yeshua, the third paragraph of the Shema becomes a proclamation and pledge of messianic redemption. More specifically, it points us beyond Yeshua's atoning suffering and death to his victorious resurrection. In Luke's account of the transfiguration, we learn that Moses and Elijah "appeared in glory and spoke of his departure (*exodus*), which he was to fulfill in Jerusalem."³⁷ The resurrection of Yeshua "fulfills" the exodus from Egypt by recapitulating Israel's journey from slavery to freedom, from death to life, and by ensuring and effecting Israel's ultimate eschatological redemption. If "the One who brought you out of the land of Egypt" serves as an expanded form of the divine Name at Sinai, then "the One who raised Yeshua from the dead" is the same Name articulated afresh in light of God's redemptive action on Yeshua's behalf.³⁸

Hashem lays claim to Israel's loyalty and love through the exodus from Egypt. He does so in an even greater manner through the resur-

---

36. Hammer, *Entering Jewish Prayer*, 128.

37. Luke 9:31.

38. Romans 4:24; 8:11. Robert Jenson notes the importance of these two ways of identifying the God of Israel, and their relationship to one another: "To the question 'Who is God?' the New Testament has one new descriptively identifying answer: 'Whoever raised Jesus from the dead.' Identification by the Resurrection neither replaces nor is simply added to identification by the Exodus; the new identifying description *verifies* its paradigmatic predecessor. For as the outcome of the Old Testament it is seen that Israel's hope in her God cannot be sustained if it is not verified by victory also over death ... Thus, 'the one who rescued Israel from Egypt' is confirmed as an identification of *God* in that it is continued 'as he thereupon rescued the Israelite Jesus from the dead'" (Jenson, *Systematic Theology*, vol. 1, 44).

rection of Yeshua. Because God has raised Yeshua from the dead, and ensured Israel's eschatological future in him, God calls for all to acknowledge Yeshua and affirm the renewal of the covenant accomplished in him.

Thus, for us as Messianic Jews, the three paragraphs of the Shema point to the heart of all that we believe: the vicarious love and obedience of Yeshua which renews God's covenant with Israel; his atoning suffering and death as the bearing of Israel's exile; and his resurrection from the dead as the pledge of Israel's future redemption. The Shema likewise expresses the heart of all that we seek to embody in our lives: love of God and neighbor; obedience to the *mitzvot*; and solidarity with Israel even in its infidelity. Finally, the Shema helps us realize that we can only live in love, obedience, and solidarity through participating in the life and death of Yeshua, the perfect one-man Israel.

THE BLESSINGS ACCOMPANYING THE SHEMA: IN PRAISE OF THE GOD OF THE COVENANT

Who is Hashem?

The three paragraphs of the Shema begin and end with an acknowledgement of Hashem as Israel's only God. The body of the paragraphs then consists of Israel's affirmation of the relational and behavioral consequences of this acknowledgement. In this way the Shema emphasizes Israel's response of covenant fidelity.

In contrast, the blessings that accompany the Shema focus on the identity of the God Israel worships. They answer the question, "who is Hashem?" by praising Hashem's sovereignty and compassion. Their answer presents Hashem as the Creator and Redeemer, who has chosen Israel in love to be God's covenant partner and given Israel the Torah as a sign of that love. They also point to the eschatological goal of God's action in creating the world and establishing a covenant with Israel. These blessings thus provide a cosmic, historical, and eschatological context for Israel's loving response to God in the Shema.[39]

---

39. The Shema is recited twice daily, once in the morning and once in the evening. On both occasions blessings precede and follow the recitation. While the wording and length of these blessings vary in the two services, the themes remain the same. Since the morning blessings are longer and more elaborate, and since the morning service as a whole plays a more prominent role in the liturgical rhythm of Jewish daily prayer, my

Hashem, Creator of the World

The first blessing before the morning Shema answers the question "who is Hashem" by presenting Israel's God as the Creator of all things. The One whom Israel worships is not a tribal deity restricted to a particular land or people, but *Adon Olam*, the Master of the universe.

Since this blessing accompanies the *morning* recitation of the Shema, it emphasizes God's creation of the heavenly luminaries (i.e., the sun and the stars). Each morning the sun dispels the darkness of night, and we experience the world as though it had been created anew. According to this blessing, our experience reflects what is actually happening: in his goodness God daily renews the work of creation (*uvtuvo mechadesh bechol yom tamid ma'aseh vereishit*). Thus, God's role and work as Creator is not restricted deistically to the initial temporal events that gave rise to the universe, but instead includes God's continual loving care for the natural world.

Jews in the pre-modern era often associated the luminaries—sometimes referred to in Scripture as the army (*tzava*) of heaven—with angelic powers.[40] This association explains the insertion of the angelic *kedushah* (sanctification) in the first blessing before the Shema. Drawing upon the classic prophetic theophanies of Isaiah 6 and Ezekiel 1, the *kedushah* depicts the angelic worship of God that takes place in the heights of heaven. The insertion of the *kedushah* in a blessing that celebrates God as Creator underlines the response of praise that creation owes to the One who is the source of its being.

The *kedushah* also sets the stage for the recitation of the Shema. The threefold angelic sanctification of the divine Name is described as their "acceptance of the yoke of the kingdom of heaven" (*vechulam mekablim aleyhem 'ol malchut shamayim*)—the same language employed in rabbinic texts to characterize Israel's recitation of the Shema. Thus, Israel's affirmation of the covenant in the Shema corresponds to the angelic worship of the Creator. Israel's earthly service mirrors the angels' heavenly service. Furthermore, as the hosts of heaven assume a priestly role of representing the worship of all creation, so Israel's response to Hashem

---

comments on the blessings that accompany the Shema will concentrate on the form these blessings take in the morning service.

40. Genesis 2:1; Deuteronomy 4:19; 17:3; Isaiah 40:26. See Mullen, "Hosts, Host of Heaven," 301–4.

involves more than its own relationship to the Creator. Israel is a priestly people, and its self-offering to Hashem represents the entire world.

Similarly, the final paragraph points forward to the blessing that follows the Shema. In that blessing we will read of the deliverance at the Sea of Reeds, and Israel's subsequent praise of God in the Song of Moses: "Who is like You, O Hashem, among the gods; who is like You, majestic in holiness, awesome in praises (*nora tehillot*), doing wonders (*oseh feleh*)?"[41] Here, in the final paragraph of the first blessing, Hashem is called "awesome in praises" (*nora tehillot*), "the Lord of wonders" (*Adon hanifla'ot*). At the Sea Israel first acknowledges Hashem's sovereignty, and enters into the priestly service that it shares with the angelic host. At the Sea Israel also receives a foretaste of the vision of God that will be given in fullness only at the eschaton, and its response likewise anticipates that day when God's Name will be sanctified on earth as it is in heaven.

Like all the blessings of the Shema, the first blessing concludes with a prayer for redemption. Continuing with the imagery of light, we pray that God might "cause a new light to illumine Zion," and that we might "all soon share a portion of its radiance" (*or chadash al tzion ta'ir venizkeh chulanu meheyrah le'oro*). We look for that day when creation will be definitively renewed, and when Zion will take its place at its center. The universal concerns of this first blessing are thus bound inseparably to Hashem's particular relationship with the people of Israel. Creation will only reach its goal when Israel attains its allotted destiny.

Creation Through Yeshua

As we have seen, the Shema expresses Israel's response to Hashem. When we recite it in Yeshua, we concentrate on his fulfillment of that response in his self-offering to God, and we participate in his self-offering through the gift of his Spirit.

The blessings that accompany the Shema praise God for the divine acts that make such a response possible and necessary. When reciting these blessings in Yeshua, we remember that antecedent to his role as our representative before God, he is already God's representative to us. Messiah is the agent by whom God accomplishes all God's works.

---

41. Exodus 15:11.

God creates all things through the divine Word and Wisdom that became incarnate in Yeshua.[42] The first blessing before the Shema begins by celebrating God's acts of creation in the words of Psalm 104:24: "O Hashem, how manifold are Your works! In wisdom You have made them all (*kulam bechochmah asita*); the earth is full of Your creatures." In accordance with the teaching of the Apostles, we see the *Chochmah* of this psalm as the divine Wisdom that became flesh in Yeshua. Even when his role in God's creative work is not overtly alluded to, we recognize it and bless Hashem for Messiah's universal mediation.[43]

In accordance with the Jewish mystical tradition, Messianic Jews likewise see the Name of God as a distinct reality, inseparably one with God yet also possessing its own differentiated identity.[44] The numerous references to God's Name in this blessing, and in Jewish prayer as a whole, point us again to Messiah Yeshua as the eternal self-expression of the ineffable God.

Messiah is also "the image of the invisible God"—both before and after his incarnation.[45] According to John, the enthroned human form that Isaiah saw was Yeshua.[46] This may explain the significance of John 1:18: "No one has ever seen God; it is God the only Son, who is close to the Father's heart, who has made him known." This verse follows a reference to the gift of the Torah through Moses. It implies that the God who Moses encountered in visible form was "God the only Son."[47]

Thus, the threefold sanctification of God found in the *kedushah* (and included in the first blessing of the Shema) includes for us the angelic recognition of the holiness and glory of the Son. He mediates God's creative work, and he likewise mediates God's self-revelation to the world created through him.

---

42. John 1:1–3; 1 Corinthians 8:6; Colossians 1:15–16; Hebrews 1:1–4.

43. "Universal mediation" means that God does nothing apart from the mediation of the Son and the Spirit.

44. Danielou, *The Theology of Jewish Christianity*, 147–63; Longenecker, *The Christology of Early Jewish Christianity*, 41–46; Fossum, *The Name of God and the Angel of the Lord*, 76–191, 239–56.

45. Colossians 1:15; see 2 Corinthians 4:4.

46. John 12:41.

47. "Christ is greater than Moses as the one whom Moses saw is greater than Moses; in the Fourth Gospel, the glory witnessed by Israelite prophets was that of Jesus himself" (Keener, *The Gospel of John: A Commentary*, vol. 1, 419). Paul hints at something similar in 2 Corinthians 3:12—4:6.

The image woven throughout the first blessing of the Shema is that of light: the light of the first day of creation, spoken into existence before the sun, moon, and stars; the light of the fourth day, identified with the luminaries (*me'orot*); the light of the last day, which will shine on a redeemed Zion. According to the Apostolic Writings, Yeshua is the true light that is the source of all other light, the light of life.[48] To praise God for light is to praise God for Yeshua.

To understand and pray the *Siddur* in this way is neither arbitrary nor eisegetical. It is to pray the traditional Jewish liturgy in the same way that the early Messianic Jews prayed the Psalms, and read the Torah and the Prophets. We find Yeshua everywhere in the tradition because he is there. We know this not simply through a grammatical historical reading of the prayers themselves, but through the knowledge implicit in Yeshua's resurrected life and the gift of his Spirit.

Hashem, God of Israel

Who is Hashem? The final lines of the first blessing hint at a truth that becomes the main point of the second blessing preceding the morning Shema (known by its opening words, *Ahavah Rabbah*): Hashem is not only the Creator of the universe, sanctified by the angels in heaven, but also the One who loves and chooses the people of Israel.

As its opening and closing lines indicate, *Ahavah Rabbah* emphasizes God's love and compassion. While God loves all creation, the second blessing of the Shema focuses on God's particular love for the descendants of Abraham, Isaac, and Jacob, Sarah, Rebecca, Rachel, and Leah. It thereby establishes a context for the first paragraph of the Shema and its call to Israel to love Hashem wholeheartedly. The One whom Israel loves is the One who first loved Israel.

How has Hashem loved Israel? Hashem has singled out the people of Israel from among the nations of the world, established a covenant with them, and given them a way of life that expresses that covenant and reflects the character of the divine covenant partner. In short, God has given Israel the gift of the Torah—a gift of love that depends upon and is inseparable from the gifts of election and covenant.

While the second blessing accompanying the Shema acknowledges in praise the God who loves Israel "with great and exceeding mercy"

---

48. John 1:4–9, 8:12; 2 Corinthians 4:6.

(*chemla gedolah vitayrah*), it departs from the pattern of the other two blessings in the emphasis it gives to petition. Above all, this blessing involves a request that we—the people of Israel—might receive inner divine illumination and strength in order to be able to live out the Shema in truth: "Illumine our eyes with the light of Your Torah, cause our heart to cleave to Your *mitzvot*, and unite our heart to love and fear Your Name."[49] As we prepare to acknowledge Hashem's "unity" and pledge our lives to love Him completely, we first ask Hashem to "unite our heart"—that we might not be divided in our basic loyalties, but might offer ourselves in genuine love as a living sacrifice.

In making such a petition, Israel recognizes that it is unable to fulfill the Torah apart from God's inner empowerment. It is unable to love God unless God lovingly enables it to do so. We confess by means of this prayer that God's greatest gift of love to Israel is the capacity to love God in return.[50]

Like all three of the blessings that accompany the Shema, *Ahavah Rabbah* includes a prayer for redemption. It focuses on the re-gathering of Israel to its land. However, according to this prayer the re-gathering is not an end itself, but has the purpose of enabling Israel to fulfill its destined vocation: "You have chosen us from all nations and languages, and drawn us near to Your great Name in truth, to acknowledge You and Your Oneness/Uniqueness in love."[51] Thus, even this prayer for redemption is oriented to Israel's recitation of the Shema, here presented in eschatological terms as the consummation of a renewed creation.

Yeshua, God's First Beloved

For the most part, our way of entry into this second blessing should be obvious. We see Yeshua as the living Torah, the supreme interpreter of the Written Torah and the One to whom it bears perpetual witness. Moreover, he is the One who has given us his own Spirit so that through him and in him we might observe the *mitzvot* and faithfully fulfill the covenant. The second blessing of the Shema provides us the opportunity to pray that we may be bound to Yeshua by his Spirit, so that his fulfillment of the Shema might become our own.

---

49. Translation mine.
50. A similar message is found in 1 Chronicles 29:14.
51. Translation mine.

Less obvious, but just as important, is the connection between Israel's election and that of Messiah Yeshua. In many ways, Ephesians 1:3–6 presents a messianic version of *Ahavah Rabbah*:

> Blessed be the God and Father of our Lord Yeshua the Messiah, who has blessed us in Messiah with every spiritual blessing in the heavenly places, just as he chose us in Messiah before the foundation of the world to be holy and blameless before him in love. He destined us for adoption as his children through Yeshua the Messiah, to the praise of his glorious grace that he freely bestowed on us in the Beloved.

Here we have a blessing formula that speaks of God's loving choice, as in the final words of *Ahavah Rabbah*.[52] If the "us" in these verses is "Israel" or "we Jews," as it appears to be in the verses that follow (Ephesians 1:11–13), the parallel becomes exact: God chooses Israel in love, to live a life that is "holy and blameless" (i.e., in conformity to the Torah).

The added words, however, provide the essential messianic hermeneutical key: the One who chooses Israel is "the God and Father of our Lord Yeshua the Messiah," and the choice is enacted "in Messiah." In other words, God first chooses Messiah Yeshua in love, and then brings Israel into that election (just as he will later bring the nations to share in Israel's election). The love that the Father has for the Son ("the Beloved") is extended to Israel, whose covenant gives it the status of adopted children.

We pray the traditional form of *Ahavah Rabbah*, in concert with other Jews throughout the world and through centuries past, but we pray it in light of Ephesians 1. In this blessing we acknowledge Messiah Yeshua not only as the goal of Jewish history, but also as its hidden origin and enduring center.

Hashem, Redeemer of Israel

Who is Hashem? We learn in the first two blessings of the Shema that Hashem is the Creator of all things who enters into a loving covenantal relationship with the people of Israel and enables them to live in a manner worthy of the One who has chosen them. Hashem is the earth's

---

52. "The One who chose his people Israel in love" (*Habocher be'amo Israel be'ahavah*).

sovereign who invites Israel to lovingly acknowledge that sovereignty and serve as its effective sign among the nations of the world. It does so through the recitation and living out of the Shema.

The third paragraph of the Shema concludes by identifying Hashem as the One who "brought you out of the land of Egypt." The blessing following the Shema picks up these words, and makes them an essential feature of the identity of Israel's God. Hashem's sovereignty in Israel's life implies not only authority to rule over Israel but also a commitment to act redemptively on Israel's behalf.

Throughout this lengthy blessing, one word receives special emphasis: *emet* (truth).

> Your teaching is *true* and enduring ... *True* it is that the eternal God is our King, that the Rock of Jacob is our protecting shield ... For our ancestors, for us, for our children, for every generation of the people Israel, for all ages from the first to the last, His teachings are *true*, everlasting. *True* it is that You are the Lord our God, even as You were the God of our ancestors ... You are, in *truth*, Lord of Your people, their defender and mighty King.

The "teaching" (*davar*) whose truth is confessed is that found in the first verse of the Shema: Hashem is the world's and Israel's only sovereign. The three paragraphs of the Shema focus on the covenantal obligations this sovereignty imposes on Israel. The final blessing accompanying the Shema underlines the fact that this sovereignty likewise imposes covenantal obligations on Hashem. God's *truth* means God's covenant faithfulness.

As the Shema relives the decisive moment of Israel's covenantal commitment to Hashem at Sinai, so the blessing following the Shema recalls the decisive moment in which Hashem manifests covenant fidelity to Israel—the exodus from Egypt and particularly its climax, the passage through the Sea. Moreover, as creation and covenantal election are divine acts that God renews daily, so the exodus recurs again and again in Israel's national life and in the life of individual Jews. Most importantly, as creation and covenantal election reach their consummation at the end of the age (as implied by the petitions for redemption inserted in the first and second blessings of the morning Shema), so God's acts of deliverance in Egypt and throughout history point forward to God's definitive intervention at the eschaton. Thus, the celebration of God's redemptive love for Israel in the third blessing culminates in a prayer for the redemption yet to come: "Rock of Israel, rise to Israel's defense; fulfill Your promise to deliver Judah and Israel."

Beyond serving as a vivid illustration of the exodus from Egypt mentioned in the final words of the third paragraph of the Shema, Israel's passage through the Sea also echoes the angelic *kedushah* and anticipates Israel's covenantal acknowledgement of God's sovereignty realized at Sinai and renewed daily in the Shema.

> With a new song the redeemed ones praised Your Name at the seashore, all of them in unison gave thanks, acknowledged [Your] sovereignty (*yachad kulam hodu vehimlichu*), and said: "Hashem shall reign for all eternity."[53]

Our earlier discussion of the first blessing pointed to its use of language from this third blessing to establish an implicit correspondence between the role of the angels on high and of Israel on earth. Here the third blessing returns the compliment and alludes to the language employed in the first blessing:

> Then they all accept upon themselves the yoke of heavenly sovereignty (*kulam mekablim alayhem ol malchut shamayim*) ... All of them as one proclaim His holiness (*kedushah kulam ke'echad 'onim*).[54]

Here Israel's unified acknowledgement of divine sovereignty at the Sea points beyond the angelic *kedushah*, the Sinai theophany, and Israel's daily recitation of the Shema to the eschatological fulfillment of divine sovereignty at the final redemption. Like *Ahavah Rabbah*, this blessing of God the Redeemer envisions the goal of redemption as a world in which Hashem's exclusive sovereignty is lovingly embraced by all.

Hashem's self-revelation reaches its consummation with the final demonstration of divine covenant fidelity to Israel. Eschatological redemption thus manifests definitively the identity of God, even as the exodus from Egypt publicly manifests the divine Name for the first time. Hashem becomes known by all as the One presented in the three blessings of the morning Shema. As a result, Hashem's sovereignty is acknowledged by all in fulfillment of the Shema itself.

---

53. Scherman (translator), *The Complete ArtScroll Siddur*.
54. Ibid.

Redemption through Yeshua

Messianic Jews believe that God liberates Israel and all creation through the work of Messiah Yeshua. The God who raised Yeshua from the tomb is the One who will give life to Israel and deliver the world from its bondage to the powers of death.

We pray the third blessing of the morning Shema in light of Revelation 15:2–3: "And I saw what appeared to be a sea of glass mixed with fire, and those who had conquered the beast and its image and the number of its name, standing beside the sea of glass with harps of God in their hands. And they sing the song of Moses, the servant of God, and the song of the Lamb." The book of Revelation repeatedly employs imagery from the exodus to depict the greater liberation at the end of the age. Here the victorious followers of the Lamb stand "beside the sea of glass," just as Israel stood beside the Sea of Reeds; and they sing a song that is simultaneously the song of Moses (Exodus 15) and the song of the Lamb. They do not sing two songs, but one: it is the song of Moses, sung now with explicit recognition that God redeems Israel from Egypt-Babylon through the death and resurrection of Yeshua.

The book of Revelation presents Yeshua as the lion of the tribe of Judah who establishes his messianic reign through becoming the slaughtered lamb. He obtains the right to open the scroll of God's redemptive plan by offering his life as a sacrifice.[55] *He is "the faithful martyr-witness" whose fulfillment of the three paragraphs of the Shema serves as the basis of God's fulfillment of the three blessings of the Shema.*[56] He is also the One who enables his followers to participate in his self-offering, so that their "martyrdom-witness," joined to his own, brings final deliverance and judgment to the world:

> When he opened the fifth seal, I saw under the altar the souls of those who had been slaughtered for the word of God and for the testimony (*martyria*) they had given; they cried out with a loud voice, "Sovereign Lord, holy and true, how long will it be before you judge and avenge our blood on the inhabitants of the earth?" They were each given a white robe and told to rest a little longer, until the number would be complete both of their fellow servants and of their brothers and sisters, who were soon to be killed as they themselves had been killed. (Revelation 6:9–11)

55. Revelation 5:1–14.
56. Revelation 1:5.

> But they have conquered him by the blood of the lamb and by the word of their testimony (*martyria*), for they did not cling to life even in the face of death. (Revelation 12:11)

Thus, the three paragraphs of the Shema are both the goal of the final redemption and the means by which it is achieved. God liberates his people and the world so that all might lovingly acknowledge the exclusive divine sovereignty, and God also accomplishes that liberation through the perfect covenantal witness of Messiah Yeshua, the one-man Israel. Furthermore, the liberating witness of the Messiah finds a necessary echo in the witness of his servants, who "complete what is lacking in Messiah's afflictions" (Colossians 1:24).

The third blessing of the Shema both remembers God's past redemptive work and prays for its consummation at the end of the age. For us, this twofold orientation involves praising God for sending Yeshua and raising him from the dead, while at the same time praying for the final liberation that is the ultimate goal and fruit of his redemptive self-offering. This prayer leads naturally into the *Amidah* (central prayer of Jewish liturgy)—but that is a topic for another discussion.

CONCLUSION

The Shema and its blessings, understood in light of Messiah Yeshua, provide us with a summary narrative framework for the good news. The first two blessings describe God's work of creation and God's covenantal election of Israel and the gift of the Torah, all accomplished through the mediation of the divine Son; the three paragraphs of the Shema describe Yeshua's work of fulfilling the Torah through his life, death, and resurrection; and the final blessing describes God's future redemption of Israel and the world as the result of Yeshua's fulfillment of the Shema and of the ongoing participation in that fulfillment by those who belong to Yeshua.

Yeshua is thus the fulfillment of the covenant—both from God's side, and from Israel's side. The blessings of the Shema emphasize the former, the Shema itself emphasizes the latter.

At the same time, the Shema and its blessings provide us not only with a narrative, but also with a script intended to shape our involvement in a dramatic performance.[57] We are part of the story! As such, we are summoned to identify with Yeshua in his vicarious fulfillment of the covenant on Israel's behalf, and to participate in it. We do so ritually as we recite the Shema daily, and holistically as we live out the meaning of the Shema in all our daily conduct.

The redemptive power of Yeshua's Shema will only be realized when the fullness of Israel and the fullness of the nations have identified with and entered into his vicarious fulfillment of the covenant. Thus, our part in the drama is essential, though radically dependent on the part played by our Messiah.

This way of understanding the Shema makes it both the text of our covenantal response to God and simultaneously the centerpiece of the wondrous works of God that we celebrate in the accompanying blessings. When Yeshua fulfills the covenant from Israel's side, he is *at the same time* fulfilling the covenant from God's side.

When we recite the Shema and its accompanying blessings, we are praying *in Israel*. According to the Messianic interpretation of this prayer offered here, any genuine recitation of the Shema and its blessings constitutes also a prayer *in Yeshua*. As we learn how to enter into this prayer consciously, explicitly, with messianic *kavannah* (direction of the heart) inspired by the Spirit of the Messiah, we bear witness to the truth of Yeshua's mysterious centrality to Jewish life, and the mysterious centrality of Jewish life to God's purposes for history and the world.

---

57. On the relevance of the metaphor of "drama" for our understanding of Scripture, tradition, theology, and practice, see Vanhoozer, *The Drama of Doctrine*.

Part III

Yeshua-faith from a Jewish Perspective

5

Beginning with the End: The Place of Eschatology in the Messianic Jewish Canonical Narrative

Christianity and Judaism have each developed different "canonical narratives," or theological frameworks by which to understand the Bible and God's work in the world. While a canonical narrative seeks to order the stories and events within the biblical canon, it also establishes a trajectory whereby Scripture connects to our experience and points forward to the world to come. In an attempt to develop a coherent and authentic Messianic Jewish canonical narrative, Kinzer assesses how both Judaism and Christianity have, in different ways, tended to either overemphasize or underemphasize the continuity between the world as we experience it and the reality of the eschaton. Kinzer posits significant continuity between the canonical narratives of Judaism and Christianity, showing how Yeshua's incarnation, life, death and resurrection extend the *kedushah* (holiness) that characterizes Israel as a people. Just as the Sabbath in Judaism offers a proleptic foretaste of the world to come, so Yeshua's gathering of a multinational *ekklesia* (community of believers) that shares in Israel's vocation points forward to God's sanctification of the whole world. Rather than supplanting Israel's call to represent God in the world, Yeshua (and the community he founds) executes the next chapter in creation's movement toward consummation and final redemption.[1]

A "CANONICAL NARRATIVE," as defined by R. Kendall Soulen, is "an interpretive instrument"—a hermeneutical tool—that orders the Bible's complex story line so as to present it as "a theological and nar-

---

1. Presented at the Hashivenu Forum in 2002. See p. 29, n. 2.

rative unity."[2] While the Bible describes people and events set in the distant past, its narrative transcends that past. It includes prophetic and apocalyptic material, and even its accounts of historical events are told for the purpose of shedding light on the future. Therefore, our canonical narrative must deal with the future as well as with the past.

The title and topic of this essay might lead one to expect discussion of end-times scenarios, millennial controversies, or the imminence of Messiah's coming. However, that is not my purpose here. Instead, I will inquire into how the Bible's eschatological vision shapes—and is shaped by—the entire biblical narrative. How is the description of the creation of the world informed by convictions concerning its ultimate consummation? How do the election of Israel and the Sinai covenant and its institutions relate to creation's destined fulfillment? How are the enfleshment of the primordial Human and his death and resurrection a preview of the eschaton? How do the gift of the *Ruach* (Spirit), the exile of the *Shekhinah* (divine presence), and the intertwined histories of the Christian church and the Jewish people point to that final breakthrough that will simultaneously renew, transform, and transcend history?

This last question demonstrates an aspect of the canonical narrative that we could easily overlook. We are not just attempting to understand the story told by the Bible. We are also seeking to place the history of the last two thousand years within the framework of that story. Thus, the canonical narrative is a hermeneutical tool both for reading the Bible and also for interpreting history in the light of the biblical narrative—or, rather, as an integral part of that narrative.

We come to these questions with a unique perspective. We are Jews, rooted in Jewish soil. That soil is Israel's experience of a continuous covenant existence through the centuries, and the literary, liturgical, and institutional embodiments of that experience. At the same time, we are Messianic—loyal students and followers of Yeshua the Messiah, who have accepted the Apostolic Writings (New Testament) as the authentic witness to his mission and message. We believe that Yeshua began a decisive new phase in the outworking of the divine plan, and that the nations of the world have been drawn into Israel's orbit with its covenantal center. Our construal of the canonical narrative should both reflect and reinforce our identity as Messianic Jews.

---

2. Soulen, *The God of Israel and Christian Theology*, 13.

THREE ESCHATOLOGICAL HORIZONS

David Novak employs the term "eschatological horizon" to characterize the way a theology envisions the relationship between this world (*Olam Hazeh*) and the world to come (*Olam Haba*).[3] This term and the concept it expresses provide a useful tool for analyzing the role of eschatology in the varied readings of the canonical narrative. A theology operates with a low eschatological horizon when it minimizes the difference between life in this world (at least among the faithful) and life in the world to come. In contrast, a theology with a high eschatological horizon accentuates the radical disjunction between these two orders of existence.

Utilizing Novak's terminology, I will argue that three versions of the canonical narrative provide negative examples for us as we seek to develop our own Messianic Jewish perspective on the role of eschatology in the story of Hashem's dealings with the world and with human beings.

(1) *Excessively Low Eschatological Horizon (Jewish).* This view is found in both a traditional and a modern form. The traditional form sees the messianic age as a restored Davidic empire that brings peace to the world, but does not alter its fundamental ontological structure. The modern form builds upon a utopian vision of human progress, and aims for a world of peace and justice but without any dramatic, extraordinary divine intervention.

(2) *Excessively Low Eschatological Horizon (Christian).* The Christian low eschatological horizon differs markedly from the Jewish version. It exaggerates the transformation of the world's ontological structure that has already occurred in the *ekklesia* through the death and resurrection of Messiah and thereby minimizes the distance between *Olam Haba* and *Olam Hazeh*. Rather than fashioning the world to come in the image of this world, it tends to spiritualize the future world and in like manner spiritualize and idealize life in Messiah in the present world.

(3) *Excessively High Eschatological Horizon (Jewish).* This view maximizes the distance between Jewish life under the Torah of this age and life in the world to come, both by emphasizing the transformed character of the future world and by denying the eschatological

---

3. Novak, "Beyond Supersessionism," 58, 60.

nature of Jewish life in this world. Ironically, this perspective on Jewish life is shared by those Christians who have an excessively *low* eschatological horizon in relation to their own life in the present age. While minimizing the difference between Christian life in this world and the life of the redeemed in the world to come, they maximize this distinction for Jewish life!

I will look at each of these views in reverse order, and contrast them with how a Messianic Jewish understanding of the canonical narrative should set its eschatological horizon.

JUDAISM AND PROLEPTIC ESCHATOLOGY

The intense rivalry and polemics between Jews and Christians over the centuries have had many regrettable consequences. One of the less recognized of those consequences is the distortion brought to both rabbinic Judaism and Christianity as each sought to distance itself from the other. From the Jewish side, Michael Wyschogrod notes that "the temptation here is to make the contrast [between Judaism and Christianity] as sharp as possible, thereby, at times, distorting Judaism."[4] Many Jewish thinkers have succumbed to this temptation when dealing with eschatology and Jewish existence in this world. Arthur Cohen is a case in point: "The Jew is the 'between-man,' between time and eternity, between the sadness of the world and the joy of redemption. He neither believes that in this time and history has the Kingdom of God been foretasted nor does he know when it is that God appoints this time and history for redemption."[5]

To deny that Jewish life provides any "foretaste" of "the Kingdom of God" is to posit such a lofty eschatological horizon that the sky cannot even be glimpsed. Is this true to the Torah or to rabbinic tradition? Nancy Fuchs-Kreimer sees the weakness of such a perspective: "In Judaism, we have stressed the communal nature of redemption and the 'not yet' quality of its futurity. In my judgment, many Jews have underemphasized the idea that at least a taste of redemption is already here. The idea surfaces in the notion that the Sabbath is a foretaste of the Messianic Time, but many Jews do not put sufficient weight on this concept and spend more time speaking of past and future than of the present."[6] The Torah itself

---

4. Wyschogrod, *The Body of Faith*, xxxv.
5. Cohen, "The Natural and the Supernatural Jew," 198.
6. Fuchs-Kreimer, "Redemption: What I Have Learned from Christians," 283.

presents Jewish life in this age as an anticipation or *prolepsis* of the life of the age to come. It does this, as Fuchs-Kreimer notes, through the institution of the Sabbath, but, even more fundamentally, through the reality that underlies the Sabbath and that is associated intimately with Israel's life—*kedushah* (holiness).

The creation narrative of Genesis 1:1—2:3 tells us six times that God, beholding what he had made, saw that it was good (vv. 4, 10, 12, 18, 21, 25). After completing the work in six days, in keeping with the numerical symbolism of the narrative, God looks upon the whole, and finds it *very* good (1:31). Thus, the world was good in all its parts, and very good in its totality. However, the climax of the narrative comes not on the sixth day but on the seventh. Ceasing from his work, "God blessed the seventh day and made it holy" (2:3). The world, untarnished by any evil, was very good. But it was not yet holy. It was *chol*—profane, secular.

The divine sanctification of the seventh day does not in itself alter the world's profane character. God does not command Adam and Eve to keep the Sabbath, nor does the book of Genesis show us anyone doing so. The Sabbath in Genesis 2:1–3 is not an institution but a hope, a promise, a pledge indicating the appointed destiny for this world that was created "very good." The seventh day thus represents a consummation of the created order that transcends the conquest of evil and the restoration of a world that is entirely good. It represents a world that is holy, i.e., filled with the divine presence, like the innermost shrine of the desert sanctuary or Jerusalem temple. Thus, we see from its initial appearance in the biblical text that holiness, *kedushah*, is itself an eschatological concept referring to an eschatological reality.[7]

The Sabbath does not become a human institution until after Israel has departed from Egypt. The *kedushah* associated with the Sabbath is likewise associated with the people of Israel and the Sinai covenant.

---

7. This is clearly the perspective of the Priestly account of creation in Genesis 1:1—2:3, for whom the category of *kedushah* is fundamental. The creation account of Genesis 2 shares a similar perspective, but expresses it in different images and concepts. Here the tree of life serves a parallel function to the Sabbath: it represents the consummation that is Adam and Eve's destiny but not yet their possession. In this light the customary rabbinic linkage between the tree of life and the Torah (based on Proverbs 3:18) takes on new significance. The Sabbath, as the central *mitzvah* (commandment) of Israel's Torah, symbolizes the proleptic eschatological holiness inherent in the Torah as a whole.

Only with the establishment of Israel as a holy people (Exodus 19:6) does *kedushah*, that eschatological destiny of consummated creation, descend to earth and become a signpost pointing the way to the world's ultimate fulfillment.[8] Thus, already in Genesis 1—2, we have allusions to Israel's role in the divine plan. Even before Adam and Eve eat from the tree of the knowledge of good and evil and are expelled from the garden, Israel has an honored place in the divine purpose, a role in bringing the world from goodness to holiness, from infancy to maturity, from potential splendor to actualized glory.

Kedushah as an eschatological reality is also seen in the institution of the *Mishkan* (tabernacle) and the *Bet Mikdash* (temple). Just as the Sabbath consummates the six-day creation, so the narrative describing the construction of the *Mishkan* is patterned after Genesis 1, with the implication that Israel's "work," directed by the divine command, completes God's work in creation.[9] The Sabbath could even be called "a temple in time."[10] Though the phrase is less immediately intelligible, it might be even more appropriate to call the temple a "Sabbath in space."[11] Both the holy day and the holy place are signs of the covenant between Hashem and Israel (Exodus 31:13, 16–17; Numbers 10:33; Deuteronomy 10:1–8). Both are also eschatological signposts. They show that the world has not yet attained its appointed goal of unrestricted *kedushah*, for only one day, one place, and one people are set apart as holy. Yet, they also show that holiness has pitched its tent in this world, granting a foretaste now of the life of the world to come.

The eschatological character of *kedushah* can be seen most vividly in Zechariah 14 and Revelation 21. The final chapters of Zechariah

---

8. Sarna, *Genesis*, 14; Soulen, *The God of Israel*, 118. It is surely significant that the various forms of the Hebrew root *koph-dalet-shin* appear nowhere else in the book of Genesis. They are not seen again until Hashem's revelation to Moses at the burning bush (Exodus 3:5), and then with the first commandments given to Israel—in Egypt (Exodus 12:16; 13:2) and at Sinai (Exodus 19:6, 10, 14, 23).

9. Levenson, *Sinai and Zion*, 142–45.

10. "Judaism teaches us to be attached to *holiness in time*, to be attached to sacred events, to learn how to consecrate sanctuaries that emerge from the magnificent stream of a year. The Sabbaths are our great cathedrals; and our Holy of Holies is a shrine that neither the Romans nor the Germans were able to burn; a shrine that even apostasy cannot easily obliterate: the Day of Atonement... Jewish ritual may be characterized as the art of significant forms in time, as *architecture of time*... The seventh day is like a palace in time with a kingdom for all" (Heschel, *The Sabbath*, 8, 21).

11. Heschel argues for the superiority of the Sabbath to the temple (Ibid., 79–83).

contain prophecies pointing to Jerusalem's desperate conflict with the nations at the end of the age. The battle ends when Hashem himself appears, "and all the holy ones with him" (14:5). The coming of Hashem brings not only Israel's deliverance, but also a transformation of the created order, in which the distinction between day and night that derives from the first day of creation in Genesis 1 is removed, and "there shall be continuous day" (14:7). More significantly, the presence of Hashem brings a new *kedushah* to the city, a *kedushah* that swallows up all that is profane and renders the distinction between holy and profane obsolete. Thus, the bells of the horses in the city are as holy as the high priest's crown, and every pot and pan in Jerusalem and all of Judah become as holy as the bowls in front of the altar (14:20–21). This demonstrates the eschatological character of *kedushah*, and implies that the world to come is "that day that is entirely Shabbat."[12]

The final chapters of the book of Revelation convey the same message. As in Zechariah, darkness is swallowed up by light (22:5) and the profane by the holy. The new Jerusalem is the holy city (21:2), in which the divine presence resides (21:3) and into which no unclean thing may enter (21:27). The twelve stones that represent the twelve tribes of Israel and that adorn the high priest's breastplate now adorn the foundations of the wall of the city (21:19; see Exodus 28:15–21). Like the holy of holies, the city is a perfect cube (21:16); this explains why there is no temple in the city (21:22), for the city as a whole has become the inner sanctuary of the divine presence. Like the Sabbath, which distinguishes between holy and profane time, the temple implies a distinction between levels of holiness, and between holy and profane. But in the new Jerusalem there is only *Shabbat*, there is only the holy of holies. Once again, the eschatological character of *kedushah* becomes evident.

By presenting Israel as a holy nation in the midst of a profane world, Tanakh points to Israel's life in this world as a foretaste or anticipation of the life of the world to come. *Olam Haba* does not involve an entirely unprecedented divine invasion from without; smaller invasions have already occurred, to make us aware of what lies ahead. Rabbinic tradition grasps this biblical truth, and extends it in various ways. Above all,

---

12. "In the renewed world that is the target of eschatological hope the difference between God and creature will remain, but that between the holy and the profane will be totally abolished (Zech. 14:20–21)" (Pannenberg, *Systematic Theology*, vol. 1, 400.).

rabbinic tradition recognizes the eschatological character of *Shabbat*.[13] The Mishnah offers this midrash on the superscription to Psalm 92: "On the Sabbath they sang *A Psalm: a Song for the Sabbath Day*; a Psalm, a song for the time that is to come, for the day that shall be all Sabbath and rest in life everlasting."[14] In accordance with this midrash, we pray in the *Shabbat birkat hamazon* (grace after meals) that we might inherit "the day that shall be all Sabbath and rest in life everlasting." Thus, the Mishnah (and the liturgical tradition that builds upon it) acknowledges that the definitive *Shabbat* is eschatological in nature. This implies that our experience of *Shabbat* in this world anticipates the life of the world to come. Such an inference finds explicit support in the following midrash:

> R. Hanina [or, Hinena] b. Isaac said: There are three incomplete phenomena (*novelet*): the incomplete experience of death is sleep; an incomplete form of prophecy is the dream; the incomplete form of the next world is the Sabbath (*novelet ha'olam haba Shabbat*). (*Gen. Rab.* 17:5)

The word *novelet* refers primarily to unripe fruit that falls from a tree. However, it can also refer to a lesser member of any general category. Jacob Neusner offers an amplified translation, rendering the word as "partial realization of a complete experience."[15] When Israel observes *Shabbat* in this world, it tastes in a partial and preliminary way the powers of the age to come. This is true because "the Sabbath possesses a holiness like that of the future world" (*Mek. Exod.* 31:17).

Rabbinic tradition likewise views the land of Israel as an anticipatory sign of the world to come. Thus, the Mishnah interprets Isaiah's prophecy that Israel "shall inherit the land" (Isaiah 60:21) as meaning that it will "have a share in the world to come" (*m. Sanh.* 10:1). Abraham Joshua Heschel states emphatically the proleptic eschatological character of the land: "There is a unique association between the people and the land of Israel . . . The Jew in whose heart the love of Zion dies is doomed to lose his faith in the God of Abraham who gave the land as an earnest of the redemption of all men."[16] In similar language, the Conservative

---

13. Heschel, *The Sabbath*, 73–76; Greenberg, *The Jewish Way*, 129; Hammer, *Entering Jewish Prayer*, 212–18.

14. *M. Tamid* 7:4.

15. Neusner, *Genesis Rabbah, vol. 1*, 184.

16. Heschel, *God in Search of Man*, 425.

movement's prayer book calls the State of Israel *reshit tzemichat ge'ulataynu*—"the first-fruits of the sprouting of our redemption."[17] The language adopted by Heschel ("earnest") and *Sim Shalom* ("first-fruits") in reference to the land resembles that employed by Paul in reference to the *Ruach HaKodesh* (Holy Spirit).[18] Just as Paul sees the gift of the *Ruach* as a foretaste of the future inheritance, so Jewish tradition as a whole sees the gift of the land in a similar light.

The daily liturgy also grants Jews an anticipatory experience of the world to come. It does this through *Pesukey deZimra*, the collection of biblical hymns recited each morning before the Shema and its blessings. The centerpiece of this collection consists of Psalms 145–150. These Psalms were composed in the wake of the return from exile in Babylon. In later tradition, however, they are seen as pointing forward to the ecstatic praise of the world to come. The following midrash on Psalm 145:1 ("I will bless Your name for ever and ever") illustrates this mode of interpretation: "One day it will not be as it is today, when, if He does wonders for Israel, they sing His praise, but if He does not, they do not sing His praise. In the time-to-come Israel will never cease singing, but will ceaselessly sing praises and blessings, as it is said, *And I will bless Your name for ever and ever* (Ps 145:1). We shall have no vocation other than blessing You with new blessings."[19] Similarly, Psalm 146:7, "The LORD will loose the bonds," receives an eschatological reading: "What is meant by *bonds* in *will loose the bonds*? The bonds of death and the bonds of the nether-world."[20] The last verse of Psalm 146 and the first verse of Psalm 147 are linked in the following eschatological midrash:

> When the Holy One, blessed be He, reigns, everything will sing praises to Him . . . *The LORD will reign for ever, your God, O Zion, to all generations. Praise the LORD! Praise the LORD; for it is good to sing praises to our God; for it is pleasant, and praise is fitting* (Ps 146:10—147:2). That is, when the Holy One, blessed be He, is King, it will be proper to praise Him. Why? Because everything will belong to the kingdom of the Holy One, blessed be He. Then

---

17. *Siddur Sim Shalom*, 416. The translation included here is my own. *Sim Shalom* itself translates the phrase as "with its promise of redemption" (ibid., 417). This phrase originated in Israeli religious Zionism.

18. See 2 Corinthians 1:22, 5:5; Ephesians 1:14; Romans 8:23.

19. Braude (translator), *The Midrash on Psalms, vol. 2*, 362.

20. Ibid., 367.

all will sing, all will shout praises, all will laud Him because all will see Him reigning.[21]

Since these Psalms are consistently read this way in the midrashic tradition, Heinrich Guggenheimer can say that their recitation before the statutory morning prayers is "intended as a preparation for the life in the World to Come."[22] This view finds support in the texts that conclude *Pesukey deZimra* (Exodus 15; Psalm 22:29; Obadiah 1:21; Zechariah 14:9), all of which have a clear eschatological import. It receives further confirmation from the opening and closing *berachot* (blessings), that refer to Hashem as "Life of the Worlds" (*chay ha'olamim*)—Life of this world and Life of the world to come. Thus, just as *Shabbat* provides a weekly taste of the coming age, so every morning the observant Jew enters in a preliminary and preparatory way into the ecstatic praise offered on that day that will be completely *Shabbat*.

In the Torah itself, *Shabbat* and the *Mikdash* serve as joint expressions of the eschatological *kedushah* given to Israel in this age. The destruction of the *Bet Mikdash* in 70 A.D. and the subsequent exile from Jerusalem raised serious questions for the rabbinic tradition. Had Israel lost its *kedushah*? With no temple, no high priest, and no sacrifices, and with a life lived in the impure lands of the *goyim* (nations), how could Israel maintain its holiness? The answer of the rabbis is striking. They did not merely claim that Israel maintains its holiness, despite its loss of the temple system and the land. They went further and asserted that Israel's holiness was never entirely dependent on these factors. Taking up themes emphasized by the Pharisees while the temple still stood, and based upon certain strands of biblical teaching, the rabbinic movement reconstructed Israel's sense of holiness along more universal lines.

> The questions taken up by the Mishnah, in the aftermath of the destruction of the Temple, are whether and how Israel is still holy. The self-evidently valid answer is that Israel is indeed holy, and so far as the media of sanctification persist beyond the destruction of the holy place—and they do endure—the task of holy Israel is to continue to conduct that life of sanctification that had centered upon the Temple. Where does holiness reside now? It is above all in the life of the people, Israel. The Mishnah may speak of the holiness of the Temple, but the premise is that the people—

---

21. Ibid., 372.
22. Guggenheimer, *The Scholar's Haggadah*, 316.

that kingdom of priests and holy people of Leviticus—constitute the center and locus of the sacred.[23]

The sect of the Pharisees and the profession of the scribes—together with surviving priests who joined them—framed a Judaism to take the place of the Judaism of Temple and cult. It emerged as a Judaism in which each of the elements of the Judaism of Temple and cult would find a counterpart: (1) in place of the Temple, the holy people, in whom holiness endured even outside of the cult, as the Pharisees had taught; (2) in place of the priesthood, the sage, the holy man qualified by learning, as the scribes had taught; (3) in place of the sacrifices of the altar, the holy way of life expressed through the carrying out of religious duties (*mitzvot*, "commandments"), and acts of kindness and grace beyond those commanded (*maasim tovim*, "good deeds"), and, above all, through studying the Torah.[24]

Every Jew has priestly obligations, every meal partakes of the holiness of a sacrificial banquet, in every place Hashem makes his presence known. In thus refashioning Jewish life for *galut* (exile), the rabbis extended Israel's sense of *kedushah* into realms formerly considered profane. In ways analogous to those adopted by the followers of Yeshua, rabbinic Judaism seized the opportunity provided by the exile and advanced toward the ideal of eschatological holiness found in Zechariah 14, rather than accepting with resignation a state of irreparable impurity.

The extension of *kedushah* into new realms was carried even further within the Hasidic movement. "The Holy strives to include within itself the whole of life. The Law differentiates between the holy and the profane, but the Law desires to lead the way toward the messianic removal of the differentiation, to the all-sanctification. Hasidic piety no longer recognizes anything as simply and irreparably profane: 'the profane' is for hasidism only a designation for the not yet sanctified, for that which is to be sanctified. Everything physical, all drives and urges and desires, everything creaturely, is material for sanctification."[25] Martin Buber recognizes that the Torah itself distinguishes clearly between holy and profane, yet he also sees a "messianic" (i.e., eschatological) impulse within the Torah (evident, as seen above, in Zechariah 14) toward the

---

23. Neusner, *A Short History of Judaism*, 57.
24. Ibid., 53.
25. Buber, "The Two Foci of the Jewish Soul," 126–27.

progressive removal of this distinction. This sets the stage for the new Hasidic teaching regarding worldly engagement.

> The Hasidic way of life . . . stressed the idea of *avodah be-gashmiyyut*, "divine worship through the use of material things." This involved a positive embrace of things of this world as means toward the greater service of God . . . In the essential Hasidic doctrine, God is to be worshiped not only by the study of the Torah, prayer, and the observance of the precepts but also, and particularly, by engaging in worldly pursuits with God in mind . . . When attending to his material needs for the sake of God, the *hasid* is carrying out acts of divine worship.[26]

In the Hasidic worldview, Israel participates in the divine drama leading to redemption by living within the profane world in such a way as to lift it to the level of holiness. *Kedushah* is an eschatological reality, and Israel shares in that reality in anticipation and also extends that reality as part of the process of preparing for the final redemption.

In light of the above, the place of proleptic eschatology within the Torah and within traditional Jewish thought must be reconsidered. When we tell Israel's story, the eschatological horizon must not be placed so high that we miss the significance of *kedushah*. Israel waits for her redemption, but she also experiences now a foretaste of what she waits for.[27]

JEWISH PROLEPTIC ESCHATOLOGY AND THE MISSION OF YESHUA

Once the note of eschatological anticipation is heard in the Torah and in rabbinic Judaism, Messianic Jews cannot avoid the question: how is this proleptic eschatology related to that introduced by Yeshua's birth, death, and resurrection? How we answer this question will determine the basic contours of our Messianic Jewish canonical narrative. The usual strategy of Christian theology has been to ignore the eschatological character of Israel's *kedushah*, and to accentuate the discontinuity between Israel's

---

26. Jacobs, "The Uplifting of Sparks in Later Jewish Mysticism," 115–16.

27. Franz Rosenzweig is one thinker who has not missed the significance of eschatological anticipation in Judaism. Stéphane Mosès calls such anticipation "one of the most central concepts in the system of *The Star of Redemption*. Anticipation is the experience through which man lives the future within the present itself, without negating the reality of the future . . . For the Jewish people . . . the anticipation of the Redemption will thus be the central experience of its religious life" (Mosès, *System and Revelation*, 175).

covenant existence before Yeshua's coming and the eschatological newness that Yeshua brings. Messiah is thus exalted by the lowering of Moses and Israel. However, I have argued that such a strategy does violence to the biblical text and to traditional Jewish understanding of it. Our attempt to shape a Messianic Jewish canonical narrative must proceed along different lines.

The Incarnation

The place to begin is with Yeshua's identity as the individual embodiment of the people of Israel. This theme was enunciated clearly by Jewish theologian Will Herberg, who noted that Yeshua "appears in early Christian thinking as, quite literally, an incarnate or one-man Israel, the Remnant-Man."[28] More recently, N. T. Wright has claimed that this notion is central to the Apostolic Writings' understanding of Yeshua's role.[29] Both David Stern and Daniel Juster have recognized that Yeshua "embodies" (Stern) and "represents" (Juster) Israel.[30] However, the full implications of Yeshua's representative role have not yet been incorporated into a coherent Messianic Jewish canonical narrative.

An essential feature of Israel's covenantal identity is to be a holy people (Exodus 19:6). As seen above, Israel's holiness has an eschatological character. It is also connected to the divine presence (the *Kavod* or *Shekhinah*) that abides with and in Israel. After the ratification of the covenant (Exodus 24), Moses ascends Mount Sinai to receive instructions concerning the building of the *Mishkan*—Hashem's mobile sanctuary in the wilderness. The reason for this institution is stated at the outset: "They shall make me a holy place, and I shall tent among them" (Exodus 25:8). The Holy One seeks a people among whom he can dwell, and the *Mishkan* serves as the localized sign and instrument of his presence. Far from being an added blessing, the gift of the divine presence constitutes a central element in Israel's vocation and identity: "For how shall it be known that Your people have gained Your favor unless You go

---

28. Herberg, "Judaism and Christianity: Their Unity and Difference," 244. Of course, for Herberg Yeshua functions as a one-man Israel for the sake of the nations, not for the sake of Israel itself.

29. Wright, *The Climax of the Covenant*, 18–40; Wright, *The New Testament and the People of God*, 402, 407, 416–17; Wright, *What Saint Paul Really Said*, 106. Wright takes the extreme opposite position from Herberg: for him Yeshua in effect *replaces* Israel.

30. Stern, *Messianic Jewish Manifesto*, 105, 107; Juster, *Jewish Roots*, 47–48.

with us, so that we may be distinguished, Your people and I, from every people on the face of the earth?" (Exodus 33:16; NJPS).

While the *Mishkan* and the Jerusalem temple represent the earthly home of the divine presence, that presence is not confined to these structures. The prophet Ezekiel sees the *Kavod* (enthroned on a chariot-like structure that symbolizes its mobility) departing from the temple, and appearing among the exiles in Babylon (Ezekiel 1:10). Ezekiel's conviction that the divine presence went into exile with the dispersed people of Judah after the destruction of the first temple reappears in rabbinic literature as the conviction that the *Shekhinah* continues to dwell with exiled Jews after the destruction of the second temple.

Israel's experience of the abiding presence of Hashem anticipates the consummation of the world, when "the land will be filled with the knowledge of God as the water covers the sea" (Isaiah 11:9). That anticipatory experience is brought to a new height in the coming of Yeshua, the one-man Israel, in whom the divine Word becomes flesh. The Apostolic Writings begin their story by narrating the birth of Yeshua, who is Immanuel, "God with us" (Matthew 1:23), and conclude by describing the new Jerusalem as "the dwelling of God" (Revelation 21:3). While the enfleshment of the *Memra* (Word) is a new and unique event, it should nonetheless be viewed in continuity with what precedes it—as a concentrated and intensified form of the divine presence that accompanies Israel throughout its historical journey. Thus, contrary to the common Christian canonical narrative, the divinity of Yeshua can be seen not as a radical rupture and disjunction in the story but as a continuation and elevation of a process initiated long before. As we will see later, the incarnation, like the building of the *Mishkan*, also needs to be viewed in terms of proleptic eschatology—it points forward to a reality that is not yet fully in our grasp.

The Character of Yeshua's Life

Yeshua's enfleshed *kedushah* stands in continuity with the holiness of the *Mishkan* and the *Bet Mikdash*—but there is also something new about his *kedushah*. The character of his life and mission displays a dynamic, outgoing, prophetic *kedushah* that will eventually lead to the sanctification of the entire created order (as envisioned in Zechariah 14 and Revelation 21). The holiness of Sinai, the *Mishkan*, and the Jerusalem temple required fences, boundaries, and guards, so that the holy might not be defiled by contact with the impure or insufficiently holy. Such contact leads to the destruction of those who bring it about. Thus, Nadav and Abihu are consumed for offering "strange fire" (Leviticus 10:1-3), Korah and his Levitical companions are annihilated for assuming prerogatives belonging solely to the *Kohanim* (Numbers 16:1-11, 16-22, 35), and Uzzah dies when he tries to prevent the ark from falling (2 Samuel 6:6-7). When the Philistines capture the ark and bring it as a trophy into Ashdod and Gath, the cities are struck with disease (1 Samuel 5).

Thus, Hashem's *kedushah* present in Israel through the priestly system threatens an impure world. At the same time, a holy person or object that comes into contact with impurity is thereby profaned, and cannot approach the holy God and the sanctuary until he, she, or it is purified. Thus, impurity also threatens Israel's *kedushah*. In either case, the boundary between the holy and the impure must be preserved and guarded at all costs.

As noted earlier, many Jews in Yeshua's day understood holiness as extending beyond the priesthood, the temple, and its sacrifices, as the heritage of every Jew in every place (at least in the land of Israel). The Pharisees seem to have held such a view. The *Yachad* (community) of the Dead Sea Scrolls saw itself as the temple, the locus of true *kedushah*, and so all who shared in the life of the community had access to the angelic assembly. It is thus appropriate to call the Pharisees and the *Yachad* "holiness movements."[31] Nevertheless, the traditional concern for separating the holy from the impure remains strong in these movements; in fact, it rises to new heights.

With Yeshua something new appears on the scene. It becomes most evident in what Dale Allison calls the "new channels" through which Yeshua "mediated the sacred . . . healings and meals."[32] The accounts of Yeshua's healings often highlight his unconventional contact with the sphere of impurity. Jacob Milgrom points to only three sources of impurity according the Torah: corpses/carcasses, scale disease, and genital discharges.[33] Yeshua is described as having contact with all three.

As for genital discharges, all three synoptic gospels tell the story of the woman with the hemorrhage who touches Yeshua and is healed (Mark 5:25-34; Luke 8:43-48; Matthew 9:20-22). Davies and Allison

31. McKnight, *A New Vision for Israel*, 46-48.
32. Allison, *Jesus of Nazareth—Millenarian Prophet*, 63.
33. Milgrom, *Leviticus 1-16*, 46.

comment that "it is possible that the woman comes up 'from behind' precisely because she is unclean and must accordingly try to touch Jesus without anyone observing . . . Instead of uncleanness passing from the woman to Jesus, healing power flows from Jesus to the woman."[34] Dunn rightly contends that the reader is expected to respond, "And she *touches* Jesus! And he makes no objection!"[35]

As for scale disease, again all three synoptic gospels tell about the healing of the "leper" (Mark 1:40–45; Luke 5:12–16; Matthew 8:1–4). As Dunn notes, "Given the importance of skin disease in the purity legislation (Lev 13–14), the significance of Jesus *touching* the leper would not be lost on anyone familiar with the Torah."[36] Davies and Allison once again recognize the reversal of the expected flow of impurity and sacred power: "When Jesus touches the man, leprosy does not spread to the healer; rather, healing power goes forth to conquer the disease."[37]

As for corpse impurity, we have two accounts of Yeshua raising the dead through contact that would have been considered defiling (Jairus' daughter in Mark 1:40–45, Luke 5:12–16, and Matthew 8:1–4, and the widow's son at Nain in Luke 7:11–17). As Milgrom observes, holiness is associated with life and impurity with death.[38] Here Yeshua overwhelms death with life, impurity with holiness. Just as striking is the story of the healing of the Gerasene demoniac (Mark 5:1–20; Luke 8:26–39; Matthew 8:28–34). The story is filled with images associated with impurity: impure spirits, impure animals (the grazing pigs), impure land (the Decapolis, inhabited mainly by Gentiles), and impure tombs.[39] Rather than fleeing this impurity, Yeshua wrestles with it and conquers it. Therefore, it is emblematic of Yeshua's program as recorded in the gospels that the first healing reported in Mark involves an *impure* spirit addressing Yeshua as "The Holy One of God" (Mark 1:23–26). The Holy One marches forth to make war on the kingdom of impurity.

---

34. Davies and Allison, *The Gospel according to Saint Matthew*, vol. 2, 129–30.
35. Dunn, *The Partings of the Ways*, 43.
36. Ibid., 42.
37. Davies and Allison, *The Gospel according to Saint Matthew*, vol. 2, 13.
38. "There is a common denominator to the three above-mentioned sources of impurity—death" (Milgrom, *Leviticus*, 46).
39. Lachs, *A Rabbinic Commentary on the New Testament*, 163; Dunn, *The Parting of the Ways*, 43.

The other "new channel" through which Yeshua mediates the sacred is the communal meal. Davies and Allison remark that Yeshua, "following established custom, often spoke of the kingdom of God as though it would be a great banquet (Matthew 8:11; 22:1–14; 25:1–13; 26:29). But given his 'realized eschatology,' the festive meals in which he participated were in all likelihood interpreted by himself and others as proleptic experiences of the kingdom (cf. Matthew 9:15)."[40] Just as Yeshua's works of healing were signs of the proleptic presence of *Olam Haba* and its *kedushah*, so too were his meals with his followers. Thus, it is especially significant that he ate with disreputable Jews, "tax collectors and sinners," who were certainly considered impure by the devotees of other "holiness movements" such as the Pharisees (e.g., Mark 2:13–17; Luke 5:27–32; Matthew 9:9–13). Scott McKnight sees the relevance of this fact for understanding Yeshua's approach to holiness:

> The opposition that Jesus provoked in his table practices is surely to be understood in this context; he provoked the Pharisees and other holiness movements because he had a different vision for the nation, because he understood holiness in different categories, and because he had a different perception of how the God of Israel was now at work among his people. It might be said that these other holiness movements had a different *ordo salutis*, in which repentance leads to holiness, which permits fellowship. Jesus affirmed, rather, that fellowship leads to both repentance and holiness.[41]

Yeshua's approach to meals parallels his practice of healing. Yeshua's contact with the impure does not defile him, but instead transmits purity, holiness, and life to the impure ones around him.

Yeshua's life and mission thus display a new type of *kedushah*, a prophetic, invasive holiness that needs no protection, but reaches out to sanctify the profane. In this respect, Yeshua's approach has much in common with the Hasidic perspective. As we have already noted, Buber explains that in Hasidic piety, the profane is merely that which has yet to be sanctified. Yeshua mediates the divine presence as the fleshly *Mishkan*, but he is not surrounded by a series of concentric barriers designed to restrict access to a privileged few. Instead, he anticipates and prepares

---

40. Davies and Allison, *The Gospel according to Saint Matthew*, vol. 2, 101; see also Dunn, "Jesus, Table-Fellowship, and Qumran," 263.

41. McKnight, *A New Vision for Israel*, 48–49.

the way for the sanctuary of the new Jerusalem, in which the city and the holy of holies are one and the same.[42]

Yeshua's Death and Resurrection

Just as the Apostolic Writings portray the divine enfleshment in the priestly imagery of the *Mishkan*-temple, so they portray the death of Yeshua in the priestly imagery of atoning sacrifice. And just as the meaning of the *Mishkan* can only be understood in relation to Israel's covenantal identity as a holy people, so also the meaning of the sacrificial system established in the Torah can only be understood in relation to Israel's corporate summons to *kiddush Hashem*, to sanctify the divine Name. According to Genesis 22, the sacrificial system of the Torah is founded on the *Akedah*—the willingness of Abraham to offer his son Isaac as a burnt offering. This is evident through the reference to "the mount of Hashem" in verse 14 and through the Chronicler's identification of Moriah as the Jerusalem temple mount (2 Chronicles 3:1).[43] Thus, the Torah teaches that temple sacrifice is meant to be an expression of the wholehearted commitment and self-giving love typified by Abraham and Isaac when they ascend Moriah.

In post-biblical Jewish tradition, the *Akedah* takes on a new significance: it becomes the model for martyrdom.[44] This is first seen in texts dealing with the martyrs of the Maccabean period (4 Maccabees 16:20). At a later date, the *Akedah* is associated with the martyrs who suffered under Roman persecution (as seen in Gen Rab 56:3, which compares Isaac's carrying the wood for the sacrifice to one who carries his own execution stake). Israel's martyrs, suffering for *kiddush Hashem*, show the same commitment to God and the same self-giving love as Abraham and Isaac. In this way the *Akedah* links martyrdom with the temple sacrifices, and makes it possible to see martyrdom as likewise having atoning efficacy (4 Maccabees 17:21–22).

---

42. This need not imply abolition of all the lines of differentiation established by the Torah's approach to impurity and holiness. However, it does imply that these lines no longer function as levels of proximity to the divine.

43. Levenson, *The Death and Resurrection of the Beloved Son*, 114–23. Rabbinic tradition recognized this relationship between the *Akedah* and the sacrifices, as seen by the morning preliminary service in which the *Akedah* is read just before a set of texts concerning sacrifice, and as seen by the importance of the *Akedah* during the ten Days of Awe that culminate in *Yom Kippur*.

44. Ibid., 187–99; Spiegel, *The Last Trial*.

Wyschogrod has argued that Israel's suffering, modeled on the *Akedah*, has always been the true sacrifice intended by the Torah: "Is it not possible that the rabbis understood that the destruction of the temple and the cessation of its sacrifices, rather than signaling the termination of sacrifices as such, restored the people of Israel to its role as the sacrifice whose blood is to be shed in the Diaspora when the holy service in Jerusalem is suspended? If there is no need for sacrament in Judaism, it is because the people of Israel in whose flesh the presence of God makes itself felt in the world becomes the sacrament."[45] Accordingly, the traditional *Yom Kippur* (Day of Atonement) liturgy includes not only a retelling of the temple sacrifices offered on that day, but also a martyrology. This fits the reading of Isaiah 53 that applies it to the suffering of the Jewish people.

If Yeshua is the perfect one-man Israel, then his death as a martyr under the Romans sums up all of Israel's righteous suffering through the ages, provides the ultimate expression of the commitment to God and self-giving love shown first in the *Akedah*, and effects definitive atonement.[46] Since Yeshua represents and embodies Israel, Isaiah 53 is fulfilled by him *and* by the people as a whole.[47] A Messianic Jewish version of the canonical narrative will see the death of Yeshua in continuity not only with Israel's temple system but also in continuity with Israel's ongoing life in this world. As with the incarnation, so with Yeshua's atoning death: the Messiah epitomizes and elevates Israel's story, rather than ending it and beginning something entirely new.

But what does martyrdom have to do with eschatology? In order to answer this question, it is best to move on and speak also about Yeshua's resurrection. Just as martyrdom first became a significant theme in Jewish life as a result of the persecutions during the Maccabean period, so resurrection likewise emerged as a major motif during the same period—and precisely in relation to the martyrs. Second Maccabees 7, which describes the execution of seven Jewish brothers, provides both the first martyrology and one of the earliest explicit statements of hope

---

45. Wyschogrod, *The Body of Faith*, 25.

46. The treatments of this topic by Davies (*Paul and Rabbinic Judaism*, 259–84) and Schoeps (*Paul*, 128–49) are still valuable.

47. "The controversy over whether Isaiah 53 refers to Israel or to a then unborn Messiah dissolves when it is remembered that Israel's Messiah embodies his people" (Stern, *Messianic Jewish Manifesto*, 107).

in the resurrection of the dead. Daniel 12:1–3, the most explicit text in Tanakh dealing with resurrection, likewise addresses (at least as its initial frame of reference) the situation of the Maccabean martyrs. Daniel and the Apostolic Writings prophesy that persecution and martyrdom will characterize the events leading up to the end of the age, and will in fact prepare the way for the renewal of all things—a renewal that features the resurrection of all the righteous.

N. T. Wright captures these connections effectively in the following paragraph:

> Why did the belief in the resurrection arise, and how did it fit in with the broader Jewish worldview and belief-system which we have sketched in the preceding chapters? Again and again we have seen that this belief is bound up with the struggle to maintain obedience to Israel's ancestral laws in the face of persecution. Resurrection is the divine reward for martyrs; it is what will happen after the great tribulation. But it is not simply a special reward for those who have undergone special sufferings. Rather, the eschatological expectation of most Jews of this period was for a renewal, not an abandonment, of the present space-time order as a whole, and themselves within it. Since this was based on the justice and mercy of the creator god, the god of Israel, it was inconceivable that those who had died in the struggle to bring the new world into being should be left out of the blessing when it eventually broke upon the nation and thence on the world.[48]

Wright continues by noting that the hope for resurrection was primarily a hope for national renewal and restoration:

> The old metaphor of corpses coming to life had, ever since Ezekiel at least, been one of the most vivid ways of *de*noting the return from exile and *con*noting the renewal of the covenant and of all creation. Within the context of persecution and struggle for Torah in the Syrian and Roman periods, this metaphor itself acquired a new life. If Israel's god would "raise" his people (metaphorically) by bringing them back from their continuing exile, he would also, within that context, "raise" those people (literally) who had died in the hope of that national and covenantal vindication. "Resurrection", while focusing attention on the new embodiment of the individuals involved, retained its original sense of the restoration of Israel by her covenant god.[49]

---

48. Wright, *People of God*, 331–32.
49. Ibid., 332. See also van Buren, *According to the Scriptures*, 27–28.

This background makes it possible to understand Yeshua's death and resurrection as the eschatological one-man Israel. Just as Yeshua dies as the ultimate Jewish martyr, engaged in the eschatological conflict that will result in the renewal of the covenant and of all creation, so he rises from the dead as the pledge of Israel's national resurrection and the first-fruits of all who sleep. This perspective on Yeshua's resurrection is articulated by R. Kendall Soulen: "Jesus, the firstborn from the dead, is also the first fruits of God's eschatological vindication of Israel's body. In light of Jesus' bodily resurrection, it is certain not only that God will intervene on behalf of the whole body of Israel at the close of covenant history but also that by this very act God will consummate the world."[50]

Whereas the enfleshment of the *Memra* in Yeshua intensifies and elevates an eschatological reality already anticipated in Israel's life, and Yeshua in his death embodies and sums up all of Israel's martyrs through the ages and prepares the way for *Olam Haba*, in his resurrection he establishes a proleptic eschatological reality unprecedented in Israel's history. However, as Soulen makes clear, that proleptic eschatological reality can only be understood in relation to Israel's destined future, of which it is a pledge.

Like the resurrection, the founding of the *ekklesia* as a twofold community, consisting of a Jewish corporate component and an associated multi-national extension of Israel, represents an unprecedented reality in Israel's history. Like the resurrection, this new element in the divine scheme also constitutes a proleptic eschatological reality, for it anticipates the final renewal of creation when Israel and the nations will be bound together in a relationship of mutual blessing among those who continue to be different. Once again, Soulen states it well:

> The resurrection anticipates the eschatological outcome of covenant history and reveals its character *in nuce* as God's vindication of Israel's body to the blessing of Israel, the nations, and all creation. But the resurrection does not have only this ultimate eschatological point of reference. The resurrection also inaugurates something new within the open-ended story of God's work as the Consummator of creation ... the new thing is the church, the table fellowship of Jews and Gentiles that prays in Jesus' name for the coming of the God of Israel's reign.[51]

---

50. Soulen, *The God of Israel*, 166.
51. Ibid., 169.

Thus, certain features of Yeshua's identity and mission (his incarnation and his atoning death) are in continuity with Israel's past history, whereas other features (his resurrection and the founding of the twofold *ekklesia*) are pledges of Israel's promised future.

Jewish Tradition

The Messianic Jewish canonical narrative must place the person and work of Yeshua within the context of the proleptic eschatological reality of Israel's life according to the Torah and Jewish tradition. But what is the status of that tradition itself within our narrative? What of the Jewish people as a whole after Yeshua's death and resurrection and the founding of the *ekklesia*? What are we to make of the rabbinic extensions of *kedushah* noted above? Many in the Messianic Jewish movement have rejected them as human attempts to refashion Judaism in the absence of the temple. Is this the only option for us?

This is not the place to assess the rabbinic tradition as a whole from a Messianic Jewish perspective. However, I would offer a brief proposal for how we might affirm the value of that tradition and incorporate it within the Messianic Jewish canonical narrative. I have already pointed out how some of the rabbinic extensions of *kedushah* parallel certain tendencies seen in the Yeshua tradition and in the life of the *ekklesia*. Just as the Apostolic Writings portray the *ekklesia* as a holy people in and among whom the Holy One resides as he did in the *Mishkan* and the temple, so rabbinic tradition sees Israel as a holy people among whom the *Shekhinah* rests. Just as the Yeshua tradition treats each member of the community as a priest, so does the rabbinic tradition (though a few distinctive priestly prerogatives remain). Just as the Yeshua tradition sees prayer, *tzedakah* (charity), and good deeds as equivalent to temple sacrifices, so does the rabbinic tradition. Just as Yeshua's approach to *kedushah* was expansive and invasive, involving contact with the impure in order to mediate to them his own holiness, so the Hasidic movement has taken as its mission the transformation of the profane into the holy. The main difference on these matters between the two movements is the basis for the development. The Yeshua tradition sees the extension of *kedushah* as deriving from the person and work of Yeshua—his identity as the enfleshed *Memra*, his atoning death, his resurrection, and his gift of the *Ruach*. The rabbinic tradition employs creative exegesis to assert that what appears to be a development is not really a development at all.

If we view the ongoing life of the Jewish people as a providential blessing for the world, and if we believe that Israel maintains a distinctive national holiness despite its refusal to accept Yeshua as the Messiah (Romans 11:16), and if we believe that there is even a mysterious divine purpose behind that refusal (Romans 11:25–36), then we should seek an explanation that is as favorable as possible to these parallel trajectories. I propose that we see Yeshua at work not only in the *ekklesia* but also among the very rabbis who reject his claims. The power of Yeshua's death and resurrection extends beyond the boundaries of the *ekklesia*.

David Stern suggests something like this in his *Messianic Jewish Manifesto*: "This concept, that the Messiah embodies the Jewish people, should not seem strange to believers, who learn precisely that about Yeshua and the Church . . . But the Church has not clearly grasped that the Holy One of Israel, Yeshua, is in union not only with the Church, but also with the Jewish people."[52] Stern draws upon the notion that Yeshua is the one-man Israel, and comes to this radical but sensible conclusion. Try though it may, Israel cannot escape its Messiah. Wanted or unwanted, noticed or unnoticed, acknowledged or unacknowledged, he still rules over his people. Therefore, we should not be surprised to find signs of his presence and activity within the people and tradition of Israel.

LIFTING THE CHRISTIAN ESCHATOLOGICAL HORIZON

We have seen that both Jewish and Christian thinkers have often understated the note of eschatological anticipation sounded in the Torah and rabbinic tradition, and overstated the discontinuity between the epoch inaugurated by the coming of Yeshua and Jewish life under the Torah. Thus, the Messianic Jewish canonical narrative needs to lower the eschatological horizon to allow for the foretaste of redemption and consummation given in Israel's life of *kedushah*.

On the other hand, the traditional Christian canonical narrative has another problem: while understating the continuity between Yeshua's coming and Jewish life, it overstates the continuity between life in Messiah in this age and life in Messiah in the age to come. In fact, it often so accentuates the redemptive power of Yeshua's incarnation, death, and resurrection, and the richness of life in the Spirit and in the church, that the future redemption drops out of the picture completely

---

52. Stern, *Messianic Jewish Manifesto*, 108.

or survives merely as an anticlimactic wrap-up of an already completed story.

Jewish critiques of Christianity have often seized upon this defect. Leo Baeck provides just such a critique, though he wrongly directs it not only at later Christian theology but also at the apostle Paul:

> The romantic faith in salvation also furnishes us with the very opposite of the ancient messianic idea which was still the idea of Jesus, too: the idea of the days to come, the idea of the promised kingdom . . . the messianic idea out of which Christianity had developed and from which it has received its name was now pushed back more and more and eventually annulled historically. The place of the kingdom of God on earth, the ancient biblical ideal, was taken over by the kingdom of the Church, the romantic *civitas Dei*.[53]

> This Messianic expectation had been done away with by Paul in its essential features. Since for him the coming of the Messiah and the redemption was something which had already been fulfilled, was already an actual possession of the present, the idea of the great future hope had consequently lost its significance.[54]

Sometimes the critique of Christianity is secondary, and serves mainly as a foil to clarify the Jewish perspective on the final redemption, as in the following citations from Wyschogrod and Novak:

> Christianity sees before it a completed salvation history. Creation to resurrection constitutes a totality of promise and fulfillment that is available to viewing and therefore to thought. Israel's story is incomplete. It is replete with great peaks and deep disappointments, but it is, above all, incomplete. The redemption implicit in the very first promise to Abraham is still in abeyance. The Exodus, Sinai, the Temple are all peaks and previews of what is in store for Israel and humanity in the fulfillment. But that fulfillment has not yet occurred, and we are therefore dealing with an uncompleted tale whose outcome we know because of our trust in the source of the promise. Nevertheless, however great our trust, we must not confuse promise with fulfillment, especially for man, who lives in time and for whom the future is shrouded in darkness.[55]

---

53. Baeck, "Romantic Religion," 86–87.
54. Baeck, "Judaism in the Church," 105.
55. Wyschogrod, *The Body of Faith*, 69. Wyschogrod thus acknowledges proleptic

And by not seeing the redeemed future as any kind of projection from a present state of affairs, Israel cannot claim to be any more redeemed than anyone else. This lack of redemption, either Jewish or universal, is a point Jews have always emphasized when the adherents of other religions and ideologies have made triumphalist claims against us, claiming that the world is already redeemed. But what God will finally do with the world is as mysterious as what God has been doing with Israel in the past and the present. Against the hidden horizon of the final redeemed future, everything past and present is ultimately provisional. God has not yet fulfilled his own purposes in history.[56]

Occasionally, a Jewish author simply contrasts the Jewish orientation to a future redemption yet awaited and the Christian orientation to a past redemption already accomplished, without any explicit praise of one or attack on the other, as in the following paragraphs from Franz Rosenzweig:

> The [Jewish] people . . . lives in its own redemption. It has anticipated eternity. The future is the driving power in the circuit of its year. Its rotation originates, so to speak, not in a thrust but in a pull. The present passes not because the past prods it on but because the future snatches it toward itself. Somehow, even the festivals of creation and revelation flow into redemption. What gives the year strength to begin anew and link its ring, which is without beginning and end, into the chain of time, is this, that the feeling that redemption is still unattained breaks through again, and thereby the thought of eternity, which seemed contained in the cup of the moment, brims up and surges over the rim.[57]

> There is no festival of redemption as such in Christianity. In the Christian consciousness, everything congregates around the beginning and for beginning, and the clear distinction which exists for us between revelation and redemption is obscured. Redemption has already taken place in Christ's earthly sojourn, at the very least in his crucifixion, properly speaking already at his birth . . . With us the ideas of creation and revelation contain a compulsion to merge in the idea of redemption for whose sake, in the final analysis, everything prior has occurred. In Christianity, correspondingly, the

---

eschatology in Israel's life in this world even as he emphasizes the height of the eschatological horizon.

56. Novak, *The Election of Israel*, 255.
57. Rosenzweig, *The Star of Redemption*, 328.

> idea of redemption is swallowed back into creation, into revelation; as often as it erupts as something independent, just so often it loses its independence again. The retrospect to cross and manger, the eventuation of the events of Bethlehem and Golgotha into one's own heart, there become more important than the prospect of the future of the Lord. The advent of the kingdom becomes a matter of secular and ecclesiastical history. But it has no place in the heart of Christendom...[58]

Whether the critique is explicit or implicit, it is evident that Jewish authors see the subordination of the final redemption to the finished work of Messiah as a problematic feature of the Christian canonical narrative.

Soulen's *The God of Israel and Christian Theology* agrees with these Jewish assessments of the Christian canonical narrative. He seeks to craft a new canonical narrative that overcomes supersessionism and facilitates constructive dialogue with contemporary Judaism, and in order to do so he must confront the traditional Christian low eschatological horizon. In a review of Soulen's book, Novak sees this as the heart of Soulen's project:

> Perhaps the main stumbling block to a better, and more fruitful, theological relationship with Judaism and the Jewish people has been the tendency of many Christian theologians to see the Christ event as the end of history. In this view, the Jews, like all the rest of the world who have not accepted Jesus as the Christ, are still struggling within history. Christians, conversely, are already beyond history and its vicissitudes and are living in eschatological time...
>
> This, more than anything else, it would seem, has led to what becomes the bete noir of Soulen's book: "supersessionism."[59]

How does Soulen reshape the canonical narrative? He does so by reconfiguring the first and second comings of Yeshua, so that the former is subordinated to the latter rather than the reverse. Instead of seeing the final coming of the kingdom as a public manifestation of what in principle was already accomplished in the death and resurrection of Yeshua, he presents the death and resurrection of Yeshua as an anticipation or *prolepsis* of what will occur definitively only at the end. "If Jesus

---

58. Ibid., 368.
59. Novak, "Beyond Supersessionism," 57.

is the proleptic enactment of God's eschatological fidelity to the work of consummation, then Jesus is by this very fact the carnal embodiment of God's end-time fidelity toward Israel and toward Israel's future as the place of unsurpassable blessing for Israel, for the nations, and for all creation. By its nature, then, Jesus' resurrection from the dead anticipates a future event whose character as victorious fidelity can no longer be in doubt."[60]

Thus, the good news is not merely a proclamation of what has already occurred, but also and preeminently an announcement about how Yeshua's death and resurrection will lead to the coming reign of Israel's God: "The gospel is good news about the God of Israel's coming reign, which proclaims in Jesus' life, death, and resurrection the victorious guarantee of God's fidelity to the work of consummation, that is, to fullness of mutual blessing as the outcome of God's economy with Israel, the nations, and all creation."[61] Soulen takes the traditional Christian canonical narrative, centered in the incarnation, and re-orders it so that it is closer to the traditional Jewish narrative, oriented to the final redemption. "The necessary correction . . . is a frank reorientation of the hermeneutical center of the Scriptures from the incarnation to the reign of God, where God's reign is understood as the eschatological outcome of human history at the end of time."[62]

Novak perceives the nature of Soulen's revision of the Christian canonical narrative, and agrees that it is crucial to Soulen's goal of overcoming supersessionism:

> Soulen seems to be constituting what I would call "the highest possible eschatological horizon." This comes out when he says, "The Church is not a community that issues directly into God's reign . . . A hiatus separates the Church and God's eschatological reign" . . . Clearly, when Christian theologians constitute a "lower" eschatological horizon, which usually has meant seeing the Eschaton as the *extension* of the Church's reign on earth, it has been most susceptible to the types of supersessionism so opposed by Soulen . . . Conversely, when Christians regard themselves within history but not its masters, they become most like the Jews.[63]

60. Soulen, *The God of Israel*, 166.
61. Ibid., 157.
62. Ibid., 138.
63. Novak, "Beyond Supersessionism," 58, 60.

While Soulen's revised narrative requires some modification (e.g., he seems to present Yeshua's death and resurrection primarily as a pledge of God's final reign, rather than as a means of bringing it to pass), his work does point the way that we should follow.

Another theologian who seeks to raise the eschatological horizon of the Christian canonical narrative is Wolfhart Pannenberg. Like Jürgen Moltmann, Pannenberg restructures Christian theology so that the eschatological future takes on special prominence.[64] He emphasizes the proleptic character of Yeshua's work, and his treatment of the *ekklesia* in relation to the divine reign employs such expressions as "provisional representation," "advance representation," "exemplary anticipation," "provisional sign," and "preliminary sign."

> The presence of God's kingdom and of his eschatological fellowship of salvation in the church is sacramental . . . But the final form of such participation and fellowship is still invisible in this transitory world and comes into it only through faith, hope, and love. It is thus of the nature of the church that it points beyond all that is provisional and imperfect in its own form to the future of the fellowship of God's kingdom. Of this kingdom the church is only a provisional representation and one that in the life of its members is often hidden and distorted beyond recognition.[65]

Pannenberg strives both to emphasize the proleptic eschatological nature of the *ekklesia* (and of Israel) and to guard against any tendency to blur or erase the distinction between the *ekklesia* and the coming kingdom. In his view, this tendency posed a dangerous temptation for the early church. "From the very first the Christian church had to fight the temptation to equate its own fellowship exclusively with that of the end-time elect and thus to see itself as an initial form of the kingdom of God. When this happens, a sense of the provisional nature of its own form of

---

64. Jürgen Moltmann would also be worthy of study in this context. Haynes, *Prospects for Post-Holocaust Theology*, 103–60, provides an excellent summary of how Moltmann's writings contribute to the development of a post-supersessionist Christian theology. Haynes notes that "Moltmann's understanding of the unfinished nature of reconciliation . . . has implications for the church-Israel relationship . . . Moltmann's eschatological Christology reopens the reconciliation which is completed in Barth's theology by incorporating a 'not yet' element absent in Barth" (ibid., 112–13).

65. Pannenberg, *Systematic Theology*, vol. 3, 464.

life is easily lost, and with it a reference beyond its own particularity to the universality of the race that is the target of God's saving purpose."[66]

Pannenberg claims that the first test of the church's sense of its own identity in relation to the eschaton arose in its dealings with the Jewish people.

> In its relations with the Jewish people the church had to decide for the first time whether it would view its own place in God's history with the human race along the lines of a provisional sign of a still awaited consummation, or view itself as the place of the at least initially actualized eschatological consummation itself. The decision went in favor of the second alternative and it came to expression in the church's claim to be exclusively identical with the eschatologically "new" people of God. The dangerous and destructive consequences of this choice mark the further history of Christianity. They take the form of dogmatic intolerance, the result of a false sense of eschatological finality that fails to see the church's provisional nature, and an endless series of divisions that follow from dogmatic exclusiveness.
>
> It is important to realize that this painful false development began with a primary mistake in the church's relation to the Jewish people.[67]

Pannenberg's thinking has much in common with that of Soulen. However, they have different starting points. Soulen begins with the problem of supersessionism, and this leads him to a new emphasis on eschatology. Pannenberg begins with a new emphasis on eschatology, and in working out the implications of this restructuring of Christian theology he sees its importance for the relationship between the *ekklesia* and the Jewish people. Regardless of the starting point, they agree that the Christian canonical narrative must be redesigned so that special attention is given to the final consummation.

Pannenberg's eschatological rethinking of ecclesiology also leads him to a rethinking of the nature of the New Covenant itself:

> Jeremiah in 31:31-32 and Isaiah in 59:21 promise the new covenant not to another people but to Israel as the eschatological renewal and fulfillment of its covenant relationship with its God. When at the Last Supper that he held with his disciples on the night of his arrest Jesus related the promise of the new covenant

66. Ibid.
67. Ibid., 476.

> to the table fellowship with his disciples that he sealed with his self-offering, he was not snapping the link of this promise to the people of Israel. Instead, he was showing that fellowship with himself is for the whole Jewish people the future of salvation that breaks in already in the fellowship of the band of disciples. The later inclusion of non-Jews in the Christian community on the basis of the confession of Jesus that is sealed by their baptism does nothing to change this.
>
> The Christian church is not exclusively identical with the eschatological people of God. It is only a provisional form of this people and a preliminary sign of its future consummation that will embrace not only members of the church but the Jewish people and the "righteous" of all the nations who stream in from every culture to the banquet of the reign of God.[68]

Pannenberg's treatment of the New Covenant reveals how significant his eschatological orientation can be for a Messianic Jewish rereading of the canonical narrative. The New Covenant itself is an eschatological reality, promised preeminently to Israel as a whole, but now "breaking in" sacramentally among "the band of disciples."

Traditional Christian theology lowered the eschatological horizon by overstating the finished nature of Yeshua's work and by exaggerating the eschatological powers inherent in the church. At the same time, it tended to individualize and spiritualize the eschaton so that it became virtually indistinguishable from the destiny of the soul after death. The Christian church thus suffered a diminished vision of its true hope—to be resurrected as a community and to inhabit a renewed creation. As the "last things" were individualized and spiritualized, the eschatological horizon was lowered once again—now not through the inordinate exaltation of the eschatological potential of life in this age, but through the downgrading of the nature of the future hope. In this scheme, if one turns from earthly concerns and cultivates the life of the soul in this world, one already partakes of the life of the world to come.

As we seek to develop a Messianic Jewish canonical narrative, we should follow the lead of Soulen and Pannenberg. Without detracting from the significance of Yeshua's incarnation, death, and resurrection, we should raise our eschatological horizon so that life in this age, while anticipating life in the world to come, is never confused with it.

---

68. Ibid., 477.

LIFTING THE JEWISH ESCHATOLOGICAL HORIZON

Jewish thought has its own problematic version of an excessively low eschatological horizon. It arises through a lowering of expectations for the messianic era. Novak has discussed the two types of eschatological views common in Jewish tradition. He calls the first position "extensive eschatology" and the second "apocalyptic eschatology." Novak describes them, and then explains why he favors the latter.

> In the first position, the extensive one, the future is an extension *from* the covenantal present *into* its fulfilled future . . . The future of the covenant is that the political conditions now absent for the full normative authority of the covenant, the Torah, will be finally made present. Most immediately, Israel will at long last dwell in security in her land. As for the rest of the world, they will either be subordinate to Israel or become part of the people through their conversion to Israel and its Torah.
>
> In the second position, the apocalyptic one, the future is far more radical. It is the transcendent interruption *into* the present *from* somewhere else. As such, it will radically alter the relationship between Israel and God, including that which has been codified in the Torah already revealed. It assumes that the future will bring an ontological change much more radical than the mere improvement—even vast improvement—of political conditions for the Jews.
>
> In terms of biblical texts themselves, the apocalyptic position has greater support by far. On theological grounds, it is convincing because it helps mitigate the error that Israel often assumes from her covenantal experience, namely, that she possesses within herself the power to carry the covenant from the present into its future completion. And on philosophical grounds, it enables us to appreciate the finite fragility of the present through the affirmation of the future that transcends it.
>
> The final and future redemption will radically change Israel's relationship with God and with the world, especially with the nations of the world. Israel's future redemption will have literal cosmic effects. It will be an invasion from the future into the present, not a transition from the present into the future. This doctrine is the very antithesis of any ideal of "progress"—ancient, medieval, or modern.[69]

Extensive eschatology renders the eschatological horizon too low in relation to Jewish life in this world. Wyschogrod's view is the same. "The

---

69. Novak, *The Election of Israel*, 153–54, 157.

difference between the world as we know it and the world as foreseen by the prophets is too great for a more or less normal evolution to account for the transition of the former into the latter. The apocalyptic dimension of messianism stresses the extraordinary magnitude of the coming transformation, which is seen as cataclysmic, since nothing ordinary can put an end to the tired and broken world of history as we have known it."[70] Whether consisting of a hope for a restored Davidic monarchy in the land of Israel within an otherwise unchanged cosmic order, or a more universal humanistic Jewish hope for a just and peaceful world order, extensive eschatology lowers the horizon too far.

CONCLUSION

We have argued to this point for rediscovery of proleptic eschatology in Jewish life, renewed attention to the continuity between Israel's *kedushah* and Yeshua's incarnation, death, and resurrection as proleptic eschatological events, and increased awareness of the preliminary and provisional nature of life in Messiah in this age in relation to the eschatological fullness of the life of the world to come. At this point it will be helpful to summarize the place of eschatology in the Messianic Jewish canonical narrative in light of these assertions, and to draw some final conclusions from the nature of that narrative.

Eschatology becomes part of the story from the very beginning. The world is created good, but not yet holy. It has an appointed destiny that transcends its original constitution. Thus, eschatology is consummation before it is redemption. The eruption of evil makes redemption a necessary component in the consummation of all things. The world is now wounded and needs to be healed, it is now broken and needs to be made whole. But the final consummation involves more than restoration to a pristine state.

The covenant with Abraham, Isaac, and Jacob and its embodiment at Sinai initiates the move from the sixth to the seventh day, from the profane to the holy, from the imperfection of this world to the fullness of the world to come. Through Israel, the world takes its first preliminary steps towards its consummation. The divine presence pitches its tent within this people, and the sacrifices ordained by the covenant enable Israel to assume its role as the world's *Kohanim* (priests), offering itself to God in worship so that the world might be sustained, redeemed, and renewed.

---

70. Wyschogrod, *The Body of Faith*, 255–56.

In Yeshua the tent of the divine presence takes a new form. As the true Israelite, blameless and holy, Yeshua sums up all that Israel was intended to be. He becomes the perfect temple, priest, and sacrifice, offering himself to God on behalf of Israel, the nations, and the entire creation. Yeshua dies not only as a sacrifice but also as Israel's perfect martyr, who, like Isaac in the *Akedah*, embodies all of Israel's martyrs in himself, and whose blood is shed both to atone for sins and to prepare the way for the coming of *Olam Haba*. That new world is anticipated and proleptically realized in the resurrection of Israel's perfect martyr, and the gift of the *Ruach* and the founding of a twofold *ekklesia* that extends Israel's heritage among the nations likewise represent anticipations of the renewed world to come.

That twofold *ekklesia* suffers a profound disruption early in its history, so that one of its two component parts is lost or at least hidden from view, and the Jewish people as a whole chart a course through history that appears to ignore the One who perfectly embodies their destiny. This disruption brings the brokenness of the present world into the very heart of the preliminary realization of the world to come, and serves as a continual reminder of the provisional nature of that realization. Nevertheless, the twofold *ekklesia* never completely loses its twofold nature, for it always includes Jews and is always headed by a resurrected Jew.[71] Similarly, the Jewish people never succeed in eluding the grasp of their resurrected brother. Like Joseph dealing with his siblings, he is never far from them, and continues to effect the divine purpose in their midst. Guided by his counsel enfolded in the ontological depths of its corporate being, the Jewish people do not retreat from their vocation after the destruction of the temple, but press on to express the power of eschatological *kedushah* in every aspect of their life, even in exile. At the end, God will make Yeshua known to his brethren and to all of creation, not only as temple, priest, and sacrifice, but also as messianic King, the eschatological ruler of Israel and the nations. At that point the New Covenant will be realized in its final and definitive form.

Accepting a version of the canonical narrative like this one will have certain consequences for our lives as Messianic Jews. First, it will highlight the importance of *kedushah* as an eschatological category.

---

71. "It is extremely doubtful whether there has ever been a time when the living membership of the church included no Jews. Yet even if there were such a time, the presence of the church's living Lord, the Jew Jesus Christ, ensures that the church remains essentially a table fellowship of Jews and Gentiles" (Soulen, *The God of Israel*, 173).

When we observe *mitzvot* in general and certain *mitzvot* explicitly associated with *kedushah* in particular (such as *Shabbat* and *kashrut* [Jewish dietary laws]), we are not only identifying with our people and its history; we are also entering into a dimension of existence in which *Olam Haba* is experienced corporately as a proleptic reality. As we separate the holy day from the profane days, and as we separate pure food from impure food and treat our daily meals as sacred sacrificial banquets, we both affirm Israel's calling to be a holy people and take our stand as a preliminary sign of *Olam Haba* within the present order of *Olam Hazeh*. We also testify to the incarnation, death, and resurrection of Messiah Yeshua, who has brought this *kedushah* to a new level through the gift of the Spirit of Holiness, imparted to Jew and Gentile alike on the basis of Yeshua's faithfulness.

Second, when we express our love and unity with those who are members of the multinational expression of the twofold *ekklesia*, we are likewise participating in the proleptic *kedushah* of the world to come. As Soulen points out, this twofold *ekklesia* serves as a preliminary sign of the shalom of *Olam Haba*, when Israel and the nations will share in the economy of mutual blessing among those who are and remain different.

Third, this form of the canonical narrative stresses that the world to come entails the perfect realization of all that is good in this world and the overcoming of all evil that thwarts such realization. This will not occur through an evolutionary process, but through a future invasion of divine power and *kedushah*, just as in the election of Israel and in the resurrection of Yeshua. However, this invasion from beyond will bring the world to its ultimate goal. Thus, a vivid eschatological awareness is not in conflict with a sensitive appreciation for all that is good and beautiful in this world. Neither is it in conflict with energetic efforts to thwart evil and realize the good in the midst of the present age; in fact, it demands just such efforts, for the invasion from beyond has already begun with the election of Israel and the coming of Yeshua. Our sincere attempts to mend the world can bring to *Olam Hazeh* an anticipatory encounter with the redemptive power of *Olam Haba*.

Fourth, the proleptic experience of eschatological realities occurs in a variety of ways. We have only spoken briefly of the *charismata* (spiritual gifts), but it is clear from the Apostolic Writings that they are to be seen as a foretaste of the powers of the age to come (Hebrews 6:5; Matthew 11:2–6, 12:28)—especially as they mediate healing to the sick, wholeness to the broken, and *kedushah* to the profane and impure. Messiah's *tevilah* (baptism) and *zikkaron* (Eucharist) likewise signify and convey eschatological realities in a proleptic manner. As noted above, *Shabbat* and *kashrut* have an eschatological significance, as do other traditional Jewish holidays (such as Passover, *Sukkot*, and the High Holy Days) and rites (such as grace after meals and the wedding ceremony).[72] We should be careful not to restrict proleptic eschatological experience to those areas that we find most comfortable, but should seek to be open to the full range of what is given.

Finally, our joy in the eschatological *kedushah* of traditional Jewish life, our convictions about the eschatological power of Yeshua's resurrection, and our experience of the eschatological renewal imparted through the Spirit of Holiness, should not dim our awareness of the proleptic quality of all these realities. From him who has given so much, much is still to be expected. The gift serves as a pledge, pointing us forward to that which lies beyond. As Rosenzweig states, "The present passes not because the past prods it on but because the future snatches it toward itself."[73]

The canonical narrative is the unfinished story of the world's creation, reconciliation, redemption, and consummation through Israel and its Messiah. It is the One Story that encompasses all our individual stories and gives them meaning and purpose. The Story remains unfinished—but the role we play gives us a preliminary and provisional taste of what is to come, and even confers the privilege of participating in its ultimate realization. Because of this, we are convinced that the plea of the *Kaddish* is far more than a utopian wish; it is an inspired invocation whose answer is assured by the resurrection of Israel's hidden Messiah:

> May His great Name be magnified and sanctified
> throughout the world which He created
> according to His will.
> May He establish His kingdom in your lifetime and during your days,
> and within the life of the entire house of Israel,
> speedily and soon; and say,
> Amen.

---

72. On the eschatological dimensions of the grace after meals and the Jewish wedding ceremony, see Neusner, *An Introduction to Judaism*, 3–8, 22–30.

73. Rosenzweig, *The Star of Redemption*, 328.

6

Final Destinies: Qualifications for Receiving an Eschatological Inheritance

> Kinzer explores the topic of individual "salvation," mining the biblical texts for guidance and challenging some of the most common prevailing viewpoints and verbiage. Examining the traditions of Peter and James, Paul, and John, Kinzer finds several distinctives regarding what one must do to be "saved." First, the Apostolic Writings (New Testament) are unequivocal in warning against presumption about insiders and outsiders with regard to the kingdom of God. Second, salvation has much more to do with faith as a life of obedience than faith as affirmation of propositional truth. Third, especially according to the Johannine tradition, eternal life starts *now*; it is a reality we live in, not a state we enter upon death. Finally, each person is accountable for the light they have seen and the truth that has been unveiled to them. Kinzer defines salvation as a life of obedience to the Torah as definitively interpreted by Yeshua, and final judgment as God's just and merciful assessment of each person's deeds in consideration of their circumstances and limitations.[1]

In *What Does It Mean To Be Saved?*, Regent College professor John Stackhouse points to a misunderstanding of salvation that he sees as endemic in the evangelical world:

1. Presented at the Borough Park Symposium in 2007 and published in *Kesher* 22 (Spring/Summer 2008), 87–119. The Borough Park Symposium first met in October 2007 in New York City with the following mission statement: "The purpose of the symposium is to provide a forum for members of the broader Messianic Jewish community to articulate their beliefs with an expectation that they will receive a respectful hearing, but without the expectation that agreement concerning these beliefs will be achieved. The Symposium is designed to provide an internal platform for leaders to better understand each another and the various positions held within the Messianic movement." The Borough Park Symposium met again in New York City in April 2010.

> In his gracious but penetrating response to the essays in this volume, Oxford professor John Webster wonders whether it is particularly North American evangelicals who need to be reminded that the Bible presents salvation as offering more than getting souls to heaven. My experience of teaching soteriology for several years at Regent College—an international graduate school of Christian studies whose students come from thirty-five countries on every continent except Antarctica—leads me to think that evangelicals far and wide also need their horizons expanded. Over and over, students have betrayed an understanding of salvation that amounted to a sort of spiritual individualism that is little better than Gnosticism.
>
> In fact, we could make an important start simply by teaching that salvation is *not* about "Christians going to heaven." Salvation is about God redeeming the whole earth ... Salvation is about heading for the New Jerusalem, not heaven: a garden city on earth, not the very abode of God and certainly not a bunch of pink clouds in the sky ... And salvation is not only about what is to come but also about what is ours to enjoy and foster here and now.[2]

According to Stackhouse and his colleagues, evangelicals too often view salvation in negative terms (what we are saved *from*), and as forensic, individualistic, private and pietistic, and spiritualized. In contrast, the authors argue that salvation should be viewed primarily as positive, transformative, communal, relational, cosmic, and embodied.[3]

Even if salvation is far more than "souls going to heaven," we cannot divorce soteriology from eschatology, nor should we minimize the significance of identifying the criteria by which individuals qualify for the final installment of the eschatological gift. Let us formulate our question in a manner that avoids soteriological ambiguity or confusion: what qualifications must individual human beings possess to inherit life in the world to come? Underlying this general question is a more specific one: do we have grounds for hope that some who do not explicitly acknowledge Yeshua before death will be among those who inherit life in the world to come?[4] Within the Messianic Jewish movement the driving

---

2. Stackhouse (editor), *What Does It Mean To Be Saved?*, 9–10.

3. Most Messianic Jews would also consider salvation as dealing prominently with nations, and in particular with the nation of Israel.

4. The distinction between implicit and explicit faith goes back to the Middle Ages. For its use by Thomas Aquinas, see Levering, *Christ's Fulfillment of Torah and Temple*, 23–24, 92–93.

concern is even more specific: do we have grounds for hope that there will be among the redeemed in the world to come Jewish people who do not explicitly acknowledge Yeshua in this life?

I call this the question of final destinies. In my view, the good news proclaimed and lived by the apostles is primarily concerned with final destiny (in the singular)—the eschatological consummation of covenant history and the created order in Messiah Yeshua by God's Spirit. However, that singular destiny is manifold and diverse, and encompasses the destinies of unique individuals. It is these eschatological destinies that will occupy my attention in this paper.

A thorough and compelling response to this question of final destinies would include at least four elements: (1) a study of the explicit biblical teaching on the topic, which would focus on the Apostolic Writings (since reward and judgment in the world to come is not a major theme in Tanakh); (2) a consideration of broader theological issues that have a bearing on the question;[5] (3) an examination of the practical implications of the available responses;[6] (4) a summary of the various responses to the question that have been offered through the centuries, and the reception they have received in the community of faith.[7]

I will pursue here only the first of these inquiries: a study of what the Apostolic Writings have to say about final destinies. Even on this point I will need to limit myself to the first two sub-questions: What qualifications must individual human beings possess to inherit life in the world to come? Do we have grounds for hope that some who do not

---

5. Relevant theological issues include the meaning and significance of God's attributes of mercy and justice and the relationship between them; the divinity of Yeshua and his mediatorial role in creation, revelation, and redemption; the validity of the traditional doctrine of "original sin" and its implications for a free human response to God's gracious initiative; the implications of the paradigmatic cases of infant mortality and those with severe mental limitations; the nature of Israel's enduring covenant and the ecclesiological bond between the Jewish people and the Christian church.

6. Practical implications include how the embrace of the various responses affect the following: motivation for outreach; the power and attractiveness of our presentation of the good news; our relationships with those who are outside the Yeshua-faith community (especially our fellow Jews); our attitudes towards the Jewish people through history and the Jewish religious tradition; the formation of personal character that bears the image of Yeshua.

7. For an excellent recent volume that covers much of this ground, written by an evangelical theologian with a missionary background, see Tiessen, *Who Can Be Saved?*.

explicitly acknowledge Yeshua before death will be among those who inherit life in the world to come? Our answers to these sub-questions will have implications for the third sub-question (i.e., the case of Jewish people who lack explicit Yeshua-faith), but we will not examine this as a topic in its own right.

Within the Apostolic Writings, I find three distinct ways of approaching this topic. They correspond roughly to three spheres of apostolic influence and activity: (1) the apostolic tradition of Peter and James (as reflected especially in the synoptic gospels and the general letters); (2) the apostolic tradition of Paul (as displayed in the letters which bear his name); and (3) the apostolic tradition of John (as embodied in the gospel and letters of John).[8] I will begin with the tradition of Peter and James, and then take up the traditions of Paul and of John.[9]

THE TRADITION OF PETER AND JAMES

The tradition that derives from Peter and James has much to say on the topic of final destinies—the reward and punishment of individuals in the world to come. It is usually overshadowed by the traditions of Paul and John, and read only in the light of their distinctive terminologies and emphases. This is unfortunate, and constitutes an oversight that we as Messianic Jews (to whom this tradition is especially addressed) are especially well suited to overcome. When studied on its own terms and taken seriously in its own right, the tradition of Peter and James challenges many popular assumptions and raises important questions.

One of the primary themes in this tradition's approach to final destinies is the warning against presumption: the misplaced confidence that *we* will be rewarded at the end, while *others* (who do not possess

8. Some texts (i.e., Acts, Hebrews, and Revelation) demonstrate an overlap of traditions. On the present topic, Revelation shares the perspective of the tradition of Peter and James. Acts and Hebrews are also closest to this tradition, though they likewise have elements in common with the tradition of Paul.

9. My focus in this paper on biblical "traditions" has a twofold purpose: (1) to facilitate the discerning of family resemblances among various strands of teaching in the Apostolic Writings, so as to enable an exegetical treatment that takes account of similarities and differences in language, conceptuality, and focus; and (2) to underline the fact that books whose authors are not themselves apostles (e.g., Mark, Luke) rely upon authoritative apostolic testimony. I am certainly not aiming to ascribe authority to underlying "traditions" apart from the canonical text—and context—in which they are embodied and transmitted. I am also not asserting any grand claims regarding the composition of the individual books. My purpose is in large part heuristic.

our qualifications) will be punished. The threatening words of John the Immerser, with which the story of Yeshua's mission begins, are typical:

> John said to the crowds that came out to be immersed by him, "You brood of vipers! Who warned you to flee from the wrath to come? Bear fruits worthy of repentance. Do not begin to say to yourselves, 'We have Abraham as our ancestor'; for I tell you, God is able from these stones to raise up children to Abraham. Even now the ax is lying at the root of the trees; every tree therefore that does not bear good fruit is cut down and thrown into the fire" (Luke 3:7-9; see Matthew 3:7-10).[10]

Descent from Abraham—a Jewish genealogy—will not provide automatic entry into the final banquet. Similarly, Gentile descent will not ensure automatic exclusion: "I tell you, many will come from east and west and will eat with Abraham and Isaac and Jacob in the kingdom of heaven, while the heirs of the kingdom will be thrown into the outer darkness, where there will be weeping and gnashing of teeth" (Matthew 8:11-12).

In Matthew's version of this saying, it is evident that those who "come from east and west" are Gentiles, since the words are uttered in response to the faithfulness of a Gentile centurion (Matthew 8:5-10). Accordingly, the "heirs of the kingdom" are Jews. Like the warning of John the Immerser, this teaching serves as an admonition against presumption based on Jewish identity.[11] Of course, it does not imply that *all* the "heirs of the kingdom" will be excluded, but instead contrasts the final destinies of many Gentiles with that of many Jews in order to challenge the comfortable assurance and exclusivism of the people of the covenant.

Yeshua's admonition against presumption extends beyond the claims of Jewish identity. He issues the same warning to his own disciples, and makes clear that their confession of faith in him as Lord, their public association with him, and even their mighty deeds done in his name will be insufficient to ensure their final destiny: "Not everyone

---

10. All biblical citations are based on the NRSV, with my own modifications.

11. The parallel in Luke has a different context, which leads to a different meaning. There the warning is issued to those who heard and saw Yeshua personally, those among whom he lived and worked: "Then you will begin to say, 'We ate and drank in your presence, and you taught in our streets'" (Luke 13:26). Those "thrust out" of the presence of the patriarchs are not "the heirs of the kingdom," as in Matthew, but "you yourselves" (i.e., those who knew Yeshua; Luke 11:28). In this context, those who "come from east and west, and north and south" are not necessarily Gentiles, but those from outside the land of Israel, who could not have known Yeshua personally.

who says to me, 'Lord, Lord,' will enter the kingdom of heaven, but only the one who does the will of my Father in heaven. On that day many will say to me, 'Lord, Lord, did we not prophesy in your name, and cast out demons in your name, and do many deeds of power in your name?' Then I will declare to them, 'I never knew you; go away from me, you evildoers'" (Matthew 7:21–23). This is an extremely significant text. It is not addressed to casual hearers of Yeshua, but to those who speak and act publicly in his name—and do so effectively! It is addressed to leaders of the Yeshua-movement—to us! Like the "heirs of the kingdom" in general, we must guard against the presumption that our participation in and apparently fruitful leadership of the community of the (renewed) covenant ensures our final destiny.[12]

Just as hopeful passages regarding the final destiny of Gentiles stand side by side with stern rebukes of Jewish presumption, so the tradition of Peter and James includes hopeful passages regarding non-Yeshua-followers that contrast with the above warning to his disciples. Of special significance is the parable of the sheep and goats (Matthew 25:31–46). As Davies and Allison note, the gospel of Matthew highlights the importance of this "word-picture of the Last Judgment" by placing it at the conclusion of Yeshua's fifth and final discourse.[13] It is thus the climax of Yeshua's public mission. The beginning of the "word-picture" describes the scene: "When the Son of Man comes in his glory, and all the angels with him, then he will sit on the throne of his glory. All the nations will be gathered before him, and he will separate people one from another as a shepherd separates the sheep from the goats, and he will put the sheep at his right hand and the goats at the left" (Matthew 25:31–33). Whoever "all the nations" may be, they certainly include multitudes that were not part of the Yeshua-believing community during their lifetime. This is confirmed by the fact that they do not recognize Yeshua as the one they helped (25:37) or failed to help (25:44). Yet, many among them inherit the life of the world to come.

The "word-picture" of the sheep and the goats deals with people who have not consciously known Yeshua during their lifetimes. In another saying Yeshua even opens up the possibility of a happy ending for those who have opposed him: "Therefore I tell you, people will be forgiven for every sin and blasphemy, but blasphemy against the Spirit

---

12. This is a common theme in the tradition of Peter and James. See, for example, 2 Peter 2:21; Hebrews 2:1–3, 10:26–31, 12:25–26.

13. Davies and Allison, *The Gospel according to Saint Matthew*, vol. 3, 418.

will not be forgiven. Whoever speaks a word against the Son of Man will be forgiven, but whoever speaks against the Holy Spirit will not be forgiven, either in this age or in the age to come" (Matthew 12:31–32; see Luke 12:10).[14] Some Pharisees had asserted that Yeshua expelled demons by means of demonic power (i.e., magic). Yeshua sees this as an act of "speaking against the Holy Spirit," that is, attributing deeds that are manifestly good (and thus the work of God) to an evil source. It is to call good evil. According to Yeshua, this constitutes a basic rejection of God. In contrast, merely to speak against Yeshua is a less serious offense. It can be forgiven—that is, some of those who do it may inherit the life of the world to come.[15]

If being a Jew or a public follower of Yeshua is insufficient for inheriting the life of the world to come, and if being a Gentile or one outside the Yeshua-believing community does not exclude one from that life, what are the qualifications for a happy final destiny? The teaching of the tradition of Peter and James shows remarkable consistency in answering this question. Yeshua's words in Matthew 7:21 are emblematic of this answer: "Not everyone who says to me, 'Lord, Lord,' will enter the kingdom of heaven, but only the one who does the will of my Father in heaven." What counts are actions (i.e., words and deeds) that conform to the divine will. Sometimes this tradition places particular emphasis on the action component:

> "For the Son of Man is to come with his angels in the glory of his Father, and then he will repay everyone *for what has been done*." (Matthew 16:27)

> "I tell you, on the day of judgment you will have to give an account for every careless word you utter; for by your words you

---

14. Some exegetes imply that this text may refer only to the period of Yeshua's earthly mission, when he operated "incognito" (France, *The Gospel according to Matthew*, 210). However, would the community have preserved such a saying if it had no application to their lives? Such a reductionist explanation derives more from a preconceived doctrinal position that seeks to evade the force of the text than from serious theological exegesis.

15. On the basis of this text, Athol Dickson asks the following questions regarding the final destinies of Jewish people who do not believe in Yeshua: "Is it possible for people of this age who were taught since birth to 'speak against the Son of Man' to be forgiven for doing exactly as they have been trained to do? . . . Will a gracious God consider their situation, look into their hearts to see if they truly love him, and forgive 'their words spoken against the Son of Man?'" (Dickson, *The Gospel according to Moses*, 253). C. S. Lewis concluded from this text that "honest rejection of Christ, however mistaken, will be forgiven and healed" (Lewis, *God in the Dock*, 111).

will be justified, and by your words you will be condemned." (Matthew 12:36–37)

If you invoke as Father the one who judges all people impartially *according to their deeds*, live in reverent fear during the time of your exile. (1 Peter 1:17)

And I saw the dead, great and small, standing before the throne, and books were opened. Also another book was opened, the book of life. And the dead were judged *according to their works*, as recorded in the books. And the sea gave up the dead that were in it, death and Hades gave up the dead that were in them, and all were judged *according to what they had done*. (Revelation 20:12–13)

Sometimes the tradition emphasizes that the deeds required are those that conform to the will of God as expressed in the commandments (*mitzvot*) of the Torah, i.e., righteous deeds:

Then someone came to him and said, "Teacher, what good deed must I do to have eternal life?" And he said to him, "Why do you ask me about what is good? There is only one who is good. *If you wish to enter into life, keep the mitzvot.*" (Matthew 19:16–17)

"For I tell you, unless your *righteousness* exceeds that of the scribes and Pharisees, you will never enter the kingdom of heaven." (Matthew 5:20)

The most important commandments that lead to life are those that summon us to love God and neighbor:

Just then a lawyer stood up to test Yeshua. "Rabbi," he said, "what must I do to inherit eternal life?" He said to him: "What is written in the Torah? What do you read there?" He answered, "You shall love the Lord your God with all your heart, and with all your soul, and with all your strength, and with all your mind; and your neighbor as yourself." And he said to him, "You have given the right answer; *do this, and you will live.*" (Luke 10:25–28)

Blessed is anyone who endures temptation. Such a one has stood the test and will receive *the crown of life that the Lord has promised to those who love him*. (James 1:12)

Has not God chosen the poor in the world to be rich in faith and to be heirs of *the kingdom that he has promised to those who love him*? (James 2:5)

> You do well if you really fulfill *the Torah of the kingdom* according to the scripture, *"You shall love your neighbor as yourself"* ... So speak and so act as those who are to be judged by *the Torah of liberty*. (James 2:8, 12)

The love that fulfills the Torah is not a sentiment, but an action done in the context of a relationship—a relationship with God, and a relationship with other human beings.

We may specify further the character of the love of neighbor commanded by Yeshua that serves as a key criterion for the inheritance of life. In so doing, we come to the heart of the teaching of Peter and James regarding final destinies. From what has been said thus far, one might think that the tradition of Peter and James presents an unattainable ideal of perfectionism that fails to take account of human sinfulness and our constant need for divine mercy. In reality, these texts demonstrate a vivid awareness of our dependence on God's mercy, expressed concretely in the forgiveness of sins. But the way we avail ourselves of this mercy is by showing mercy ourselves:

> "Blessed are the merciful, for they will receive mercy." (Matthew 5:7)

> "And forgive us our debts, as we also have forgiven our debtors ... For if you forgive others their trespasses, your heavenly Father will also forgive you; but if you do not forgive others, neither will your Father forgive your trespasses." (Matthew 6:12–15)

> "Do not judge, so that you may not be judged. For with the judgment you make you will be judged, and the measure you give will be the measure you get." (Matthew 7:1–2)

> For judgment will be without mercy to anyone who has shown no mercy; mercy triumphs over judgment. (James 2:13)[16]

Yeshua also conveys this central teaching through the parable of the unforgiving servant (Matthew 18:23–35). A king forgives an enormous debt owed him by one of his ministers, but that same minister fails to forgive a tiny debt owed him by one of his slaves. The parable concludes in this way:

> "Then his lord summoned him and said to him, 'You wicked slave! I forgave you all that debt because you pleaded with me. Should

---

16. Texts on *tzedakah* (charity) show the same principle at work (e.g., Luke 6:38; 16:9–13, 19–31; 19:8–90).

you not have had mercy on your fellow slave, as I had mercy on you?' And in anger his lord handed him over to be tortured until he would pay his entire debt. So my heavenly Father will also do to every one of you, if you do not forgive your brother or sister from your heart." (Matthew 18:32–35)

All of the above texts provide classic examples of the traditional rabbinic principle of "measure for measure" (*middah keneged middah*). According to this principle, God will treat us in the same way we have treated others. Yeshua takes up this principle, but he applies it to only one feature of our conduct: if we want God to be generous and merciful toward us, we must be generous and merciful to others. This reflects Yeshua's sense that all human beings are in desperate need for mercy. Strict justice will not produce a good result for anyone. This does not lead him to emphasize faith rather than deeds, but instead to emphasize one aspect of how we act toward others—our generosity and readiness to forgive.[17]

According to the tradition of Peter and James, Yeshua also teaches that the final judgment that determines final destinies takes account of the unique circumstances, challenges, and opportunities of each individual. The judge assesses not only what the individual has done, but also the relationship between what they have done and what they were given. This aspect of the final judgment is especially prominent in the parable of the talents (Matthew 25:14–30), placed immediately before the parable of the sheep and goats. A master entrusts property to three servants: the first servant receives five talents, the second receives two talents, and the third receives one.[18] The first servant goes into business, and produces an additional five talents for his master. The second servant does the same, and likewise doubles the initial investment. The response of the master in both cases is the same: "Well done, good and trustworthy slave; you have been trustworthy in a few things, I will put you in charge of many things; enter into the joy of your master" (25:21, 23). The third servant returns the deposit without addition, and is rebuked for it. If he had produced one additional talent—thus doubling the master's initial investment—he would have received the same commendation as the

---

17. See Boccaccini, *Middle Judaism*, 217–20. Boccaccini exaggerates the difference between the Yeshua tradition and rabbinic thought on this topic, but his exposition of the teaching of the Yeshua tradition on forgiveness is superb.

18. A talent was worth more than fifteen years' wages of a laborer.

other two servants. Thus, the master's pleasure is dependent not simply on what each servant produces, but on what they have done with what they were given.

This principle of relative accountability is likewise reflected in another saying of Yeshua dealing with masters and slaves: "That slave who knew what his master wanted, but did not prepare himself or do what was wanted, will receive a severe beating. But the one who did not know and did what deserved a beating will receive a light beating" (Luke 12:47–48a). The slave who did not know what was expected of him is still held accountable—presumably because he should have known! His ignorance is culpable. Nevertheless, his punishment is light in comparison to the slave who knew what his master wanted, and did not do it. The principle of justice illustrated by this example is then stated explicitly: "From everyone to whom much has been given, much will be required; and from the one to whom much has been entrusted, even more will be demanded" (Luke 12:48b). Yeshua here teaches that the final judgment will take account of what each of us knew and did not know, of the resources each of us had or lacked. The perfect justice of God will be administered in light of God's all-seeing eye.

The tradition of Peter and James calls for faith in Yeshua as God's elect servant, and insists that the afflicted are healed when they trust in him (e.g., Mark 2:5; 5:34, 36; 6:5–6; 10:52; Matthew 8:10, 13; 15:28).[19] Nevertheless, this tradition nowhere presents explicit faith in Yeshua (or lack of such faith) as a criterion of judgment in the last day.[20] What then

---

19. In keeping with the usage of the synoptic gospels, Acts 4:9 employs the verb "be saved" (*sosotai*) to refer to bodily healing. It also attributes this healing to the "name" of Yeshua and to "the faith of his name" (3:16). This is the context for Peter's claim, "There is salvation in no one else, for there is no other name under heaven given among mortals by which we must be saved" (Acts 4:12). Obviously, "salvation" has wider meaning here than just physical healing. However, it must include such manifestations of saving power. Given this fact, John Taylor's interpretation of the text has merit: "He was saying that Jesus of Nazareth is the source of every act of healing and salvation that has ever happened. He knew perfectly well that vast numbers of people had been healed without any knowledge of Jesus, yet he made the astounding claim that Jesus was the hidden author of all healing. He was the totally unique savior because he was totally universal" (Tiessen, *Who Can Be Saved?*, 85).

20. Of the two possible exceptions, Revelation 21:8 and Mark 16:16, the *apistois* who are cast into the lake burning with fire are not "the unbelievers" (KJV, NASB, NIV) but "the faithless" (RSV, NRSV, NEB, ESV), "the unfaithful" (CEV), or "the untrustworthy" (Stern). JB properly paraphrases as "those who break their word," while TEV has "the traitors." This reading is supported by Revelation's universal use of the positive form of the adjective (*pistos*) to mean "faithful" rather than "believing" (1:5; 2:10; 2:13;

is Yeshua's role in the determination of final destinies? In order to understand the perspective of the tradition of Peter and James on this question, we must attend to the eschatological expectations displayed in this tradition. John the Immerser had proclaimed an imminent judgment on Israel as part of the birth pangs of the messianic age (Matthew 3:1–12). Yeshua came to renew Israel's covenant (Luke 22:20) and to restore the twelve tribes (Matthew 19:28), but first he had to take upon himself the judgment that belonged to Israel so that Israel and the nations might receive divine forgiveness (Matthew 20:28; 26:28). As his death involves the bearing of Israel's judgment, so his resurrection anticipates and secures Israel's ultimate eschatological resurrection (Matthew 27:52–53).

Yeshua's redemptive work thus focuses first on Israel's—and the world's—final destiny. The destinies of individuals receive their particular meaning only within the framework of that singular but multifarious national and cosmic destiny. The mission of Yeshua thus has a direct bearing on the life and destiny of every individual. But does the tradition of Peter and James provide any further insight into what this entails?

This tradition tells us three additional things about Yeshua and the final destinies of individuals that are of great importance. First, Yeshua himself will be the judge who determines each destiny (Matthew 7:22–23; 10:33; 16:27; 25:31–33). His teaching and his example, which provide God's definitive interpretation of the essential requirements of the Torah, will serve as the standard of judgment,[21] and his atoning sacrifice will make available God's forgiveness. But every individual will also encounter him face to face to receive his personal verdict on their lives.

Second, those who hear his call to discipleship, leave all to follow him, and remain faithful to the end will inherit the life of the world to come (Matthew 19:21, 29; Mark 8:35). Following Yeshua is the perfect observance of the Torah (Matthew 19:16–21), and thus qualifies one for that inheritance. Those who live in a manner that acknowledges be-

---

3:14; 17:14; 19:11; 21:5; 21:6). The other possible exception to this generalization (Mark 16:16) will be treated later, for reasons to be explained at that point.

21. Wolfhart Pannenberg notes that the Beatitudes allot the inheritance of the kingdom to categories of people whose character reflects the teaching and example of Yeshua, regardless of whether they have ever heard of him: "The message of Jesus is the norm by which God judges even in the case of those who never meet Jesus personally . . . all to whom the Beatitudes apply will have a share in the coming salvation whether or not they ever heard of Jesus in this life. For factually they have a share in Jesus and his message, as the day of judgment will make manifest" (Pannenberg, *Systematic Theology*, vol. 3, 615).

fore the world their relationship to Yeshua will have that relationship acknowledged by Yeshua, the judge before the Father (Matthew 10:32). Even those who hear that call at the end of their lives, and respond sincerely, will be with Yeshua in paradise (Luke 23:39–43). However, if one becomes a disciple and then, in a situation of stress, denies knowing Yeshua (like Peter in Matthew 26:69–75) and fails to repent (unlike Peter), then Yeshua the judge will deny that person before the Father (Matthew 10:33). This accords with the principle of accountability, "From everyone to whom much has been given, much will be required" (Luke 12:48b).

Finally, as noted above, some who were not conscious and explicit followers of Yeshua will be welcomed at the end by Yeshua the judge with the words, "Come, you that are blessed by my Father; inherit the kingdom prepared for you from the foundation of the world" (Matthew 25:34). But, according to this crucial "word-picture of the Last Judgment," these heirs of the kingdom actually had a history of responding faithfully to the personal call of Yeshua, and were inheriting the kingdom because of that response. That call had come through Yeshua's family members—the hungry, the thirsty, the stranger, the naked, the sick, the imprisoned (Matthew 25:35–36, 40). Apparently, what Yeshua had said of the apostles also applies to the needy: "Whoever welcomes you welcomes me" (Matthew 10:40).[22] Thus, even those who are never conscious of Yeshua's presence or call (Matthew 25:37–38, 44), which comes to all people, are judged by how they respond to that call.

To summarize: the apostolic tradition of Peter and James challenges the presumption of Jews and Yeshua-believers regarding final destinies and insists that the final judgment will involve a just and merciful assessment of everyone's deeds. While the judgment will take account of the particular circumstances, gifts, and limitations of each individual, it will also scrutinize the deeds of all according to the Torah as definitively interpreted by Yeshua. That definitive interpretation places special emphasis on the requirement that we show mercy to others, giving and

---

22. Exegetes disagree over the identity of Yeshua's "family members" in Matthew 25. Some see them as disciples of Yeshua, either apostles or other suffering members of the community (see, for example Keener, *A Commentary on the Gospel of Matthew*, 604–6). Others, such as Davies and Allison, see them as the needy in general. While I incline to the latter view, it is significant, regardless, that (1) the sheep and goats are those outside the covenant community, and (2) they did not know that they were encountering Yeshua when they cared for his "family members."

forgiving. Yeshua himself will be the judge, and his assessment of our deeds will also reveal how we related to him during our lives—explicitly or implicitly.

THE TRADITION OF PAUL

It is enlightening to read Paul in light of the tradition of Peter and James rather than the reverse. We find that Paul employs his own distinct conceptual framework and addresses a situation unlike that described in the gospels (e.g., a mission outside the land of Israel, among Gentiles, which focuses on the establishment of stable Yeshua-faith communities). However, his message on the topic of final destinies departs little from that of the tradition of Peter and James.

The tradition of Peter and James sets the question of the final destinies of individuals within the broader context of the final destiny of Israel's eschatologically renewed national life.[23] The tradition of Paul paints on an even vaster canvas. Creation as a whole suffers in bondage to decay, and longs for the cosmic liberation that will come when the "children of God" are glorified (Romans 8:18–23). Paul recognizes that God's saving purpose affects "all things," and that God's self-offering to *each* will be definitively bestowed when God rules over *all*: "When all things are subjected to him [Yeshua], then the Son himself will be subjected to him who put all things under him, that God may be everything to every one" (1 Corinthians 15:28). To expand our vision beyond the horizons of our narrow individual concerns, God reveals to us the ultimate goal of "all things": "For He has made known to us in all wisdom and insight the mystery of his will, according to his purpose which he set forth in Messiah as a plan for the fullness of time, to unite all things in him, things in heaven and things on earth" (Ephesians 1:9–10). Our individual destinies are wrapped up in the destiny of "all things."

But Paul does have much to say about those individual destinies. Like the tradition of Peter and James, he warns sternly against any form of presumption in the face of divine judgment. Physical descent from the patriarchs and matriarchs (Romans 9:8), the covenantal sign of circumcision (Romans 2:25–29), and possession and knowledge of the Torah (Romans 2:17–24) are all privileges of enormous value (Romans 3:1–2; 9:4–5), but they cannot guarantee the inheritance of the life of the

---

23. See McKnight, *A New Vision for Israel.*

world to come. Gentile Yeshua-believers have been grafted into Israel's tree, but they must not boast arrogantly of their spiritual superiority over Jews, or God will cut their branches from the trunk (Romans 11:17–22). They also must not revert to their past Gentile life of idolatry and sexual immorality, thinking that their immersion in the Messiah and their participation in his covenant meal will ensure their final redemption; such a return to paganism would resemble the conduct of the generation of the exodus, and would elicit the same judgment as received by those wayward Israelites (1 Corinthians 10:1–13). Paul makes clear that even he, an apostle of the Messiah, cannot presume a favorable judgment, but must persevere in faithfulness to his calling (1 Corinthians 4:4–5; 9:24–27; Philippians 3:11–14).

Paul likewise suggests that we should avoid hasty conclusions about the final destiny of those outside the community of God's manifest covenantal action in Israel and in Yeshua. In Romans 2, Paul cites the example of virtuous Gentiles in order to chasten the presumption of his fellow Jews:

> When Gentiles, who do not possess the Torah, do instinctively what the Torah requires, these, though not having the Torah, are Torah to themselves. They show that what the Torah requires is written on their hearts, to which their own conscience also bears witness; and their conflicting thoughts will accuse or perhaps excuse them on the day when, according to my good news, God, through Yeshua the Messiah, will judge the secret thoughts of all. (Romans 2:14–16)[24]

> So, if those who are uncircumcised keep the requirements of the Torah, will not their uncircumcision be regarded as circumcision? Then those who are physically uncircumcised but keep the Torah will condemn you that have the written text and circumcision but break the Torah. (Romans 2:26–27)

---

24. James D. G. Dunn underlines the significance of the reference to "my good news" in this context: "The introduction of the gospel as criterion is not at odds with the preceding argument, as though in speaking of divine judgment Paul suddenly narrowed the much broader criteria with which he had been operating to the narrower one of faith in Christ. On the contrary, his point is precisely that his gospel operates with those broader factors, with faith in Christ seen as of a piece with a less well defined responsiveness to the Creator... Faith in Christ is of course the goal of his own mission and preaching (cf. 10:14–17), but as a fuller and normative rather than exclusive expression of such responsiveness" (Dunn, *Romans 1–8*, 103).

Both of these texts have the final judgment in view, as do previous verses in the chapter (see Romans 2:5-13). Paul does not imply that such Gentiles are perfect in their conformity to the law "written on their hearts," but only that their implicit relationship with the God of Israel will culminate at the end in an explicit acknowledgement of them as servants of the Most High.[25]

For Paul, as for Peter and James, the needle that bursts all bubbles of presumption is the sober expectation that God will judge the deeds of every one at the last day:

> But by your hard and impenitent heart you are storing up wrath for yourself on the day of wrath, when God's righteous judgment will be revealed. For he will repay according to each one's deeds: to those who by patiently doing good seek for glory and honor and immortality, he will give eternal life; while for those who are self-seeking and who obey not the truth but wickedness, there will be wrath and fury. There will be anguish and distress for everyone who does evil, the Jew first and also the Greek, but glory and honor and peace for everyone who does good, the Jew first and also the Greek. For God shows no partiality. (Romans 2:5-11)

Some see these words as hypothetical and rhetorical, and refuse to take them at face value. Such rejection of the plain sense of Paul's words finds support neither in the wider canonical witness of the Apostolic Writings, nor in the remainder of the Pauline corpus, where a final judgment of our deeds is taken for granted: "Yes, we do have confidence, and we would rather be away from the body and at home with the Lord. So whether we are at home or away, we make it our aim to please him. For all of us must appear before the judgment seat of Messiah, so that each may receive recompense for what he has done in the body, whether good or evil" (2 Corinthians 5:8-10; see Romans 14:10-12). Paul's joyful expectation and hopeful confidence never degenerate into presumption, for he knows that "all of us" will give an account for what we have done.[26]

---

25. Ibid., 101.

26. The importance of this theme in Paul's teaching has recently been emphasized by VanLandingham, *Judgment & Justification in Early Judaism and the Apostle Paul*, 175-241.

Like the tradition of Peter and James, Paul implies that the final judgment will take account of the particular circumstances of each individual. One will be judged according to what one has done with what one was given. Paul sees this principle at work in the differentiated judgment of Jews and Gentiles: "All who have sinned apart from the Torah will also perish apart from the Torah, and all who have sinned within the framework of the Torah will be judged by the Torah. For it is not the hearers of the Torah who are righteous in God's sight, but the doers of the Torah who will be justified" (Romans 2:12-13).

Paul then proceeds to speak about Gentiles who "do instinctively what the Torah requires" and who show thereby that "what the Torah requires is written on their hearts" (Romans 2:14-15). In verses 12-13, "Torah" includes the detailed ordinances addressed specifically to Israel and the commandments that presume an explicit knowledge of the God of Israel; in contrast, "what the Torah requires" in verses 14-15 consists only of basic moral and religious teaching such as that later codified under the Noachide laws. Those who have been instructed and formed in the Mosaic Torah will be judged in the light of that instruction, whereas those whose knowledge of God and God's requirements is more general will be judged in light of that general knowledge.

The tradition of Peter and James stresses that observance of the Torah prepares one for the life of the world to come, and that the two love commandments constitute the core of that observance. The apostle Paul acknowledges the central role played by love of neighbor in the Torah as a universal and enduring guide to life in the Messiah (Galatians 5:14; 6:2 Romans 13:8-10), and he sees the fulfillment of this commandment as an anticipation of the life of the world to come (1 Corinthians 13:8, 13). As an essential expression of this love, the Pauline tradition echoes that of Peter and James in its teaching about forgiveness (Colossians 3:12-14; Ephesians 4:1-3, 31-32; 5:1-2). Paul focuses on the way such forgiveness responds to, participates in, and replicates the forgiving love of God in Messiah, but—unlike the tradition of Peter and James—he does not teach about the granting of forgiveness as a condition for receiving forgiveness.

The most distinctive feature of the Pauline teaching on final destinies, in comparison to the tradition of Peter and James, is the role of faith (Romans 1:16; 1 Corinthians 1:21; 15:1-2). The good news of Messiah Yeshua's obedient life, sacrificial death, and victorious resurrection brings God's salvation to Israel, the nations, and all creation, and the saving power of this good news is effective among those who respond with faith:

> "The word is near you, on your lips and in your heart" [Deuteronomy 30:14] (that is, the word of faith that we proclaim); because if you confess with your lips that Yeshua is Lord and believe in your heart that God raised him from the dead, you will be saved. For one believes with the heart and so is justified, and one confesses with the mouth and so is saved. The scripture says, "No one who believes in him will be put to shame." For there is no distinction between Jew and Greek; the same Lord is Lord of all and is generous to all who call on him. For, "Everyone who calls on the name of the Lord shall be saved." (Romans 10:8–13)

We must pay close attention to what Paul says and does not say here. Many bring to the text assumptions about what Paul means by "faith" that are unsupported by his actual words.[27]

First of all, in the Pauline letters faith involves belief in certain key truths. In Romans 10, the key truths concern the resurrection of Yeshua and his enthronement as Lord.[28] In Romans 4, Paul pictures God's giving a son to the aged Abraham and Sarah as a kind of resurrection (4:17, 19), and explicitly compares Abraham's faith in God's promise with our belief that God raised "Yeshua our Lord" from the dead (4:24). Why this focus on Yeshua's resurrection and Lordship? According to Paul, Yeshua rises from the dead as "the first fruits of those who have fallen asleep" (1 Corinthians 15:20). His resurrection is the beginning of the resurrection of the righteous, and his glorified humanity becomes the agent of the life-giving transformation of all who belong to him (1 Corinthians 15:21–22, 45, 48–49). In this context to believe that God raised Yeshua from the dead is to believe that God will also raise us from the dead in him, with him, and through him.

Second, while this faith involves belief in a set of key truths, it is far more than the intellectual affirmation of a set of propositions. Romans 4 presents Abraham as the model of faith, and his belief in God's promise of a son took the form of heroic trust over many years (4:19–21). His

---

27. For an insightful and up-to-date study of Paul's use of *pistis*, see Campbell, *The Quest for Paul's Gospel*, 178–207.

28. "It is significant that it is the Resurrection which is mentioned—an indication that for Paul the belief that God raised Jesus from the dead is the decisive and distinctive belief of Christians" (Cranfield, *The Epistle to the Romans*, vol. 2, 530).

faith (*pistis*) was thus expressed as faithfulness (another meaning of *pistis*), and could also be characterized as obedience (Romans 1:5; 16:26). Elsewhere Paul speaks about "faith working through love" (Galatians 5:6). Thus, "Paul does not regard faith in purely passive terms: rather, it has very definite moral aspects which determine how the believer should live 'by faith' or 'by the Spirit.'"[29]

Third, Paul often associates faith with water-immersion (Galatians 3:25–27; Ephesians 4:5). In fact, scholars commonly view the confession of faith referred to in Romans 10 as an integral part of the ritual of immersion in the early Yeshua-community.[30] This is significant because it implies that Pauline "faith" is enacted in a communal context. It is not merely a private, individual, and subjective experience, but an action realized in a corporate setting.

Finally, this association with immersion also implies that "faith" is one of Paul's ways of speaking about union with the Messiah.[31] Just as Paul connects "faith" and "salvation," so Paul connects union with Yeshua in the Spirit and the final destiny of life in the world to come:

> If we have been united with him in a death like his, we will certainly be united with him in a resurrection like his . . . if we have died with Messiah, we believe that we will also live with him. (Romans 6:5, 8)

> If the Spirit of him who raised Yeshua from the dead dwells in you, he who raised Messiah from the dead will give life to your mortal bodies also through his Spirit that dwells in you. (Romans 8:11)

The importance of belief in the resurrection of Yeshua becomes evident in this context. In the ritual act of immersion, and in suffering affliction for Messiah's sake (Romans 8:17), the follower of Yeshua participates in his death. We do so with hope that this participation will culminate

---

29. Barclay, *Obeying the Truth*, 236.

30. For example, see Cranfield, *Romans*, 527; Dunn, *Romans 9–16*, 607; Keck, *Romans*, 254. Dunn compares the confession of faith in Yeshua as "Lord" with the Shema: "The confession which follows functions therefore as an (or the) equivalent of the Shema (Deut 6:4): as he who says the Shema identifies himself as belonging to Israel, so he who says *kyrion Iesoun* [Yeshua is Lord] identifies himself as belonging to Jesus. As a 'slogan of identification' it would no doubt be used at baptism, but also much more widely in worship (1 Cor 12:3), evangelism (2 Cor 4:5), and parenesis (Col 2:6)."

31. Some recent Scandinavian studies of Luther have concluded that the Reformer likewise understood "faith" primarily in terms of "union with Christ." See Braaten and Jenson (editors), *Union with Christ: The New Finnish Interpretation of Luther*.

for us in the resurrection life and glory that Yeshua now possesses as "Lord."

Paul's concept of "faith" thus has enormous depth and scope. It cannot be equated with the acknowledgment of Yeshua as Lord condemned in Matthew 7:21–23, which is compatible with disobedience to God and alienation from the Messiah. It also cannot be equated with the purely intellectual assent condemned in James 2:14–26, which exists independent of any appropriate deeds. In fact, its closest correlate in the tradition of Peter and James is faithful discipleship. As noted above, that tradition proclaims that all who follow Yeshua as his disciples, and remain faithful to the end, will inherit the life of the world to come (Matthew 19:21, 29; Mark 8:35). Just as an intimate and loyal relationship with Yeshua the itinerant Master provides assurance of a happy final destiny, so union with the crucified and risen Lord—in "faith"—offers the same assurance.

If "faith"—signifying a bond of union with the Messiah—leads to a happy final destiny, what leads to a tragic ending? Several Pauline texts address this question:

> Do you not know that wrongdoers will not inherit the kingdom of God? Do not be deceived! Fornicators, idolaters, adulterers, male prostitutes, sodomites, thieves, the greedy, drunkards, revilers, robbers—none of these will inherit the kingdom of God. (1 Corinthians 6:9–10)

> Now the works of the flesh are obvious: fornication, impurity, licentiousness, idolatry, sorcery, enmities, strife, jealousy, anger, quarrels, dissensions, factions, envy, drunkenness, carousing, and things like these. I am warning you, as I warned you before: those who do such things will not inherit the kingdom of God. (Galatians 5:19–21)

> Put to death, therefore, whatever in you is earthly: fornication, impurity, passion, evil desire, and greed (which is idolatry). On account of these the wrath of God is coming on those who are disobedient. (Colossians 3:5–6)

> Be sure of this, that no fornicator or impure person, or one who is greedy (that is, an idolater), has any inheritance in the kingdom of Messiah and of God. Let no one deceive you with empty words, for because of these things the wrath of God comes on those who are disobedient. (Ephesians 5:5–6)

Paul stresses the link between Yeshua-faith and the eschatological inheritance of God's kingdom. However, when speaking about those who are excluded from that inheritance, Paul lists types of behavior that are in fundamental violation of the universally applicable norms of the Torah (in rabbinic terms, the Noachide commandments). He does not include in the list "unbelief" (i.e., lack of explicit Yeshua-faith). As we inferred earlier from our reading of Romans 2, Paul does not divide the world neatly between Yeshua-believers (who are "saved") and those who lack explicit faith in Yeshua (who are "damned"). Judgment for all will be according to deeds rather than beliefs or experiences, though beliefs and experiences shape deeds. Just as the deeds of the "righteous Gentiles" of Romans 2 demonstrate an implicit Torah inscribed on their hearts, so the deeds of some outside the visible walls of the *ekklesia* (Yeshua-believing community) may bear witness to their implicit faith in the crucified and risen Messiah.

In conclusion, Paul addresses a different audience than the tradition of Peter and James, and develops a new concept of "faith." Nevertheless, his teaching regarding final destinies bears a close resemblance to that of his fellow apostles.

THE TRADITION OF JOHN

Like the apostolic tradition of Paul, the tradition of John emphasizes "faith" as the proper response to the person and message of Yeshua. John writes his gospel with a clear and single purpose, and he conveys that purpose unambiguously at the end of the book: "But these [signs] are written so that you may come to believe that Yeshua is the Messiah, the Son of God, and that through believing you may have life in his name" (John 20:31). What does John mean by "believe"? And what does he mean by "have life in his name"?

As in Paul, faith involves the affirmation of certain truths. In John, faith focuses less on particular eschatological events enacted in Yeshua (i.e., his death and resurrection), and more on Yeshua's personal identity.[32] Faith affirms that Yeshua is the Messiah (John 11:27; 20:31; 1 John 5:1), the Son of God (John 11:27; 20:31; 1 John 5:5), who comes from and is sent by God (John 16:27; 17:8, 21). But faith sees Yeshua as more than merely a faithful servant, entrusted with a unique redemptive mission:

---

32. "Doubtless the prime interest of a gospel . . . is to set forth the *action* of God in Christ for the fulfillment of his purpose of grace . . . But the unremitting concentration of [John] the Evangelist on the person through whom God acts makes it plain that for him 'function and person are inseparable'" (Beasley-Murray, *John*, lxxxiv).

he is the Holy One of God (John 6:69), who dwells in the Father and in whom the Father dwells (John 10:38; 14:10–11). He is the One who shares the divine Name and nature (John 17:11–12), and faith in Yeshua acknowledges that he rightly proclaims, "I Am" (John 8:24; 13:19; see 8:58–59, 18:5–6). In contemporary idiom, we could say that for John the central truth affirmed by faith is the deity of Yeshua.

However, John shows no more interest than Paul in purely intellectual assent to propositional truths. One does not "have life" through affirming creedal formulas. Believing that Yeshua is the way, the truth, and the life (John 14:6) necessarily involves answering an invitation to enter and nurture a relationship. It is the proper human response to a personal encounter with the One who embodies the self-revelation of Israel's God. It involves "coming to" Yeshua (6:35), "loving" Yeshua (16:27), and "obeying" Yeshua (14:21; 15:10; 3:36; 8:51; 12:47–48). As in Paul, so in John faith serves an equivalent role to that played by discipleship in the tradition of Peter and James.[33]

What is the "life in his name" received by those who believe in Yeshua? In the apostolic tradition of Peter and James, "life" refers to a gift bestowed in the future, in the world to come (Matthew 7:14; 18:8–9; 19:16–17, 29; 25:46). Therefore, we might reasonably think that John's primary concern is to assure those who believe in Yeshua of their future destinies. However, close attention to John's usage makes clear that this is not the case. In John "eternal life" is received now, in *this* world. It is a present possession, not one merely anticipated in the future.[34]

> Whoever believes in the Son has eternal life . . . (John 3:36)

> "Very truly, I tell you, anyone who hears my word and believes him who sent me has eternal life, and does not come under judgment, but has passed from death to life." (John 5:24)

> "Very truly, I tell you, whoever believes has eternal life." (John 6:47)

---

33. "'Believe' thus refers to the proper response to God's revelation, a faithful embracing of his truth, as in OT 'faithfulness'; it is a conviction of truth on which one stakes one's life and actions, not merely passive assent to a fact" (Keener, *The Gospel of John: A Commentary*, vol. 1, 327).

34. "For the Synoptics, 'eternal life' is something that one receives at the final judgment or in a future age (Mark 10:30; Matt 18:8–9), but for John it is a present possibility" (Brown, *An Introduction to the Gospel of John*, 239).

> "Those who eat my flesh and drink my blood have eternal life." (John 6:54)

The present possession of eternal life gives confident hope for the future world (John 6:40, 54; 11:25–26). However, John focuses not on that future hope, but on the life that those who believe receive *now*.

Yeshua gives eternal life to those who believe in him (John 5:21; 10:26; 17:2). Moreover, the life he gives remains his own after he gives it away, for it is not a "thing" external to his person. Yeshua gives life by giving himself.

> "For just as the Father has life in himself, so he has granted the Son also to have life in himself . . . " (John 5:26)

> "I am the bread of life. Whoever comes to me will never be hungry, whoever believes in me will never be thirsty." (John 6:35; see 6:53–58)

> "I am the resurrection and the life." (John 11:25)

> "I am the way, and the truth, and the life." (John 14:6)

Eternal life is not merely Yeshua's gift to us—it is his presence among us and within us. This is why we need to "believe in" Yeshua in order to have that life—since "believing" means coming to him, loving him, remaining with him. When we draw near to Yeshua, we are drawing near to life. It is like the light or heat given off by a fire—one cannot have the light and heat without the fire, and one cannot have the fire apart from the light and heat.

This identification of Yeshua with "life" in John is linked to the book's emphasis on Yeshua's deity. God is the only one who has life "in himself." Yet, God has granted that Yeshua likewise have life "in himself," so that all would honor him even as they honor God. To draw near to Yeshua is to draw near to God, and to draw near to God is to have life: "And this is eternal life, that they may know you, the only true God, and Yeshua the Messiah whom you have sent" (John 17:3).

Just as John focuses on eternal life as a present reality, so he envisions judgment as occurring now and not merely in the world to come:

> For God so loved the world that he gave his only Son, so that everyone who believes in him may not perish but may have eternal life. Indeed, God did not send the Son into the world to condemn the world, but in order that the world might be saved through

> him. Those who believe in him are not condemned; but those who do not believe are condemned already, because they have not believed in the name of the only Son of God. And this is the judgment, that the light has come into the world, and people loved darkness rather than light because their deeds were evil. For all who do evil hate the light and do not come to the light, so that their deeds may not be exposed. But those who do what is true come to the light, so that it may be clearly seen that their deeds have been done in God. (John 3:16–21)

Yeshua comes as light that reveals what we have done and who we really are. Those who flee from the light are those who prefer the darkness. Their judgment is not a future verdict, but a present reality—for in fleeing from the One who is the light and the life, they condemn themselves to darkness (the absence of light) and death (the absence of life).[35]

While believing in Yeshua is the way one receives life (since, as noted above, he *is* the life, and believing means "coming to him"), the reason why people "come to the light" is "that it may be clearly seen that their deeds have been done in God." The converse is also true: those who disbelieve run away from the light in order that "their deeds may not be exposed . . . because their deeds are evil." One's response to Yeshua reveals who one truly is: if we reject the One who is truth, we show that we are false; if we reject the One who is goodness itself, we show that we are evil. Thus, John dismisses neither the significance of deeds (in supposed contrast to "faith") nor the significance of the way one has lived *before* believing in Yeshua.[36] In this text, judgment is still according to deeds, and belief or disbelief is not so much the basis of judgment as it is *the judgment itself, rendered by the one being judged*!

In the apostolic tradition of Peter and James, no explicit connection is made between "faith in Yeshua" and final destinies. In the tradition of Paul, Yeshua-faith is linked to "salvation," but judgment is rendered according to deeds that violate the Noachide commandments (with no reference to the absence of Yeshua-faith). In the tradition of John, as seen above, faith in Yeshua leads to "eternal life," and disbelief in Yeshua brings condemnation—but both outcomes are viewed primarily as present realized conditions rather than future destinies (though they have

---

35. See Brown, *Gospel of John*, 239.
36. See Tiessen, *Who Can Be Saved?*, 145.

definite implications for the world to come). Nonetheless, the novel linkage between "disbelief" and judgment deserves comment.

> Those who believe in him are not condemned; but those who do not believe are condemned already, because they have not believed in the name of the only Son of God. (John 3:18)

> Whoever believes in the Son has eternal life; whoever disobeys the Son will not see life, but must endure God's wrath. (John 3:36)

Who are those who "do not believe in the name of the only Son of God"? Does this refer to every person in the world who is not explicitly a believer in his name? The second passage above would imply that more than this is meant by "do not believe," as it is the one who "disobeys the Son" who endures "God's wrath," and disobedience requires knowledge of a command and a Commander.

This inference draws support from other texts in John. In John 6:36, Yeshua says, "But I said to you that *you have seen me* and yet do not believe." In the verses that follow, Yeshua contrasts these disbelievers with those who believe: "every one who *sees the Son* and believes in him has eternal life" (John 6:40). Just as belief in Yeshua is preceded by an encounter with him in which the person "sees the Son," so disbelief is preceded by a similar encounter. Elsewhere John describes this personal encounter with auditory rather than optical imagery: "I do not judge anyone who *hears my words* and does not keep them, for I came not to judge the world, but to save the world. The one who rejects me and does not receive my words has a judge; on the last day the word that I have spoken will serve as judge" (John 12:47–48). The disbeliever hears the words of Yeshua, and rejects Yeshua and his words. Once again, this contrasts with the believer in Yeshua: "Truly, truly, I say to you, he who *hears my word* and believes him who sent me, has eternal life" (John 5:24).[37]

Thus, the Gospel of John says little about *non*-believers, but much about *dis*-believers![38] It deals harshly with those who see the light, recognize it as light, and then turn their backs and run away from the

---

37. This perspective provides the necessary context for interpreting other Johannine verses, such as John 8:24: "I told you that you would die in your sins, for you will die in your sins unless you believe that I am he." As Tiessen notes, "it is important to remind ourselves that Jesus made the statement specifically to people to whom he was revealing his identity. It is critical that we not overextend such statements to the unevangelized, who are, by definition, without such revelation" (Tiessen, *Who Can Be Saved?*, 85).

38. Ibid., 134.

light. It speaks of the condition of those who have encountered Yeshua and rejected him—not of those who have never encountered him at all. What does this mean for our day? To hear and see Yeshua is not just to read a book about him, hear a preacher speak about him on TV, watch a movie about his life, or receive a tract and a memorized speech from a missionary on the street. What we actually perceive in such contacts is shaped by our communal commitments and our personal and family history. To see Yeshua, in the Johannine sense, is to see *the light*, and to recognize its brightness. Such an encounter is required for genuine belief *or* disbelief to occur.

What does this mean for Jewish people who do not believe in Yeshua? Whatever was the case with his own generation who clearly "saw him" and "heard him," and said an emphatic "no" to him, we cannot assume that all future generations of Jews who lack explicit belief in him have encountered him and given that same negative response. Only God can distinguish between a disbeliever and a non-believer; however, even if the distinction were evident to human eyes, the extraordinary circumstances of Jewish history would incline one to extreme caution in assessing the destinies of individual Jews.

What does the tradition of John have to contribute to an inquiry into the future destiny of non-believers in Yeshua? Its assumptions appear to be similar to those discerned above in the traditions of Peter and James and of Paul. Just as the realized judgment enacted in this world through an encounter with Yeshua leads to life or condemnation depending on the previous deeds of the person who sees Messiah's light, so the final judgment will be based on deeds: "Do not be astonished at this; for the hour is coming when all who are in their graves will hear his voice and will come out—those who have done good, to the resurrection of life, and those who have done evil, to the resurrection of condemnation" (John 5:28–29).

The prologue to the gospel of John also states that all things were made through the Word who becomes incarnate in Yeshua (John 1:13, 9, 14). In him is the life that is the light of all people (John 1:4–5, 9). Many writers in the early church understood this to mean that the Son of God had acted in a revelatory and salvific manner outside the history of the people of Israel.[39] It is evident that the tradition of John itself assumed that the Son of God had acted similarly in Israel's own history (John

---

39. Ibid., 48–52.

12:41). In this perspective, all human beings encounter Yeshua's light in some measure, and all will be held accountable for how they respond to the light they receive.

In conclusion, we find that the tradition of John has less explicit teaching about final destinies than the traditions of Peter and James or of Paul. It speaks much about "eternal life" and "condemnation," but these are seen primarily as present realized conditions rather than anticipated future recompense. Belief and disbelief in Yeshua are not so much qualifications for future destinies as they are the judgments that individuals render on themselves in the present by turning towards or away from the light that is revealed to them.

While John differs from the traditions of Peter and James and of Paul in the singularity of its focus on faith in Yeshua as the One in whom God dwells uniquely, and in its predominantly realized eschatological horizon, it offers no teaching on future destinies that conflicts with the other apostolic traditions we have examined.

MARK 16:9–16

The final text to consider, Mark 16:9–16, cannot be assigned to any particular stream of apostolic tradition. While attached to the ending of the gospel of Mark, a scholarly consensus recognizes that it does not belong to the original composition.[40] Its canonical value has been disputed, but we will not here enter that debate.

Mark 16:15–16 offers the only example in the Apostolic Writings of a passage that explicitly connects final condemnation to lack of faith in the good news: "And he said to them, 'Go into all the world and proclaim the good news to the whole creation. The one who believes and is immersed will be saved; but the one who does not believe will be condemned.'"

Does this text teach that all those who do not believe in Yeshua in this life are destined for final destruction? In context, it is evident that the point of the passage is far more limited. The previous verses tell us what is meant by "not believing." Miriam of Migdol (Mary Magdalene)

---

40. See Kernaghan, *Mark*, 343–44. Even conservative scholars who argue for its early dating and canonical value agree that it does not belong in Mark: "It may be compared with the story of the woman taken in adultery, in John viii, as an example of an early tradition which may very well be genuine and is undoubtedly primitive, but does not belong to the actual Gospel text as it stands" (Cole, *The Gospel according to St. Mark*, 259).

sees the risen Yeshua, and goes to tell his followers of her encounter. Though they had been with him for three years, had loved and served him, and had heard him speak of his coming death and resurrection, "they would not believe" (Mark 16:11). Two more come to them with the same report, and still "they did not believe" (Mark 16:13). Finally, Yeshua appears to them himself and admonishes them for their "lack of faith" (Mark 16:14). He then commands them to "proclaim the good news to the whole creation" (Mark 16:15). In this context, it is evident that "the one who does not believe" is one who hears the good news, encounters through it a compelling testimony to the risen Lord, and nevertheless stubbornly and persistently refuses to become a disciple (i.e., be immersed and enter the community of those who love, serve, obey, and trust him).

The teaching on belief and disbelief in Mark 16:9–16 resembles what we have found in the tradition of John. Condemnation awaits those who willfully disbelieve, that is, reject the light that has dawned upon them. These words do not refer to those who lack genuine knowledge or experience of Yeshua, but to those who, like the disciples, know him—see the light—and then refuse to accept what he has done for them. Mark 16:16 does not categorize the whole world into the two groups of "believer" and "non-believer," and consign the latter to eternal perdition. It instead describes the two responses offered by people who have genuinely encountered Yeshua.

CONCLUSION

At the beginning of this paper I stated that a thorough and compelling response to the question of final destinies would include at least four elements, and that I would here be dealing with only the first of those elements. Therefore, any conclusions drawn at this point must be provisional, to be tested and refined by further theological, practical, and historical reflection. Nevertheless, our study of the explicit biblical teaching on the topic provides us with a preliminary hypothesis that deserves serious consideration.

According to this hypothesis, the apostolic teaching (as witnessed especially by the traditions of Peter and James and of Paul) begins by warning us against presumption regarding our own "salvation" and the damnation of others. It is striking how often the apostolic instruction has been understood by evangelicals in exactly the opposite form: as assuring our salvation and the salvation of others like us (in opinions, experiences, or community affiliations), and the damnation of those unlike us. I think that Søren Kierkegaard was on the right track in his meditation on "fear and trembling": "I have never been so far in my life, and am never likely to get farther than to the point of 'fear and trembling,' where I find it literally quite certain that every other person will easily be blessed—only I will not. To say to the others: you are eternally lost—that I cannot do. For me, the situation remains constantly this: all the others will be blessed, that is certain enough—only with me may there be difficulties."[41] Kierkegaard is not here making a doctrinal statement about the salvation of "the others." Instead, he seeks to exemplify the attitude that the good news aims to evoke through its warnings concerning final destinies.

The universal apostolic teaching that all will be judged according to their deeds ought to safeguard against any measure of presumption. We find this teaching in every strand of apostolic tradition that we have examined. What counts at the end, in the final analysis, is not our lineage, ethnicity, religious affiliation, religious experiences, or religious opinions, but how we lived our lives. Did we obey the divine commandments? Did we do God's will? Did we realize God's purpose for our lives?

God's justice in this final judgment is expressed in God's holding each accountable only for what he or she has received. We are responsible to take what we know and what we are given, and to make something of it. Each must respond to the light of revelation that she or he has been apportioned. This should sober us, who have beheld Yeshua's glory, and likewise temper our assessment of the destinies of others.

God's redemptive purpose for Israel, the nations, and all creation is realized through the person and work of Messiah Yeshua and the gift of the Spirit. Since the destinies of individuals receive their character from the wider corporate and cosmic destiny in which they share, no one may attain a blessed end apart from the saving work of Yeshua. Ultimately, the happiness of the world to come will consist of an eternal community of "all things" with the Father through the Son in the Spirit. In anticipation of that day, God offers us the opportunity to enter into that eternal relationship now. This is what the tradition of Peter and James knows as discipleship, and what the traditions of Paul and John mean by "faith in Yeshua." The judgment of our actions will determine whether we have already begun

---

41. Cited in Von Balthasar, *Dare We Hope "That All Men Be Saved"?*, 88.

living in this eternal relationship, implicitly or explicitly, and whether we have continued do so, or whether we have sought the way of escape.

For those without explicit faith in Yeshua, the judgment of their works will reveal how they have responded to the light—or, better, the Light—they have been given. All creatures are created and sustained by God through the divine Word in the Spirit, whether they know it or not. All creatures—and all human beings in particular—encounter God through the Word in the Spirit every day, every hour, every moment. Yeshua is met in the person of the needy; he stands beside everyone who has been wronged, and who must decide whether to bear a grudge or let it go; he speaks to each through the Torah "written on the heart." Most significantly, Yeshua reveals himself explicitly through the proclamation of the good news, through the transmission of his teaching, and through the embodiment of his redemptive mission in the life of the community that bears witness to his name. How have we responded to Yeshua, the living Torah, in all our actions? At the end, he will ask this question of everyone.

What C. S. Lewis says about Yeshua's threats concerning hell applies equally well to the entire apostolic teaching on final destinies: "The Dominical utterances about Hell, like all Dominical sayings, are addressed to the conscience and the will, not to our intellectual curiosity. When they have roused us into action by convincing us of a terrible possibility, they have done, probably, all they were intended to do."[42] In similar manner the Dominical and apostolic promises concerning the life of the world to come rouse us to action—not by alerting us to "a terrible possibility" but by setting before us a glorious hope. May each of us respond to the Light that has illumined our lives, and may he welcome each of us with the words, "Well done, good and trustworthy servant, enter into the joy of your Master."

---

42. Lewis, *The Problem of Pain*, 119.

7

Lumen Gentium, through Messianic Jewish Eyes

Written and presented by Mark Kinzer on behalf of the Messianic Jewish participants in the Roman Catholic—Messianic Jewish dialogue group, this paper was delivered at the group's meeting in 2008. The group first met at the Camaldoli monastery in Italy in 2000 and has continued to meet each year since then. Here Kinzer interacts with the Vatican II document *Lumen Gentium* (which sets forth the role of the church as a "light to the nations") from a Messianic Jewish perspective. He praises the document for its treatment of both the body of Christ and the people of God, its exhortation to maintain unity amidst diversity, and its charitable and promising stance toward non-Catholics. He expresses concern about the document's assertion that the church is the "new people of God," explaining that the logical conclusion of such a position is that Israel according to the flesh no longer has a divine vocation in the world, and that Jews who become believers in Yeshua have no divine calling to live as Jews. *Lumen Gentium*'s language of the church as the "new Israel" reveals a supersessionist leaning, and from Kinzer's perspective, the document's treatment of the people of God suffers from an exaggerated sense of discontinuity. While the *Catechism of the Catholic Church* (1992) serves to correct some of *Lumen Gentium*'s problematic elements, the positive assertions made in the *Catechism* regarding the Jewish people are not fully integrated into its ecclesiology. Because the deficiencies that remain are largely due to omissions, Kinzer is hopeful that the Catholic Church can move forward toward further developing its teaching on the church's relation to the Jewish people.[1]

Any serious encounter between Messianic Jews and Roman Catholics leads eventually to a discussion of ecclesiology. Each poses

1. Published in modified form in *First Things* 189 (January 2009), with responses and a rejoinder by Kinzer in *First Things* 193 (May 2009).

questions that challenge the identity claims of the other. Yet, these questions may open unanticipated avenues of theological reflection that result in a deeper self-understanding for each partner in the conversation.

There is no better place to begin the discussion than with a careful reading of *Lumen Gentium*, the document of Vatican II that provides the most comprehensive and lucid teaching on the meaning and role of the church offered by any official Christian body through the centuries. At the same time, we must recognize that important developments have occurred since Vatican II in Catholic thought concerning the Jewish people. Therefore, we should supplement this reading of *Lumen Gentium* by attending also to the *Catechism of the Catholic Church* (CCC) which has included these developments in its teaching.

What does a Messianic Jew make of *Lumen Gentium* and the *Catholic Catechism* in its treatment of the church, Judaism, and the Jewish people?

APPRECIATION

There is much that this Messianic Jew admires in *Lumen Gentium*. The document wisely treats two biblical concepts as central to the identity of the church: the body of Christ and the people of God. The first concept highlights the church's union with the crucified and risen Yeshua and her identity as the continuing earthly embodiment of his presence (LG 7). Because the church is the body of Christ, she serves as a sacrament in the midst of the world, mediating to the world the reality of the risen Lord (LG 48). The second concept highlights the church's identity as a humanly structured society with continuity through time (LG 9–17). Because the church is the people of God, she lives as a community that is fully in the world though not of it. The first concept emphasizes the church's union with God through Christ in the Spirit; the second emphasizes the church's role as the communal expression in this world of a humanity renewed and transformed through the redemptive work of the Messiah. By linking the two concepts, *Lumen Gentium* asserts that the church is both a mystical reality and a fully human community, and that neither may be emphasized legitimately at the expense of the other.[2]

---

2. "But, the society structured with hierarchical organs and the Mystical Body of Christ, are not to be considered as two realities, nor are the visible assembly and the spiritual community, nor the earthly Church and the Church enriched with heavenly things; rather they form one complex reality which coalesces from a divine and a human element. For this reason, by no weak analogy, it is compared to the mystery of the

In line with this dual identity, the document describes the functions of the church in terms of the traditional threefold office of Christ as priest, prophet, and king (LG 10–13, 21, 25–27, 34–36).[3] Characterizing the church in this way implies her union with Christ as his body, since she corporately assumes the same functions that properly belong to him as her head. On the other hand, the three offices refer originally to the key leadership positions within the people of Israel, and their use in the document therefore implies a likeness to the communal and institutional reality of Israel's life. The reiterated motif of the threefold office thus confirms and reinforces the central importance of the church's dual identity as the body of Christ and the people of God.

In ascribing such importance to the church's identity as the people of God, *Lumen Gentium* raises the ecclesiological question that is of greatest concern for Messianic Jews: what is the relationship between the church and the Jewish people? The document honestly addresses this question by focusing on the transition from the Old to the New Covenant, and from biblical Israel to the church (LG 9). While I am dissatisfied with the answers provided by *Lumen Gentium*, I appreciate the way its presentation of the church places this question at the center of the ecclesiological agenda.

Messianic Jews should be challenged by the document's summons to ecclesial unity and universality, and impressed with the way this summons is balanced by the value placed on the church's inner diversity.[4] *Lumen Gentium* acknowledges the importance of regional differences (LG 13); historical differences in the customs of particular churches founded in different periods (LG 13); vocational differences between the clergy, laity, and religious (LG 18–29; 30–38; 43–47); and eschatological differences between the pilgrim church and the church in heaven (LG

---

incarnate Word. As the assumed nature inseparably united to Him, serves the divine Word as a living organ of salvation, so, in a similar way, does the visible social structure of the Church serve the Spirit of Christ, who vivifies it, in the building up of the body" (LG 8).

3. The threefold office of priest/prophet/king provides a key structural motif for the entire document. Thus, the church as the people of God is described in its priestly (LG 10–11), prophetic (LG 12), and royal roles (LG 13–16). The next unit shows how the episcopal office (with its subordinate clergy) embodies and represents these three roles (LG 21, 25–27). Finally, the document portrays the laity as participating in its own distinctive manner in the threefold office (LG 34–36).

4. "By divine institution the Holy Church is ordered and governed with a wonderful diversity" (LG 32).

48–51). This combination of unity and diversity provides a potential framework for discussing the consequences of the rebirth of the church from the circumcision.

As a Messianic Jew, I am grateful for *Lumen Gentium*'s open, hopeful, and realistic perspective on those outside the visible structure of the Roman Catholic Church, and even outside an explicit confession of faith in Christ (LG 15–16). Without minimizing the centrality of such faith, or compromising its own essential ecclesiological claims, the document makes it possible for Catholics to enter into fruitful and constructive relationships with non-Catholics. It encourages charitable and humble assessments of one's neighbor, without sacrificing the church's apostolic and evangelical task in the world (LG 17).

Perhaps the greatest strength of *Lumen Gentium* is its overall design. The document addresses some of the most distinctive and controversial teachings of Roman Catholicism—such as the infallibility and universal jurisdiction of the Pope, the immaculate conception and bodily assumption of Mary, and the seven sacraments—but it contextualizes these teachings in a spiritual and communal framework that gives new perspective on their meaning.

By beginning with a trinitarian reflection on the church's mystery as the body of Christ (LG 2–4), *Lumen Gentium* makes clear that the spiritual reality of the church takes precedence over its juridical structure. The document then proceeds to discuss the church as a human society, but it does so by characterizing the church as the people of God (LG 9–17). The church's nature as a structured community, a people, with continuity through time, involves all its members and not just its official leaders. Thus, the communal reality of the church also takes precedence over its juridical structure. Of course, *Lumen Gentium* sees the church's hierarchical structure as of immense importance, and devotes much of its space to explaining its role (LG 18–29). At the same time, by setting the discussion of the church hierarchy within the context of the church's nature as the body of Christ and the people of God, the document indicates that the hierarchical structure exists to serve ends greater than itself.[5] Similarly, by presenting the Council teaching on Mary as a

---

5. It should also be noted that *Lumen Gentium* sets its teaching on the Papacy (LG 22) in the broader context of the episcopate and apostolic succession (LG 19–21). The bishop of Rome exercises "full, supreme and universal power over the Church" (LG 22), but he does so as the head of an episcopal college—though he does not need the explicit approval of the other bishops to exercise his authority.

sort of appendix to its teaching on the church (LG 52–69), rather than devoting a special document to her, the Council indicates that Mary's primary role is to serve as a model, type, and mother for the church, rather than to function as an independent object of devotion.

Messianic Jews can and should recognize *Lumen Gentium* as a landmark achievement of the Second Vatican Council. Nevertheless, as is to be expected, not every aspect of the document elicits our unequivocal assent.

CONCERNS

While Messianic Jews can appreciate the way *Lumen Gentium* gives new prominence to the question of the church's identity in relationship to Israel, we also find the answers it gives dissatisfying. The *Catechism* helps in this regard, as it compensates for some of the deficiencies we see in *Lumen Gentium*. Nevertheless, through Messianic Jewish eyes even the *Catechism* does not go far enough.

Before explaining the concerns, let us summarize what *Lumen Gentium* has to say about the Jewish people. The document first speaks of the people of Israel at the beginning of its trinitarian introduction (LG 2), which considers the plan of God the Father, conceived "before time began":

> All the elect, before time began, the Father "foreknew and predestined to become conformed to the image of His Son, that he should be the firstborn among many brethren." He planned to assemble in the holy Church all those who would believe in Christ. Already from the beginning of the world the foreshadowing of the Church took place. It was prepared in a remarkable way throughout the history of the people of Israel and by means of the Old Covenant. In the present era of time the Church was constituted and, by the outpouring of the Spirit, was made manifest.

God's purpose—"to raise men to a participation in the divine life"— is realized in his plan "to assemble in the holy Church all those who would believe in Christ." The history of the people of Israel foreshadows and prepares for the establishment of the church, which is constituted through Christ's person, life, and work, and manifested by the outpouring of the Spirit. Thus, the church is an essentially new reality in the world. It shares some features in common with the people of Israel in the old covenant, but it is fundamentally discontinuous with it. The goal of the divine plan, conceived "before time began," is the establishment of the church, and God's dealings with the people of Israel in the old covenant were all ordered to prepare for that goal.

This view of "Old Covenant Israel" is reiterated and developed in LG 9—the document's primary paragraph on this theme. The paragraph introduces the central motif of *Lumen Gentium*—the church as the people of God. It begins by describing God's corporate purpose for humanity, and how that purpose leads to the election of the people of Israel and the establishment of God's covenant with them:

> At all times and in every race God has given welcome to whosoever fears Him and does what is right. God, however, does not make men holy and save them merely as individuals, without bond or link between one another. Rather has it pleased Him to bring men together as one people, a people which acknowledges Him in truth and serves Him in holiness. He therefore chose the race of Israel as a people unto Himself. With it He set up a covenant. Step by step He taught and prepared this people, making known in its history both Himself and the decree of His will and making it holy unto Himself.

The ultimate purpose of this election, however, does not have to do with Israel itself as a particular community, but with the new universal reality that is the church:

> All these things, however, were done by way of preparation and as a figure of that new and perfect covenant, which was to be ratified in Christ, and of that fuller revelation which was to be given through the Word of God Himself made flesh. "Behold the days shall come saith the Lord, and I will make a new covenant with the House of Israel, and with the house of Judah . . . I will give my law in their bowels, and I will write it in their heart, and I will be their God, and they shall be my people . . . For all of them shall know Me, from the least of them even to the greatest, saith the Lord." Christ instituted this new covenant, the new testament, that is to say, in His Blood, calling together a people made up of Jew and gentile, making them one, not according to the flesh but in the Spirit. This was to be the new People of God. For those who believe in Christ, who are reborn not from a perishable but from an imperishable seed through the word of the living God, not from the flesh but from water and the Holy Spirit, are finally established as "a chosen race, a royal priesthood, a holy nation, a purchased people . . . who in times past were not a people, but are now the people of God."

The covenant with Israel, which establishes Israel as a nation, is but a "preparation" and "figure" of a new and better covenant that will establish "the new People of God." This new people—whose membership is determined not by physical but spiritual birth—is the Israel mentioned by Jeremiah 31 as the recipient of the "new covenant." Thus, *Lumen Gentium* presents the church as a new reality, patterned in some ways on the people of Israel and marvelously prepared for by it, but essentially discontinuous with it. It would be natural to conclude from this characterization of the church that Israel according to the flesh no longer has a particular divine vocation in the world (beyond that of other ethnic groups), and that Jews who enter the church have no particular divine vocation—specifically as Jews—within the ecclesial sphere.

After further description of the church as a "messianic people" called to be "an instrument for the redemption of all," LG 9 proceeds to speak of it as a true people possessing all "those means which befit it as a visible and social union."

> Israel according to the flesh, which wandered as an exile in the desert, was already called the Church of God. So likewise the new Israel which while living in this present age goes in search of a future and abiding city is called the Church of Christ . . . While it transcends all limits of time and confines of race, the Church is destined to extend to all regions of the earth and so enters into the history of mankind . . .

The document here draws language from the Apostle Paul, who refers to "Israel according to the flesh" (1 Corinthians 10:18). It then goes beyond the language of Paul and the New Testament by referring to the church as "the new Israel." Such terminology, combined with the preparatory nature of Israel's calling, implies that fleshly Israel no longer retains a unique and positive vocation in the world. In a sense, it no longer even merits the title of "Israel." At the same time, by noting that "Israel according to the flesh . . . was already called the Church of God," *Lumen Gentium* hints that the historical discontinuity between the two Israels—the one in the old covenant, the other in the new—might not be as radical as first appeared.

Only one paragraph of *Lumen Gentium* (LG 16) explicitly addresses the relationship between the church and the Jewish people after the coming of Christ.

> Finally, those who have not yet received the Gospel are related in various ways to the people of God. In the first place we must recall the people to whom the testament and the promises were given and from whom Christ was born according to the flesh. On account of their fathers this people remains most dear to God, for God does not repent of the gifts He makes nor of the calls He issues.

By citing Romans 11:28–29, *Lumen Gentium* decisively rejects the notion that Israel according to the flesh has forfeited its election and no longer holds a distinctive divine vocation in the world beyond that of other ethnicities. However, the context of this rejection of supersessionism undermines to a certain extent its positive message. The Jewish people are presented as the first of many groups "who have not yet received the Gospel"—they are part of a broader category of adherents of "non-Christian religions." Such adherents, we learn, "are related in various ways to the people of God." The Jewish people, therefore, are not *part of* the people of God, i.e., the church, but are—like all human beings—*related to it* because of the church's universal vocation. Thus, at the very point at which *Lumen Gentium* seeks to make an explicitly positive statement about the Jewish people, it implicitly distances Israel from its own original status as the people of God, and implicitly treats Israel's religious tradition, rooted in divine revelation, as merely the first among many non-Christian traditions.[6]

What does a Messianic Jew make of *Lumen Gentium*'s teaching related to Israel according to the flesh? Through Messianic Jewish eyes, its overall perspective on the Jewish people—both before and after the coming of Christ—suffers from an exaggerated emphasis on discontinuity. The document's use of the term "new" underlines this emphasis. It speaks of the new people of God and the new Israel. It likewise speaks of

---

6. The relationship between Judaism and Christian faith is better captured by John Howard Yoder in his assertion that Judaism is a "non-non-Christian religion" (*The Jewish-Christian Schism Revisited*, 147, 156). This relationship is also expressed practically in the Vatican decision to relate to Judaism through an organ concerned with intra-Christian dialogue, as noted by Richard John Neuhaus: "From the Jewish side, when after the council the Catholic Church was formalizing its conversations with non-Christians, the Jewish interlocutors insisted that they not be grouped with the Vatican dycastery designed to deal with other religions but be included under the secretariat for promoting Christian unity. There were political reasons for that insistence, not least having to do with the politics of the Middle East, but that arrangement has, I believe, much more profound implications than were perhaps realized at the time" (Yoder, "Salvation is From the Jews," in Braaten and Jenson (editors), *Jews and Christians*, 68).

the church as first "constituted" in our era, apparently by the death and resurrection of Christ. The message of the document makes it evident that "new" here refers to the appearance of a reality that did not in any sense exist before. The new people, the new Israel, was foreshadowed by the old, and thus shares certain features by way of analogy, but the two realities are not integrally interconnected.

According to our thinking as Messianic Jews, this way of employing the word "new" detracts from the richness of its biblical meaning. In many biblical texts the word would be more suitably translated as "renewed." The new heavens and new earth are glorified forms of what existed before. The new humanity is the old humanity, raised from the dead and transformed. This understanding of eschatological "newness" is supported by its paradigmatic case—Yeshua's resurrection. The risen Yeshua is new, different, yet the same human being as the one who was born of Mary. In the same way, the church should be seen as a renewed Israel, a renewed people of God. It is an eschatological form of Israel, anticipating the life of the world to come through the gift of the Spirit. As an eschatological reality, it is also an expanded Israel, including within its ranks people from all the nations of the world. However, in the apostolic period it still maintained continuity with Israel according to the flesh—founded and led by observant Jews (i.e., the apostles and elders), centered in the holy city of Jerusalem, and containing at its heart a visible corporate expression of Jewish life (i.e., the Jerusalem congregation of Yeshua-believers). This continuity extended to the church's relationship to the wider Jewish world that had not yet accepted the church's status as an expanded eschatological Israel. For Peter, Paul, and James, the leaders of the Jewish people were still their leaders, and the Jewish people were still their people—the people of God.

Likewise, the new covenant of Jeremiah 31 is promised, not to the church as a distinct new reality, but to Israel according to the flesh. God promises Israel that he will renew the covenant he made with them when they came out of Egypt. Wolfhart Pannenberg states this clearly:

> Jeremiah in 31:31–32 and Isaiah in 59:21 promise the new covenant not to another people but to Israel as the eschatological renewal and fulfillment of its covenant relationship with its God. When at the Last Supper that he held with his disciples on the night of his arrest Jesus related the promise of the new covenant to the table fellowship with his disciples that he sealed with his

self-offering, he was not snapping the link of this promise to the people of Israel. Instead, he was showing that fellowship with himself is for the whole Jewish people the future of salvation that breaks in already in the fellowship of the band of disciples. The later inclusion of non-Jews in the Christian community on the basis of the confession of Jesus that is sealed by their baptism does nothing to change this.[7]

To this point, only a small portion of Israel according to the flesh has entered fully into this renewed covenant, but the promise remains for Israel as a whole, and the promise will be fulfilled. In this sense, Israel according to the flesh is itself the people of the new or renewed covenant—the people to whom that covenant uniquely and particularly belongs as a heritage.

Lumen Gentium 9 recognizes that the church is essentially "a people made up of Jew and gentile," united according to the Spirit. However, in context this expression appears to mean no more than that membership in the church is independent of restrictions based on birth or ethnicity. To say that it is "made up of Jew and gentile" simply means that it is made up of all people, and that the Jews in its midst have no privileged position. *Lumen Gentium* certainly does not intend to teach that the church must always include Jews, or that such Jews must be visibly Jewish, or that the church must always ensure that distinct Jewish life can be lived with integrity in its midst, or that Jews who are part of the church have the obligation or even permission to transmit Jewish life to the next generation. At the same time, *Lumen Gentium* does not exclude such notions.

Fortunately, many of these deficiencies are addressed in the *Catechism of the Catholic Church*. There Israel's priestly vocation appears in the present rather than the past tense: "Israel *is* the priestly people of God" (CCC 63; emphasis mine). The remainder of the sentence unambiguously identifies this "Israel" with the Jewish people, not the church.

The *Catechism* later affirms explicitly the enduring significance of the Jewish people, in paragraphs that are presented as commentary on *Lumen Gentium* 16:

> "Those who have not yet received the Gospel are related to the People of God in various ways." (Lumen Gentium 16)

---

7. Pannenberg, *Systematic Theology*, vol. 3, 477.

> *The relationship of the Church with the Jewish People.* When she delves into her own mystery, the Church, the People of God in the New Covenant, discovers her link with the Jewish People, "the first to hear the Word of God." The Jewish faith, unlike other non-Christian religions, is already a response to God's revelation in the Old Covenant. To the Jews "belong the sonship, the glory, the covenants, the giving of the law, the worship, and the promises; to them belong the patriarchs, and of their race, according to the flesh, is the Christ," "for the gifts and the call of God are irrevocable." (CCC 839)
>
> And when one considers the future, God's People of the Old Covenant and the new People of God tend towards similar goals: expectation of the coming (or the return) of the Messiah. But one awaits the return of the Messiah who died and rose from the dead and is recognized as Lord and Son of God; the other awaits the coming of a Messiah, whose features remain hidden till the end of time; and the latter waiting is accompanied by the drama of not knowing or of misunderstanding Christ Jesus. (CCC 840)

It is impossible to overstate the importance of these paragraphs. They correct the gravest problems in *Lumen Gentium*'s treatment of the Jewish people in the following three ways: (1) The distinction between the Jewish people and the church is no longer that between Israel according to the flesh and the new Israel, but instead between "God's People of the Old Covenant" and "the People of God in the New Covenant"—with the former title applied not only to Israel before the coming of Christ, but to the Jewish people throughout history. While I question whether this is the most apt title for the Jewish people, it at least leaves no doubt about the spiritual status of Israel—it remains the people of God; (2) "The Jewish faith" is distinguished clearly from all "other non-Christian religions." Like the faith of the church, Judaism is a response to God's revelation. Not only are the "gifts and call of God" irrevocable, but the core beliefs of Judaism—including the enduring role of the Torah in Jewish life—are acknowledged as God-given; (3) The relationship between the church and the Jewish people (and between Christian faith and Jewish faith) is not external to the church's identity, as one could conclude from the radical discontinuities of *Lumen Gentium*, and even from the citation of *Lumen Gentium* with which this unit begins. Instead, the Jewish people and the Jewish faith are integrally tied to the church's own identity, since the church "discovers her link with the Jewish People" by turning inward and reflecting on the mystery of her own being as the church (an allusion to *Nostra Aetate* 4). This link involves both a common origin, and a common messianic destiny.

While *Lumen Gentium* identifies the church as the "new Israel," her assumption of this title requires and involves no evident bond to the Jewish people. The *Catechism*, on the other hand, makes clear that the entry of Gentiles into the church—and their new identity as participants in the life of Israel—involves a "turning towards the Jews":

> The magi's coming to Jerusalem in order to pay homage to the king of the Jews shows that they seek in Israel, in the messianic light of the star of David, the one who will be king of the nations. Their coming means that pagans can discover Jesus and worship him as Son of God and Savior of the world only by turning towards the Jews and receiving from them the messianic promise as contained in the Old Testament. The Epiphany shows that "the full number of the nations" now takes its "place in the family of the patriarchs," and acquires *Israelitica dignitas* (is made "worthy of the heritage of Israel"). (CCC 528)

The coming of the magi to Jerusalem prefigures the response of the Gentiles to the message of the Jewish apostles of the Jewish Messiah, and the latter enables Gentiles to take their "place in the family of the patriarchs"—but only through a new bond that is established between them and the flesh and blood "family of the patriarchs."

When the *Catechism* deals directly with the Jewish people and the Jewish faith—both before and after Christ—it does not suffer from the same weaknesses as *Lumen Gentium*. However, when the *Catechism* turns its attention to the article of the Creed dealing with the church (CCC 748–975), it follows closely the scheme of *Lumen Gentium*, and hardly mentions the Jewish people. This is a failure of omission rather than commission, but it indicates that the *Catechism* has not integrated its affirmations about the Jewish people into its ecclesiology. In regards to our concerns as Messianic Jews, the *Catechism* is a great improvement, but it has not yet hit the mark.

DEVELOPMENT

Even in *Lumen Gentium*, the primary weakness in dealing with the Jewish people and the Jewish faith derives from omission. Its teaching on this topic seems problematic to a Messianic Jew more because of what it implies that what it states. This is a point of great importance, since it means that the Catholic Church could develop its doctrine on ecclesiology and the people of Israel in constructive new directions without contradicting its previous authoritative teaching.

Pure Omission

What new points need to be added to *Lumen Gentium*'s treatment of the Jewish people and Jewish faith, apart from what is already added by the *Catechism*? From a Messianic Jewish perspective, there are two omissions that require attention. First, the historic church needs to examine the significance and role of the church from the circumcision, both in its biblical origins and in its contemporary manifestations. This examination will be as challenging and troubling for Catholics as *Lumen Gentium* is for Messianic Jews—but also, hopefully, as rewarding. While the resurgence of the church from the circumcision raises difficult questions about Catholic identity, it also opens new possibilities for affirming continuity with "Old Covenant Israel" without detracting from the eschatological newness of God's redemptive work through the Son in the Spirit. Yeshua is not only "lumen gentium," a light to the Gentiles, but also "glory to your people Israel" (Luke 2:32). His body should likewise illumine both spheres, but in different ways, as Cardinal Schönborn has described so well in a recent article.[8]

Secondly, neither *Lumen Gentium* nor the *Catechism* deals with the relationship between the land of Israel and the people of Israel, nor with the implications of this relationship for the church's own identity in an age when the people of Israel once again dwell in the land. Just as the destruction of a Jewish national presence in the holy city and land in the first century opened the door for supersessionist ecclesiology, so the restoration of such a presence in the twentieth century challenges that ecclesiology. This second point is connected to the first, for the restora-

---

8. "St. Paul distinguishes between the two vocations, between those who believed in Jesus as the Messiah who came 'from circumcision' and those who converted to Christ and came 'from the Gentiles' . . . By welcoming the Gospel, the Jews are witnesses of God's fidelity to his promise, while the Gentiles are witnesses of the universality of his mercy. These two appeals in the Church reflect the twofold way of the same salvation in Christ, one for Jews and one for Gentiles. Thus the same Jesus Christ is simultaneously 'a light for revelation to the Gentiles, and for glory to your people Israel' (Luke 2:32)" (Schönborn, "Judaism's Way to Salvation," 9).

tion of a Jewish national existence in the land promised to the patriarchs and matriarchs has also led to the restoration of the church from the circumcision in the holy land and the holy city. Jerusalem was the original center of the church; could it be that Zion again has a central role to play in the life of the church? Could it be that she who became the capital of the church from the Gentiles—though Roman Catholics will be reluctant to concede that this is all that she is—must learn to share pride of place with another whose history is even more hallowed? In keeping with Romans 11, the *Catechism* recognizes that "the glorious Messiah's coming is suspended at every moment of history until his recognition by 'all Israel'" (CCC 674). If that recognition emerges gradually rather than in a sudden burst of illumination, should we not expect the reemergence of the church from the circumcision, and the reemergence of the holy land and the holy city as a center not only for pilgrimage but also for ecclesial identity?

While treatment of these two points is totally absent from *Lumen Gentium* and the *Catechism*, the paragraph of the *Catechism* cited above (CCC 674) may offer a hint whose meaning could be further developed: "The 'full inclusion' of the Jews in the Messiah's salvation, in the wake of 'the full number of the Gentiles,' will enable the People of God to achieve 'the measure of the stature of the fullness of Christ,' in which 'God may be all in all.'" The "People of God" will not reach its fullness until the Jewish people—as a corporate reality—and the church from the Gentiles come together as one flock with one Shepherd, to celebrate the glory of God through Israel's crucified and risen Messiah in the power of the Holy Spirit.

Insufficient Development

In addition to these omissions, there are three points that are central to *Lumen Gentium* whose implications are not adequately explored in that document or in the *Catechism*. The first concerns the relationship between the two primary biblical concepts employed by *Lumen Gentium*: the people of God and the body of Christ. While these two concepts are employed together in the document, the relationship between them is not developed. The *Catechism* provides some perspective on this relationship: "The images taken from the Old Testament [to speak of the Church] are variations on a profound theme: the People of God. In the New Testament, all these images find a new center because Christ has become the head of this people, which henceforth is his Body" (CCC 753).

These statements are terse, and could be understood in a number of ways. Let us consider one way of understanding them that would open up new vistas for ecclesiology. Yeshua becomes the head of the people of Israel through his death and resurrection, and—*in a certain way*—all those who are part of that people receive a new status as members of his body.[9] Those Jews who receive the good news affirm that status, and enter into the eschatologically renewed and expanded Israel. Those who do not receive the good news are put in an anomalous and precarious situation—yet Yeshua remains their king and head, whether they acknowledge the fact or not. He was born "the king of the Jews" (Matthew 2:2), he was crucified under the same title (Matthew 27:11, 29, 37), and he will bear it for all eternity. Thus, for Jews participation in the life of the people of God leads to membership in the body of their appointed messianic king. For Gentiles, on the other hand, the situation is reversed. All Gentiles who are joined to the body of Christ through faith and baptism thereby become part of an expanded people of Israel. For them, membership in the body leads to citizenship in the commonwealth of Israel.

As for how membership in Messiah's body leads to citizenship in Israel, we must reflect on the fact that Yeshua was born a Jew, was circumcised on the eighth day, and lived as a faithful Jew throughout the course of his earthly life. When he was raised from the dead, his Jewish identity carried over into his glorified existence, just as did his masculine gender. To say that Yeshua *was* a Jew is a fact of history. To say that Yeshua *is* a Jew is a fact of explosive theological consequence. The Son of God does not assume a generic human nature, but the humanity descended from Abraham, Isaac, and Jacob, Sarah, Rebecca, Rachel, and Leah. When Gentiles become part of that body, they become part of a Jewish body. They do not themselves become Jews, but they become part of the Jewish commonwealth.

A second central motif of *Lumen Gentium* points in a similar direction. This motif is the threefold office of priest/prophet/king that Christ shares with his body. While *Lumen Gentium* introduces the three-

---

9. I am deliberately employing the phrase "in a certain way," which is used in Vatican II's *Gaudium et Spes* 22: "For, by his incarnation, he, the Son of God, has *in a certain way* united himself with each man" (emphasis mine). While I am not making exactly the same point as GS 22, my use of the phrase is the same.

fold office of Christ in its section on the church as the people of God (paragraphs 10–16), it nowhere connects the theme to the life of Israel according to the flesh. Yet that is its source. The Torah defines Israel's institutions of leadership according to the offices of priest, prophet, and king (Deuteronomy 16:18—18:22). The English theologian Colin Gunton makes explicit the connection that *Lumen Gentium* leaves implicit: "Like all societies, Israel had religious, moral and political dimensions to her life, and it can be said that the offices corresponding to them were those of priest, prophet and king . . . All of them . . . are equally oriented at once to Israel's relation to God and to the social order consequent upon that. They were called in order to maintain Israel's faithfulness to the covenant."[10]

To describe Yeshua as priest, prophet, and king is to affirm that God has appointed him the definitive ruler of Israel, the one called "to maintain Israel's faithfulness to the covenant," and that the entire line of Israel's national leadership is summed up in him.

> In what he does and teaches, this Spirit-inspired prophet concentrates in himself the work of the lawgivers, prophets, kings, priests, and indeed wisdom teachers of Israel. Their work comes to a head in him.[11]

> In his person, and through the various acts and phases of his historic career, Jesus fills the offices and institutions of Israel with distinctive and definitive meaning . . .[12]

In this way, the life of the people of Israel goes beyond preparing for and foreshadowing the church; even more, Israel "provides the logic of Christology."[13]

What are the practical consequences of this connection between the threefold office of Christ and the national life of the people of Israel? It could lead to the same conclusions as those suggested above in discussing the relationship between the people of God and the body of Christ. Yeshua's divine appointment to these national offices puts him in relationship with the Jewish people as a whole, and with every Jew. He is the priest, prophet, and king from whom the priestly, prophetic, and

---

10. Gunton, *The Christian Faith*, 69.
11. Ibid., 106.
12. Ibid., 72.
13. Ibid., 80.

royal aspects of Jewish life derive. Jewish people enter into a relationship with him by virtue of being part of the people—whether they know it or not, whether they like it or not. This relationship may not be salvific—but, in a mysterious way, it founds and constitutes their covenantal identity. When Jews acknowledge Yeshua as Israel's priest, prophet, and king, they confirm their own identity as members of the eschatologically renewed people of Israel.

Thus, participation in the people of God points Jews to a relationship with Christ (though most Jews do not yet discern the meaning of the signs). For Gentiles, on the other hand, the process takes place in reverse order: relationship with Christ initiates them into the people of God.

These two central themes of *Lumen Gentium*—the church as the people of God and body of Christ, and as participant in Christ's threefold office—presume a basic truth: Yeshua sums up not only the line of Israel's leaders, but Israel's life as a whole. He is the one-man Israel, who carries the entire people in himself even more than did his ancestor Jacob. Thus, all Jewish identity "comes to a head in him." *Lumen Gentium* recognizes that this is true for Christ's relationship with the church. We should take this further, and affirm it also of his relationship with the Jewish people.

What we have found in these two themes has an exact parallel in a third central theme of *Lumen Gentium*: the Virgin Mary as "type" of the church. The document concludes with teaching on Mary because it seeks to properly contextualize her important role. Rather than viewing her as an independent object of devotion, Catholics are encouraged to see her as an individual embodiment of what the church should be as a whole:

> Wherefore she is hailed as a pre-eminent and singular member of the Church, and as its type and excellent exemplar in faith and charity. (LG 53)

> By reason of the gift and role of divine maternity, by which she is united with her Son . . . the Blessed Virgin is also intimately united with the Church. As St. Ambrose taught, the Mother of God is a type of the Church in the order of faith, charity and perfect union with Christ. For in the mystery of the Church, which is itself rightly called mother and virgin, the Blessed Virgin stands out in eminent and singular fashion as exemplar both of virgin and mother. (LG 63)

> Seeking after the glory of Christ, the Church becomes more like her exalted Type, and continually progresses in faith, hope and charity, seeking and doing the will of God in all things. Hence

the Church, in her apostolic work also, justly looks to her, who, conceived of the Holy Spirit, brought forth Christ, who was born of the Virgin that through the Church He may be born and may increase in the hearts of the faithful also. The Virgin in her own life lived an example of that maternal love, by which it behooves that all should be animated who cooperate in the apostolic mission of the Church for the regeneration of men. (LG 65)

The Virgin becomes a model for individual Catholics in her virtue and for the church as a whole in her maternal love. In that love, the church gives birth to her children through the waters of baptism, and nurtures them in the teaching of Christ her spouse.

But what of Mary's relationship to the people of Israel? Only once does *Lumen Gentium* allude to that relationship, calling her "the exalted Daughter of Zion" (55). This singular reference deserves far more attention than it receives. When Scripture presents the people of Israel as a corporate reality, it normally speaks of the community using masculine language. The community is Jacob, God's Son and representative in the world. However, when it speaks of the capital city of Jerusalem, the language is feminine. The city represents the corporate reality of the community in relationship to God, her spouse, and the people themselves are her children. Just as Yeshua embodies Israel as priest, prophet, and king, so Mary embodies Zion, mother of all the faithful.

Mary is the type of the church, but she becomes that type through her role as the individual personal representation of the holy city, and of the temple that resided at its center. By neglecting this dimension of Mary's identity, *Lumen Gentium* again accentuates discontinuity at the expense of continuity. As the church is seen as a radically new reality, prefigured by but discontinuous with the old, so the imagery of Zion appears as but figurative prophetic foreshadowing of a new multinational community in which Jews are but another redeemed ethnicity.

But is not Mary still a Jewish mother, just as Yeshua is still a Jewish Messiah? In giving birth to the Messiah, was she not an expression of Israel's entire history and life, the sum of humble and faithful Jews through the centuries—a history that was as necessary to Yeshua's conception as Mary's own fiat? If indeed Mary has a special place in the heavenly courts and if indeed she watches over her children on earth—do not her people according to the flesh have a special place in her heart among those beloved children?

While this theme, like the others mentioned in this section, is neglected in *Lumen Gentium*, it is nevertheless fully compatible with its explicit teaching. What is needed may be added as legitimate development rather than as rejection or critique. Perhaps *Lumen Gentium* is itself a "preparation" and "foreshadowing" of something greater to come!

CONCLUSION

Lumen Gentium challenges Messianic Jews—shaped to a great extent by the individualistic ethos of Protestantism—to consider the significance and implications of recognizing the continuity of the church as a real community in time, "constituted and organized in the world as a society" (LG 8). The existence of Messianic Jews challenges Roman Catholics—shaped to a great extent by the supersessionist ethos of traditional Catholic culture—to consider the significance and implications of recognizing the continuity between Israel according to the flesh and the church.

The Preacher of the Papal Household, Fr. Raniero Cantalamessa, suggests that the Messianic Jewish movement may be the beginning of the "rejoining of Israel with the Church."[14] At the same time, he recognizes that this eschatological event will have a profound impact on the church itself: "It is certain that the rejoining of Israel with the Church will involve a rearrangement in the Church; it will mean a conversion on both sides. It will also be a rejoining of the Church with Israel." If Fr. Cantalamessa is correct—and our reading of *Lumen Gentium* supports his visionary claim—such a "rearrangement" will not damage the Catholic Church, but instead enable it to realize its original catholicity in eschatological fullness.

Epilogue

Postmissionary Messianic Judaism, Three Years Later: Reflections on a Conversation Just Begun

As part of the Robert L. Lindsey Lectures, Mark Kinzer delivered the following lecture in July 2008 at Narkis Street Congregation in Jerusalem. He reviews the history of reception of *Postmissionary Messianic Judaism* and responds to the book's host of critics and reviewers. Kinzer clarifies the centrality of the claim made in chapter 2 of *Postmissionary Messianic Judaism*, namely that, according to the Apostolic Writings (New Testament), Jewish observance is obligatory for Jewish Yeshua-believers as a matter of covenant fidelity. From this claim stems a multitude of implications, first and foremost in Kinzer's thought being the notion of "bilateral ecclesiology in solidarity with Israel." If the Jewish branch of the *ekklesia* (Yeshua-believing community) is covenantally bound to live as Jews while the Gentile branch of the *ekklesia* is not, Kinzer asserts that only such an ecclesial framework is suitable. While the novelty of Kinzer's ideas in *Postmissionary Messianic Judaism* continues to generate dialogue, much conversation is still required to solidify just how those ideas are to be implemented. Kinzer makes explicit his hopes for the ongoing conversation in several different spheres and recommends serious consideration of the Catholic Church's commitment to non-schismatic development and incorporation of new communities and movements.[1]

I HAVE BEEN ASKED to speak this evening about *Postmissionary Messianic Judaism: Redefining Christian Engagement with the Jewish People*—a book published in 2005 that sums up the vision guiding my

---

1. Resources related to the Lindsey lectures (including Kinzer's lecture and its responses) can be accessed at http://www.narkis.org/Archives/Lindsey%20Lectures/LindseyLectures2008.htm.

life in its first half-century—and the discussion it has sparked.² This verb seems especially appropriate, as the conversation has at times been volatile. Gratefully, the light generated has sometimes been commensurate to the heat.

The volume received immediate attention in the Messianic Jewish congregational movement and in the world of Christian missions to the Jews. Within a year of its publication the scholarly journals associated with those two communities, *Kesher* and *Mishkan*, had printed fourteen responses to *PMJ*, with rejoinders by the author. Discussion has continued unabated in these communities since that time. Reviews of the book have also appeared in Christian and academic circles, and more are on the way. To this point, no review or response has been printed in a mainstream Jewish publication (though the book has been noticed, as we will see later).

Some readers have found *PMJ* deeply disturbing. One of the earliest reviews called it "profoundly defective" and "unbiblical."³ Another asserted, "If Mr. Kinzer's platform were to be adopted, the biblical faith of Jesus would be destroyed among both Jews and Gentiles."⁴ An evangelical biblical scholar characterized my ecclesiological proposal as "apartheid."⁵ An evangelical missionary, with better humor, suggested that this ecclesiology, "if embraced by a significant segment of the Church, should give evangelicals a few sleepless nights."⁶ A friendly reviewer commented that "many Christians might view Kinzer's proposal as being just short of theologically bizarre."⁷ A less friendly reviewer argued that "the path to postmissionary Messianic Judaism is the path to the negation of the true Messianic faith."⁸ Apparently this last author decided that he had not expressed himself with sufficient clarity or force, and so he added: "I am, therefore, afraid that postmissionary Messianic

---

2. Sources referenced in this essay can be found in the "Chronological Bibliography of Materials Related to *Postmissionary Messianic Judaism*," 202–4. Significant resources related to *Postmissionary Messianic Judaism* that have been published/presented since this lecture was delivered appear in the bibliography with asterisks beside them.

3. Robinson, "Postmissionary Messianic Judaism."

4. Maoz, "Four Comments on Postmissionary Messianic Judaism," 70.

5. Schnable, "The Identity and the Mission of Believers in Jesus Messiah," 47.

6. Daniels, "Avoiding Potholes on the Road to Jerusalem," 10.

7. Neuhaus, "On the Square."

8. Brown, "Is A Post-Missionary, Truly Messianic Judaism Possible?"

Judaism will prove to be the beginning of the road to apostasy for many Jewish (and even Gentile) believers, the beginning of the road to spiritual confusion for many more, and, generally speaking, the beginning of the road to the shriveling up and dying of true 'Messianic Judaism' for many congregations."[9] Perhaps responses of this sort are to be expected when a book is widely regarded as "challenging,"[10] "bold,"[11] and "audacious."[12]

Thankfully, this is not the entire story. Critics and fans of *PMJ* alike have found the book "fascinating,"[13] "engaging,"[14] "sophisticated,"[15] "nuanced,"[16] "lucid,"[17] and "well-written."[18] Beyond being a good read (at least in comparison to volumes of the same genre), critics and fans alike have also recognized *PMJ* to be "groundbreaking,"[19] "seminal,"[20] "important,"[21] "required reading,"[22] and a "watershed volume."[23] David Stern sees *PMJ* as an "ecclesiological breakthrough," and suggests that I may be "the Copernicus of ecclesiology."[24] (Given some of the responses to the book, I feel more like Galileo than Copernicus!)

In this paper I would like to reflect upon the conversation that has been launched by *PMJ*, addressing some of the questions that have been raised about the book and expressing hopes for future directions that the conversation might take. Before I do this, however, I would like to

---

9. Ibid.
10. Daniels, "Avoiding Potholes on the Road to Jerusalem," 10.
11. Schebera, "Postmissionary Messianic Judaism," 129.
12. Yocum, "On Mark Kinzer's *Postmissionary Messianic Judaism*," 902.
13. Maoz, "Four Comments," 69; Neuhaus, "On the Square."
14. Maoz, "Four Comments," 69.
15. Robinson, "Postmissionary Messianic Judaism: A Review Essay," 8; Brown, "Is A Post-Missionary, Truly Messianic Judaism Possible?"
16. Brown, "Is A Post-Missionary, Truly Messianic Judaism Possible?"; Soulen, "Postmissionary Messianic Judaism," 37.
17. Soulen, "Postmissionary Messianic Judaism," 37.
18. Akiva Cohen, "Four Comments," 1.
19. Harvey, "Shaping the Aims and Aspirations of Jewish Believers," 22; Harink, "A Response," 43.
20. Harvey, "Shaping the Aims and Aspirations of Jewish Believers," 22.
21. Soulen, "Postmissionary Messianic Judaism," 37.
22. Robinson, "Postmissionary Messianic Judaism: A Review Essay," 21.
23. Brown, "Is A Post-Missionary, Truly Messianic Judaism Possible?"
24. Stern, "A Response," 17.

summarize the argument of *PMJ*, and identify a crucial element in its structure that has gone largely unnoticed.

THE ROLE OF JEWISH COVENANTAL OBLIGATION IN THE ARGUMENT OF *PMJ*

As most readers recognize, *PMJ* is a book about ecclesiology. It attempts to rethink the relationship between the Christian church and the Jewish people, and in the process it posits a new way of conceptualizing the church's communal framework which I call "bilateral ecclesiology." In this framework the *ekklesia* consists of a united community that is essentially twofold, containing a Jewish sub-community that links it to the national life and history of the people of Israel, and a multinational sub-community that extends Israel's heritage among the peoples of the earth without annulling their distinctive cultural identities. Thus, the bilateral constitution of the *ekklesia* enables it to fulfill a universal vocation while maintaining solidarity with Israel.

Furthermore, *PMJ* argues that this solidarity involves an acknowledgement that the Jewish people remains a community in covenant with God, and that its corporate resistance to Yeshua-faith has not undermined this covenant nor vitiated the authority of its tradition and its teachers. Going further, *PMJ* contends that Yeshua himself dwells not only with the Christian church but also with the Jewish people, and that his presence is manifest in Jewish life whenever Jews remain faithful to the covenant. Therefore, the Jewish wing of the *ekklesia* can participate in the life of the wider Jewish community and adhere to Jewish tradition without jeopardizing fidelity to the Messiah whose name it explicitly and unashamedly confesses.

Readers have applauded or attacked these conclusions, and the evidence and reasoning summoned in *PMJ* to support them. However, few readers have noted the core of *PMJ*'s argument and the recurring role this core plays throughout the book. I am referring to chapter 2 of *PMJ*, entitled "The New Testament and Jewish Practice."

In that chapter I examine how the Apostolic Writings deal with a set of Jewish practices rooted in the Torah which by the first-century had become crucial markers of Jewish identity: circumcision, *Shabbat* (Sabbath) and holiday observance, and *kashrut* (Jewish dietary laws). I reach the following conclusion: "Our survey of the New Testament teaching on Jewish practice (for Jews) has produced a surprising result.

We have good grounds for upholding the view that the New Testament as a whole treats Jewish practice as obligatory for Jews."[25] I do not assert here merely "that Messianic Jews lived Torah observant lives during the New Testament period."[26] Instead, I contend that the Apostolic Writings consider such observance to be an obligatory expression of Jewish covenant fidelity rooted in theological conviction rather than prudential judgment.[27]

The final sentences of chapter 2 demonstrate how I view the importance of this proposition: "This conclusion has profound theological implications. In many ways, the remainder of this book is an attempt to reflect on those implications and on their significance for the church and for the Jewish people."[28] The discovery of an enduring requirement for a basic level of Torah observance for Yeshua-believing Jews is interesting and important in itself, and stands as a foundational principle of much of the Messianic Jewish congregational movement in the Diaspora. Many readers have noted *PMJ*'s emphasis on this point, and have interacted with it critically or appreciatively. However, few have grasped the integral position it holds within the structure of the argument of *PMJ*. What does the requirement of Jewish practice have to do with a bilateral ecclesiology in solidarity with Israel that affirms not only Israel's Torah but also its religious tradition? What is the relationship between chapter 2 and the expansive and controversial conclusions of the rest of the book? To answer these questions, let us review the basic outlines of the argument of *PMJ* (as contained in chapters 2-7), with an eye on the role played by the conclusions reached in chapter 2.

Chapter 3, "The New Testament and the Jewish People," takes up the question of the spiritual status of the Jewish people as a whole. The introduction to the chapter explains the implications of chapter 2 for this question: "We concluded in our previous chapter that the New Testament considers Jewish practice normative for Jews who believe in Yeshua, though not for Yeshua-believing Gentiles. We also noted the

25. Kinzer, *Postmissionary Messianic Judaism*, 95.

26. Glaser, "A Response," 31.

27. I elaborate on this point in my *Kesher* response to Glaser, 58–62. Like Glaser, Robinson (2006) sees my argument as based on the example of the apostolic lifestyle. My *Mishkan* response to him is also relevant here: "It is not the apostolic observance of the Torah that is decisive, but the apostles' evident conviction that this observance is a matter of obedience to a divine commandment."

28. Kinzer, *Postmissionary Messianic Judaism*, 96.

intimate connection between such practice and Jewish national identity. Given this connection, the obligation of Jewish practice for Jews (and not for Gentiles) implies that the New Testament regards the Jewish people as recipients of a particular calling and as servants with a distinctive role and mission in the divine purpose."[29]

Yet, it might still be possible that only Yeshua-believing Jews carry on this "distinctive role and mission," and that the rest of the Jewish people are cut off from Israel's spiritual heritage. The introduction to chapter 3 considers this possibility, and then points out "the formidable theological problems raised by this hypothesis. Since a body of Yeshua-believing Jews faithfully devoted to Jewish practice ceased to exist at some point in the first millennium, this hypothesis leads to the disturbing conclusion that the Jewish people as a whole expired at that point. Is this theologically tenable? If Jewish practice is important to God, then the Jewish people are important to God. Did he permit this people to perish?"[30] Thus, the only conclusion that makes sense is that "Jews who have not believed in Yeshua but who have loyally sustained a continual Jewish communal presence in the world through hours of deepest darkness are heirs of God's covenant with Israel."[31]

This is only the introduction to chapter 3. The remainder of the chapter consists of an exegetical study of the actual teaching of the Apostolic Writings on this question. The logical implications of chapter 2 determine the thesis to be tested, and support that thesis, but they cannot conclusively substantiate the thesis apart from a direct interpretive engagement with the text. As we will see, this is the method followed throughout *PMJ*. I formulate a thesis based largely on the implications of chapter 2, and then test that thesis by seeing whether it enables us to make good sense of the relevant scriptural texts.

With chapter 4, "Bilateral Ecclesiology in Solidarity with Israel," we reach the heart of *PMJ*, both physically (the chapter begins on page 151 of a 310 page book) and theologically. In this chapter I make the case for the ecclesiological vision that is the main point of *PMJ*. As in chapter 3, the introduction to the chapter formulates its thesis by drawing out the implications of chapter 2:

29. Ibid., 97.
30. Ibid., 98.
31. Ibid.

> Jewish practice is inherently corporate in nature. Circumcision is a social rite, performed by a trained official within the community. Sabbath observance requires social support and communal expression. The dietary laws require kosher meat processing and a network of related families following similar food customs. The practical need for communal support reinforces the underlying meaning of all Jewish practice, which is to be an effective sign marking Israel as a people set apart for God
>
> At the same time, the New Testament also emphasizes the importance of Gentiles becoming part of the ekklesia without becoming Jews . . .
>
> Only one structural arrangement would allow for distinctive Jewish communal life within the context of a transnational community of Jews and Gentiles: the one ekklesia must consist of two corporate subcommunities . . . Thus the first implications of chapters 2 and 3 is that the ekklesia is bilateral—one reality subsisting in two forms.
>
> Given . . . that faithful Jewish practice requires extensive communal support, a second implication arises out of the first: the Jewish branch of the twofold ekklesia must identify with the Jewish people as a whole and participate actively in its communal life.[32]

After articulating the thesis in its introduction, chapter 4 proceeds to test this thesis by examining the relevant texts in the Apostolic Writings. As in chapter 3, the biblical material confirms a thesis derived initially from the conclusions of chapter 2.

Chapter 5, "The Christian No to Israel: Christian Supersessionism and Jewish Practice," tells the sad story of the birth and development of Christian supersessionism from Ignatius of Antioch to Thomas Aquinas. The recounting of such a narrative has become commonplace in the post-Holocaust world of Christian theology and ecumenical relations. However, the focus of this telling differs from most others. *PMJ* does not aim to document anew the contempt for Jews and Judaism cultivated by the Christian church, or the Christian claim that the church and Christianity have replaced Israel and Judaism. Instead, *PMJ* describes how contempt and supersessionism took the form of rejecting Jewish practice for Jewish Yeshua-believers and delegitimizing the Jewish *ekklesia* whose life embodied such practice. Scholars rarely take note of this form of contempt and supersessionism because they rarely acknowledge

32. Ibid., 152.

the apostolic teaching regarding Jewish practice. Once we recognize the latter, the former becomes especially significant. What was thought to be obligatory by the apostles is now condemned as mortal sin! Thus, the Christian "No" to Israel (as expressed in the prohibition of ecclesial Jewish practice) entails a partial Christian "No" to the apostles, and to the Messiah of Israel who commissioned them.

This sets the stage for the most radical and controversial chapter of *PMJ*. Having looked at the historical Christian "No" to Israel, we now examine the historical Jewish "No" to Yeshua. The underlying premise of both chapters 6 and 7 is that Jewish practice requires a living tradition of communal application, and that any twenty-first century version of the Jewish *ekklesia* must recognize Jewish tradition as having some measure of authority. "One cannot build a contemporary Judaism exclusively on either the Bible or modern (or postmodern) sensibility. Without some connection to the historical experience of the Jewish people, Judaism evaporates into thin air."[33] But this raises the question, how can Yeshua-believers treat as in any sense authoritative a tradition that said "No" to Yeshua? This is a formidable challenge. Nevertheless, we will see that the conclusions of chapter 2 that made the question necessary also play a crucial role in answering it.

As a community, the Jewish people of the first century did not accept the messianic claims of Yeshua. This lack of a communal "Yes" has a theological significance of its own. However, it does not constitute an emphatic "No." Most Jews of the first century likely had little awareness of those claims, and little opportunity to respond to them. By the time the name of Jesus was widely known among the Jewish people, the message he proclaimed and entrusted to his apostles—in relation to the Jewish people—had been turned upside down.

> As seen in chapters 2, 3, and 4, the message of Yeshua came to the first generation of Jewish hearers as a proclamation of how the God of Israel had acted and was acting in Yeshua for the redemption of Israel and the world . . . As seen in chapter 5, the message about Yeshua that came to Jews in the second century was radically different. It spoke of how Israel's covenant and way of life had been annulled in the Messiah, and it claimed that Jewish identity and practice were of no value or even prohibited. Any Jew who was loyal to the covenant would conclude that such a

---

33. Ibid., 215.

message could not possibly come from the God of Israel. To reject such a purported Messiah would be an act of fidelity to God rather than infidelity!³⁴

Moreover, by the Middle Ages ostensibly Christian societies sometimes demanded that the Jews in their midst convert to Christianity (and abandon Jewish practice and identity), with the only alternatives to conversion being death or exile. In such a situation, who was living out the good news? The Christians who made such a perverse demand? The Jews who converted at the edge of a knife? Or those Jews who sacrificed their lives to remain faithful to the covenant? When set in the context of the enduring obligation of Jewish practice and identity, as taught by the apostles, we are compelled to accept the paradox that these Jewish martyrs were epitomizing the gospel at the very moment they were purportedly rejecting it!

At this point, some of my critics cry "foul!"

> The Jewish rejection of the church's message was a "hidden participation in the obedience of Yeshua." Creative, yes; but surely we are forgiven if we see a theological sleight-of-hand in that argument . . . In calling a no a yes, some fundamental aspect of the biblical message has been turned upside down!³⁵
>
> So, no is yes and judgment is blessing and absence is presence and hardening is redemptive. Are we actually supposed to embrace this?³⁶

I think that it is no coincidence that the loudest objections to my reasoning in these chapters come from authors who do not accept my conclusions in chapter 2. If one does not see Jewish practice and identity as obligatory for Jews according to the apostolic teaching, then my argument in chapter 6 will appear hollow. In fact, if those conclusions are false, my argument in chapter 6 *is* hollow! However, if chapter 2 points us in the right direction, then the paradox of chapter 6 is no "theological sleight-of-hand" but rather a bracing challenge to sclerotic missiological and ecclesiological paradigms. As elsewhere in *PMJ*, much stands or falls on the credibility of chapter 2.³⁷

---

34. Ibid., 224.
35. Robinson, "Postmissionary Messianic Judaism: A Review Essay," 17.
36. Brown, "Is A Post-Missionary, Truly Messianic Judaism Possible?"
37. Even in the case of chapter 6, which builds upon a theological interpretation of

Chapter 6 argues that the apparent Jewish "No" to Yeshua does not detract from the value and authority of a Jewish tradition that plays an essential role in sustaining Jewish practice through the centuries. Chapter 7, "Jewish Tradition and the Biblical Test," continues the argument of chapter 6 by proposing an understanding of that tradition and of the Apostolic Writings that renders them compatible. Both chapters depend on the conclusions of chapter 2, as no tradition of legal interpretation and application is required if Jewish practice is optional rather than normative.

While the message of *PMJ* goes far beyond the obligatory nature of Torah-based Jewish practice and identity for Jewish Yeshua-believers, one cannot underestimate the centrality of this proposition for the argument of the book as a whole. It is far more important as the basis for reaching other conclusions than as a conclusion in its own right.

THE DISCUSSION THAT HAS ENSUED

The discussion that has followed the publication of *PMJ* indirectly highlights the crucial role played in its argument by chapter 2. Most in the Messianic Jewish congregational movement in the Diaspora agree that some form of Torah-based Jewish practice is a covenantal responsibility for Jewish Yeshua-believers. As a result, bilateral ecclesiology makes sense to them, and they find little that is objectionable in the first five chapters of *PMJ*. Controversy only arises when I argue for the legitimate authority of Jewish tradition (chapters 6–7) and the practical imperative of postmissionary witness (chapters 8–9). As one major leader in the Messianic Jewish Alliance of America told me, "If only you had ended the book after chapter 5!"

In contrast, most in the sphere of Christian missions find *PMJ* troubling from beginning to end. They do not see the arguments or conclusions of chapter 2 as compelling, and therefore bilateral ecclesiology in solidarity with Israel has no resonance for them. Some of the missionaries have approved of Messianic Jewish congregations, but usually as an expedient missiological option rather than an essential ecclesiological imperative.[38] Church membership for Jewish Yeshua-believers is seen as

---

history, I seek to find at least implicit biblical corroboration. The biblical support comes from my reading of Romans 8–11 (see *Postmissionary Messianic Judaism*, 129–37).

38. Thus, in a recent issue of *The Chosen People* (Volume XIV, Issue 5, June 2008), Glaser writes: "My wife and I have attended churches for most of our lives, and our

equally viable. The overriding goal is still to bring "unsaved" individual Jews to faith in Christ and membership in the church.

At the same time, missionary respondents to *PMJ* have acknowledged the importance of the issues that the book raises, and have shown a willingness to engage those issues in a constructive way:

> What does it mean to be *Jewish*—not only of what promises are the Jewish people the recipients, but what if any covenantal *obligations* devolve on them by virtue of their being Jews? Kinzer is right to raise the question . . .
>
> In what way can it be claimed that the Jewish people remain a distinct people, if there is not some way in which that distinctiveness can be lived out and passed on to future generations?
>
> Granted that the Jewish people are still a *people* and not just a collection of individual Jews, how can or should that corporate expression of peoplehood be realized?[39]

> I know that Kinzer's book will challenge Messianic Jews like myself to rethink our understanding of who we are as Jews in the Messiah Yeshua. In addition, those of us who work in Jewish missions also need to reflect on our relationship to the Jewish community . . . Kinzer is right to remind Messianic Jews to see themselves as part of the Jewish community and behave accordingly . . . The Jewish missions community needs to start thinking as insiders rather than outsiders, and I believe this will empower our ministries to our people.[40]

> Certainly, there are many topics that [Kinzer] has put on the table in a clear and reasoned way that demand our attention, most specifically, the question of the problem of assimilation for Jewish believers and the proposed solution of a strict bilateral ecclesiology.[41]

---

daughters—who identify as Messianic Jews—were raised going to churches. Chosen People Ministries intentionally plants Messianic congregations because we believe that Jewish people should have a choice. Messianic congregations are culturally comfortable places where Jewish people can worship the Lord and bring their non-believing Jewish family and friends . . . Certainly many Jewish people will go to a church and find the Lord, but not every Jewish person who is open to the Gospel will feel comfortable in a church. So we plant Messianic congregations to give those Jewish people who prefer the comfort of a more 'Jewish' environment the opportunity to hear the Gospel, be saved and then to grow in grace as part of Jesus-focused Jewish community" (3).

39. Robinson, "Postmissionary Messianic Judaism: A Review Essay," 9.
40. Glaser, "A Response," 34–36.
41. Brown, "Is A Post-Missionary, Truly Messianic Judaism Possible?"

Robinson, Glaser, and Brown all appear to recognize that Messianic Jews are responsible to live as Jews, participate in the life of the Jewish people, and transmit Jewish life to their children and grandchildren. My question to them is this: can we fulfill such a responsibility apart from a bilateral ecclesiology in solidarity with Israel?

While the missionaries and the messianics disagree over chapters 1–5, many come into alignment in their resistance to chapters 6–9. The two concerns raised by Messianic Jews—over the legitimate authority of Jewish tradition and the practical imperative of postmissionary witness—appear again in the missionary response, though with a heightened tendency to caricature my position. "In the midst of 300 pages of often nuanced and sophisticated arguments, it is somewhat shocking to arrive at two of the book's main conclusions: first, that Jewish believers should embrace Orthdodox Judaism; and second, that our witness of Yeshua to our own people should henceforth 'be rendered in a postmissionary mode.' These suggestions are outrageous and must be categorically rejected."[42]

Let me attempt to clarify my views on these two points. First of all, *PMJ* never advocates the embrace of "Orthodox Judaism." It does argue that no modern or postmodern form of Judaism can bypass rabbinic tradition. At the beginning of chapter 6 I quote and agree with the words of Peter Ochs: "There is, in one sense, no other Judaism for Jews than that which comes by way of Rabbinic Judaism, or the Judaism of *Mishnah*, Talmud, synagogue, prayer book, and Torah study that emerged after, in spite of, and in response to the loss of the Second Temple. All of the new Judaisms that have appeared since have appeared from out of and in terms of this Rabbinic Judaism."[43]

At the end of chapter 7, I contend that this must also be true of the "new Judaism" that is emerging in the movement of which I am part. "Like every tradition transmitted and nurtured by human communities, including the Christian tradition, rabbinic Judaism is imperfect and requires continual renewal, development, and contextual reapplication. Nevertheless, it is *rabbinic Judaism* that is being renewed, developed, and contextually reapplied. We cannot affirm the election and way of

---

42. Ibid.
43. Kinzer, *Postmissionary Messianic Judaism*, 215.

life of the Jewish people without likewise affirming the tradition that has sustained them both."[44]

I have enormous respect for Orthodox Judaism, but I make no claims to be an Orthodox Jew, nor am I working to form an Orthodox version of Messianic Judaism. I do seek to live as an *observant* Jew, and I aim to foster an expression of Messianic Judaism that learns from the full breadth of Jewish tradition. Nevertheless, Messianic Judaism will always provide its own distinctive interpretation of Judaism, centered in the teaching, example, and redemptive work of Messiah Yeshua. In this way it seeks to renew, develop, and contextually reapply the rabbinic Judaism that is the common heritage of the Jewish people as a whole.[45]

The second concern voiced in both the Messianic Jewish congregational movement and in the missionary world relates to the soteriological and missiological implications of *PMJ*. Raising a question regarding the basis of salvation, Mitch Glaser writes, "I would challenge the author to offer a more explicit explanation of his views on this very important matter."[46] I attempted to do so in a paper on "Final Destinies" delivered at the Borough Park Symposium in October 2007.[47] However, the main concern in this area has not been theological but practical: does *PMJ* foster a mentality that undermines active and effective witness to Yeshua among the Jewish people? I sought to address that concern in a lecture in July 2007 entitled "Yeshua, the Glory of God and the Glory of Israel: Motives for Postmissionary Messianic Jewish Outreach."[48] To be postmissionary is not to transcend the good news, but to understand its message as the realization rather than the nullification of the Jewish people's communal identity and destiny. *To be postmissionary is always to think of individual Jews and their future in relation to the Jewish people as a whole and its future.* Postmissionary witness to Yeshua involves a new orientation to Jewish corporate life, history, and religious tradition,

---

44. Ibid., 260.

45. To understand some particulars of the form of Messianic Judaism I advocate, see the *Messianic Jewish Rabbinical Council Standards of Observance* (May 2007), available at www.ourrabbis.org.

46. Glaser, "A Response," 32–33.

47. See p. 126–55 of this volume.

48. A recording of this message is available online. See the chronological bibliography for details.

but it remains witness to Yeshua. And, I would argue, a witness that is passionate, powerful, and persuasive.

As for the Christian response to *PMJ*, the most important question revolves around the unity of the bilateral *ekklesia*.

> At the same time, Kinzer's vision of the church as a community of reconciliation between those who remain genuinely different left me with some lingering questions about how Kinzer would deal with the more traditional but nevertheless wholly justified ecclesial concern to express messianic peace through visible unity.[49]

> This creates perplexing ecclesiological questions. Are there then two churches, one for Jews and another for Gentiles?[50]

> It is not clear, for example, how this approach (which is not just an idea, but a reality embodied in a number of Messianic Jewish congregations) can hold that, by his Cross, Christ has united Jews and gentiles in one body (cf. Eph 2:11–22). It sometimes seems as though Christ has two bodies—two churches—neither of which has a universal saving mission. With that, the sense in which Christ himself has a single saving purpose for all ceases to be apparent.[51]

PMJ does assert the unity of the bilateral *ekklesia*. Employing the language of Karl Barth, chapter 4 states: "We therefore have a bilateral community: it is both 'indissolubly one' and 'ineffaceably two.'"[52] However, the chapter also cites with approval the words of David Noel Freedman, who describes a "two-house theory of Christianity" that divided Jews and Gentiles into "two classes, equal but separate."[53] In retrospect, I see Freedman's language as problematic. While the two wings of the bilateral *ekklesia* must remain distinct, they cannot be "separate."

My Christian interlocutors are therefore justified in their concerns. We must affirm and guard the unity of the *ekklesia* at the same time as we preserve its essential twofold nature. How is this to be accomplished? I did not intend in *PMJ* to propose a particular governmental or structural arrangement for the bilateral *ekklesia*. Instead, I attempted

---

49. Soulen, "A Response," 106.

50. Neuhaus, "On the Square."

51. Marshall, "Elder Brothers: John Paul II's Teaching on the Jewish People as a Question to the Church," 125.

52. Kinzer, *Postmissionary Messianic Judaism*, 175.

53. Ibid., 178.

to define the communal and relational reality that any such arrangement must foster. The discussion about ecclesial structure has yet to take place. It should be set in a dialogue between Christian and Messianic Jewish leaders who accept and embrace the need for both unity and bilateral differentiation.

Future discussion about the practical structure of a bilateral *ekklesia* would benefit from a consideration of the wisdom of the Catholic tradition. In the Protestant world, new communities and movements tend to generate new denominations. In contrast, Catholicism has a long history of incorporating new communities and movements into its institutional life without fragmentation. We see this especially in the formation of religious orders and their integration into the wider life of the church. More relevant to our situation, however, is the Catholic approach to diverse rites (such as the Byzantine, Ukranian, or Syriac). Catholicism has found a way to accommodate the particularities of various theological, liturgical, and devotional traditions within its ranks. It has the capacity to do so in part because its ecclesial structures transcend the local congregation. If the local congregation is the exclusive bearer of ecclesial identity and life, then it is difficult to conceive of a bilateral ecclesiology that will establish the level of unity required by the good news.

A second insight deriving from Catholicism concerns the centrality of the Lord's Supper/Eucharist (which my own community calls *HaZikkaron*). It seems clear from the Apostolic Writings that one of the crucial functions of this ritual is to be an expression and instrument of unity (1 Corinthians 10:16–17; 11:17–32). It is also clear that the apostles viewed the partaking of food at the same table (in contexts that likely included a eucharistic dimension) as a primary sign of the reconciliation of Jew and Gentile in one community (Galatians 2:11–14). Thus, any adequate structural and communal embodiment of bilateral ecclesiology will need to provide contexts where members of the Jewish and Gentile wings of the one *ekklesia* can gather together to celebrate *HaZikkaron* as one twofold body.

Christian readers of *PMJ* have also commented on the broader theological issues it raises in the areas of Christology and pneumatology. Thus, Peter Hocken writes:

> An important section in Kinzer's book treats the total and permanent identification of Yeshua with his own people and of Yeshua as "one-man Israel." Kinzer makes this a key plank—I think

rightly—in his advocacy of the theological and covenantal significance of rabbinic Judaism, but he does not use this to provide a christological foundation for his Messianic Jewish ecclesiology. If a biblically-based ecclesiology is based on the missions of the Son and the Spirit, a messianic and non-supersessionist understanding of the church will be based on the crucified and risen Messiah of Israel, whose glorified humanity, through which the Holy Spirit is poured out, always remains Israelite-Jewish and becomes the instrument by which the Gentile believers are grafted into the transformed commonwealth of Israel.[54]

John Yocum puts the emphasis on pneumatology:

A troubling absence from the book is mention of the gift of the Holy Spirit as constitutive of the body of Christ, and what this might mean for our understanding of the status of the people of Israel. Kinzer mounts a 'Christological test' for the validity of rabbinic Judaism, and concludes that the tradition of the Talmud and Mishnah pass that test. I would not suggest that there is such a thing as a 'pneumatological test,' since normally the presence of the Holy Spirit is tested by reference to Christ rather than vice versa; but, is not the presence of Christ possible in different modes, and is the confession of Yeshua as Messiah not intrinsically connected to his vivifying, illuminating, empowering presence through the outpouring of the Holy Spirit? Certainly the New Testament indicates that in some way Christ was present and active already in the history of Israel prior to the incarnation, but not in the mode in which He is present to those who receive the gift of the Holy Spirit after the resurrection. Is it only recognition of the intimate presence of the one *already* present in their midst that is at issue in the acceptance of Yeshua as Messiah?[55]

Hocken and Yocum pose questions of cardinal importance. If the ecclesiology I propose has merit, it must be rooted in the fundamental realities of who God is and what God has done, is doing, and will do. It will also shed new light on our understanding of these realities. Thus, I accept the friendly critique of Hocken and Yocum, and approve of the direction to which they point. In fact, I am hoping that my next book will be devoted to the topic of Christology, bilateral ecclesiology, and the God of Israel.

But this leads us to the final section of this paper.

---

54. Hocken, "A Response," 52.
55. Yocum, "On Mark Kinzer's *Postmissionary Messianic Judaism*," 904.

THE FUTURE OF THE DISCUSSION

To conclude this paper, I would like to express my hopes for the future of this conversation. I will focus less on response to *PMJ* as a book, and more on the discussion of the substantive issues the book raises. I will do so by distinguishing five spheres of conversation: (1) the Messianic Jewish congregational movement in the Diaspora; (2) the Messianic Jewish congregational movement in the land; (3) those involved with Christian missions to the Jews; (4) the Christian church; and (5) the mainstream Jewish community.

Within the Messianic Jewish congregational movement in the Diaspora, I hope for further discussion about our relation to Christian missions to the Jews, to evangelical Christianity, and to the Jewish community and its religious tradition. I argue in *PMJ* that, though Messianic Judaism originated in Christian missions to the Jews, it points beyond that world (though not beyond "mission" *per se*). In contrast with the world of Christian missions, Messianic Judaism has accepted the covenantal responsibility of Torah-based Jewish practice, and has identified itself as a distinctive Yeshua-centered form of Judaism. In this way it has taken a step away from viewing itself as merely a subset of evangelical Protestantism.

However, I think that the difficulty many Messianic Jews have in appreciating chapters 6 and 7 of *PMJ* reflects the need for serious consideration of the consequences of what we have already accepted as true. Is it possible to practice a substantive Torah-based Jewish way of life without drawing extensively on Jewish religious tradition? And is it possible to draw extensively on Jewish religious tradition without having a Christologically-grounded affirmation of the community that carried and produced this tradition, and of the tradition itself? In the long term, is it possible to accept the conclusions of *PMJ*'s chapter 2 without also embracing positions resembling those in chapters 6 and 7?

Bilateral ecclesiology in solidarity with Israel summons the Messianic Jewish congregational movement to take a step towards the Jewish world and a step away from its evangelical matrix. Only by being distinct from evangelicalism, and connected to Judaism, can such a Messianic Judaism fulfill its vocation as an ecclesiological bridge enabling the church to discover its identity in relationship to Israel and enabling the Jewish people to encounter its Messiah as it has never done before.

Within the Messianic Jewish congregational movement in the land of Israel, I hope for the emergence of serious theological discussion in general. To this point the Israeli Messianic Jewish community has had few trained scholars and little interest in theological discourse. I see signs of change in this regard, and anticipate that new insights will arise from a knowledgeable and theologically conscious Messianic Jewish community in the land.

In particular, I hope for serious theological discussion among Israeli Messianic Jews concerning the nature, significance, and obligations of Jewish covenantal identity. In the past, Israeli Messianic Jews have often thought of their Diaspora cousins as psychologically insecure members of the house of Jacob who lean on Torah-based Jewish practice—and the tradition that embodies such practice—as a crutch to sustain an untenable identity in exile. In contrast, as Israelis they have no such issues—they speak Hebrew, live in the land promised to our ancestors, and participate as citizens in a Jewish state.

Of course, this attitude reflected the views of secular Israeli society as a whole regarding Zionism and Diaspora Judaism. However, the discussion of Jewish identity in twenty-first century Israel has shifted dramatically. Numerous factors have contributed to this shift, including the failure of the secular Zionist ideology and ethos; the resurgence of orthodoxy in its various forms; the presence of hundreds of thousands of Israeli citizens who are technically Gentiles of Jewish descent; the vast numbers of Israelis living at least part of their lives in the Diaspora, and experiencing Diaspora Judaism firsthand; and the Arab challenge to Israel's status as a Jewish state. Suddenly, Jewish identity in the land seems almost as insecure as Jewish identity in the Diaspora. To provide mooring for this identity, many Israelis are recognizing the need to recover a connection to the Jewish past. It is not enough to trace our roots to King David, the Maccabees, and the Zealots. We cannot leap from 70 C.E. to 1900 or 1948, as though the eighteen intervening centuries were a historical anomaly of no consequence.

A few Israeli Messianic Jews have reached similar conclusions. They have found that it is not enough to trace their roots to the Jewish disciples of Yeshua in the Acts of the Apostles. Jewish life did not end with the destruction of the temple in 70 or with the demise of Jerusalem's Yeshua-believing community that congregated there, and it was not reborn out of thin air with the emergence of the Zionist or Hebrew Christian movements. *Jewish life extends as a continuous and unbroken line, and Jewish identity depends upon our capacity to make every section of that line a resource for our stage in the journey.* I would hope for an increase in the number of Israeli Messianic Jews who reach this conclusion, and for the development of a vibrant and fruitful conversation among them that will enrich both the Israeli Messianic movement and their cousins abroad.

Within the community of Christian missions to the Jews, I would hope for a willingness to pursue ecclesiological questions, and to see them as important in their own right and not only as subordinate matters related to missiology and soteriology. As should be clear from *PMJ*, I see Jewish communal identity as an ecclesial reality that is fundamental to the life and mission of the Christian church. Some of the responses to *PMJ* from those in the missionary community have acknowledged the importance of these questions, and have summoned their colleagues to address them. To my knowledge this has not yet occurred, but the conversation has just begun.

In particular, I am eager to hear discussion among the missionaries concerning the importance of sustaining cross-generational Jewish life for their converts. Is it important that the grandchildren of Jewish believers in Yeshua also identify and live as Jews? If so, have traditional missionary methods and models facilitated this goal, or hindered it? If bilateral ecclesiology in solidarity with Israel is not an option, how can this goal be achieved? Engagement with such issues will require that missionaries set aside atomistic approaches to ecclesiology, missiology, and soteriology, and think in more communal terms. In the process, they may discover neglected truths in a Bible that took shape in a world unfamiliar with modern Western individualism.

Within the Christian church, I hope to see a growing awareness of the importance of Messianic Judaism for Christian identity and for opening new vistas on the church's relationship to the Jewish people as a whole. Already, this has begun to happen. I have been personally involved in one noteworthy project that shows great potential, and that illustrates what could develop on a broader scale. In the fall of 2000 a small group of Messianic Jews and Roman Catholics were called together by Father (now Cardinal) Georges Cottier, the theologian of the Papal Household, to begin a conversation. The meeting was not a formal dialogue sponsored by the Vatican, but an unofficial initiative of Cardinal Cottier and some other prominent Catholic officials. We have met each year since 2000, and we have learned much from one another. Catholic participants have shown great appreciation for the spiritual significance of the Messianic Jewish movement and sincere openness to the challenging message we bring. If such encounters are possible between leaders at the highest level of the Catholic Church and Messianic Jews, may we not hope for similar relationships and conversations to develop with others in the Christian world?

Ultimately, these conversations must lead to discussion of the importance of preserving the Jewish life and identity of Jewish Yeshua-believers. Christian leaders must face this issue as much as Christian missionaries to the Jews. Even when pastors and denominations do not engage in organized and deliberate evangelistic outreach to Jews, their churches attract Jewish souls who have lost or never had an attachment to Jewish communal life. What responsibility do Christian leaders have to encourage such people to continue to live as Jews? What responsibility do they have to assist them in doing so? These are questions that Christians have never asked before. If the perspectives advanced in *PMJ* have any traction, they will be asked now.

Finally, within the wider Jewish world, I hope to see recognition that this conversation is taking place among Messianic Jews, missionaries, and Christian leaders. It has already received some attention. Thus, in an article published by the Jewish Telegraphic Agency, a respected Jewish journalist surveyed the Messianic Jewish scene and wrote the following:

> Over the past two years, some Messianic leaders have questioned whether their movement is too aligned with evangelicals. The opening volley came in 2005 when theologian Mark Kinzer published a book called "Post-Missionary Messianic Judaism," arguing that accepting Christ does not release a Jew from certain religious obligations such as keeping kosher and observing Shabbat.
>
> Kinzer ... believes that Messianic congregations have an obligation to preserve those practices—not as a form of "contextualized" Christianity but rather as what he calls an authentic Judaism. "God's covenant with Israel necessitates a certain way of life," he says. "It's not an option. Any message that alienates Jews from Judaism is not the Gospel. You haven't saved a Jewish soul."[56]

56. Yeoman, "Messianics are Praying the 'Shema,' but Preaching Jesus as the Messiah."

In a similar vein, the Jewish Daily Forward described segments of the Messianic Jewish world that advocated a closer connection to the larger Jewish community:

> A touchstone for the group has become a book, "Postmissionary Messianic Judaism: Redefining Christian Engagement With the Jewish People," authored by Mark Kinzer in 2005. Kinzer has been considerably less well received in such overtly Christian missionizing quarters as the Lausanne Consultation on Jewish Evangelism, which was founded by Christian evangelical leaders in 1980.[57]

While these articles show that *PMJ* has not gone entirely unnoticed within the wider Jewish world, very few members of that community have any inkling of the discussion that is taking place among us. I expect that to change in the coming years.

I am not anticipating that the wider Jewish community will open its arms in enthusiastic embrace of *PMJ* and the form of Judaism it advocates. However, I do believe that *PMJ* provides a platform for an unprecedented development—a genuine dialogue between Messianic and mainstream Jews. We will not compromise our convictions about Yeshua as Israel's Messiah—and I do not expect that they will compromise their convictions that we are gravely misguided on this point. Nevertheless, enough commonality exists for a conversation to begin. May it begin soon.

I am gratified that most of my readers agree that *PMJ* is a significant book. One of my most formidable critics (Michael Brown) has called it a "watershed volume." If Michael Brown is correct, the coming years will advance the overall conversation far beyond where it stands at present. I will be delighted if that is the case, even if my book is not remembered as the place where the streams began to flow in another direction.

---

57. Siegel, "Messianic Jews Find Fertile Ground in the Bible Belt."

General Bibliography

Allison, Dale C. *Jesus of Nazareth—Millenarian Prophet*. Minneapolis: Fortress, 1998.
Baeck, Leo. "Romantic Religion." In *Jewish Perspectives on Christianity*, edited by Fritz A. Rothschild, 56-91. New York: Continuum, 1996.
———. "Judaism in the Church." In *Jewish Perspectives on Christianity*, edited by Fritz A. Rothschild, 92-110. New York: Continuum, 1996.
Barclay, John M. G. *Obeying the Truth*. Minneapolis: Fortress, 1988.
Barth, Karl. *Prayer*. Louisville: Westminster John Knox, 2002; original edition 1952.
Beasley-Murray, George R. *John*. Word Biblical Commentary, vol. 36. Waco: Word, 1987.
Berkovits, Eliezer. *Not in Heaven: The Nature and Function of Halakha*. Hoboken, NJ: Ktav, 1983.
Boccaccini, Gabriele. *Middle Judaism*. Minneapolis: Fortress, 1991.
Braude, William G., translator. *The Midrash on Psalms, vol 2*. New Haven: Yale University Press, 1959.
Braaten, Carl, and Robert Jenson, editors. *Union with Christ, The New Finnish Interpretation of Luther*. Grand Rapids: Eerdmans, 1998.
———, editors. *Jews and Christians: People of God*. Grand Rapids: Eerdmans, 2003.
Brawley, Robert L. *Luke-Acts and the Jews*. Atlanta: Scholars, 1987.
Brown, Raymond E. *An Introduction to the Gospel of John*. New York: Doubleday, 2003.
Brown, Wesley H., and Peter F. Penner, editors. *Christian Perspectives on the Israeli-Palestinian Conflict*. Pasadena: WCIU, 2008.
Buber, Martin. "The Two Foci of the Jewish Soul." In *Jewish Perspectives on Christianity*, edited by Fritz A. Rothschild, 122-31. New York: Continuum, 1996.
Campbell, Douglas A. *The Quest for Paul's Gospel*. London: T. & T. Clark, 2005.
Cantalamessa, Fr. Raniero. *The Mystery of Christmas*. Sydney: St. Paul's, 1988.
Cardozo, Nathan T. Lopes. *The Written and Oral Torah*. Northvale, NJ: Jason Aronson, 1997.
Cohen, Arthur A. "The Natural and the Supernatural Jew." In *Contemporary Jewish Theology*, edited by Elliot N. Dorff and Louis E. Newman, 190-98. New York: Oxford University Press, 1999.
Cole, Alan R. *The Gospel according to St. Mark*. Grand Rapids: Eerdmans, 1961.
Cosgrove, Charles H. *Elusive Israel*. Louisville: Westminster John Knox, 1997.
Cranfield, C. E. B. *The Epistle to the Romans, vol. 2*. Edinburgh: T. & T. Clark, 1979.
Crüsemann, Frank. *The Torah*. Edinburgh: T. & T. Clark, 1996.
Danby, Herbert. *The Mishnah*. Oxford: Oxford University Press, 1933.
Danielou, Jean. *The Theology of Jewish Christianity*. London: Darton, Longman, & Todd, 1964.
Davies, W. D. *Paul and Rabbinic Judaism*. Philadelphia: Fortress, 1980; orig. pub. 1948.

Davies, W. D., and Dale C. Allison. *A Critical and Exegetical Commentary on the Gospel according to Saint Matthew.* Edinburgh: T. & T. Clark, 1997.
Dickson, Athol. *The Gospel according to Moses.* Grand Rapids: Brazos, 2003.
Donin, Rabbi Hayim Halevy. *To Pray as a Jew.* New York: Basic, 1980.
Dunn, James D. G. "Jesus, Table-Fellowship, and Qumran." In *Jesus and the Dead Sea Scrolls,* edited by James H. Charlesworth, 254–72. New York: Doubleday, 1992.
———. *The Partings of the Ways.* Philadelphia: Trinity, 1991.
———. *Romans 1–8.* Word Biblical Commentary, vol. 38a. Dallas: Word, 1988.
———. *Romans 9–16.* Word Biblical Commentary, vol. 38b. Dallas: Word, 1988.
Edersheim, Alfred. *Prophecy and History.* Grand Rapids: Baker, 1980; original edition 1885.
Falk, Harvey. *Jesus the Pharisee.* Mahwah, NJ: Paulist, 1984.
Fishbane, Michael. *Biblical Interpretation in Ancient Israel.* Oxford: Oxford University Press, 1985.
Fossum, Jarl E. *The Name of God and the Angel of the Lord.* Tübingen: Mohr, 1985.
France, R. T. *The Gospel according to Matthew.* Grand Rapids: Eerdmans, 1985.
Fuchs-Kreimer, Nancy. "Redemption: What I Have Learned from Christians." In *Christianity in Jewish Terms,* edited by Tikva Frymer-Kensky et al., 275–84. Boulder: Westview, 2000.
Greenberg, Irving. *The Jewish Way.* New York: Touchstone, 1988.
Gruber, Daniel. *Rabbi Akiba's Messiah: The Origins of Rabbinic Authority.* Hanover, NH: Elijah, 1999.
Guggenheimer, Heinrich. *The Scholar's Haggadah.* Northvale, NJ: Jason Aronson, 1995.
Gunton, Colin E. *The Christian Faith.* Oxford: Blackwell, 2002.
Halivni, David Weiss. *Peshat and Derash.* Oxford: Oxford University Press, 1991.
———. *Revelation Restored.* Boulder: Westview, 1997.
Hammer, Reuven. *Entering Jewish Prayer.* New York: Schocken, 1994.
———, translator. *Sifre on Deuteronomy.* New Haven: Yale University Press, 1986.
Harlow, Rabbi Jules, editor. *Siddur Sim Shalom.* New York: The Rabbinical Assembly and The United Synagogue of America, 1985.
Harrington, Daniel J. *The Gospel of Matthew.* Collegeville, MN: Liturgical, 1991.
Hartman, David. *A Living Covenant.* Woodstock, VT: Jewish Lights, 1997.
Harvey, Richard. *Mapping Messianic Jewish Theology: A Constructive Approach.* Milton Keynes, UK: Paternoster, 2009.
Hays, Richard B. *The Moral Vision of the New Testament: Community, Cross, New Creation. A Contemporary Introduction to New Testament Ethics.* New York: HarperOne, 1996.
Haynes, Stephen R. *Prospects for Post-Holocaust Theology.* Atlanta: Scholars, 1991.
Hengel, Martin. "The Effective History of Isaiah 53 in the Pre-Christian Period." In *The Suffering Servant: Isaiah 53 in Jewish and Christian Sources,* edited by Bernd Janowski and Peter Stuhlmacher, 75–146. Grand Rapids: Eerdmans, 2004.
Herberg, Will. *Faith Enacted as History.* Philadelphia: Westminster, 1976.
———. "Judaism and Christianity: Their Unity and Difference." *The Journal of Bible and Religion* 21 (April 1953) 67–78.
Heschel, Abraham Joshua. *God in Search of Man.* New York: Farrar, Straus & Cudahy, 1955.
———. *The Sabbath.* New York: Farrar, Straus, and Giroux, 2001; orig. pub. 1951.

Hoenig, Samuel N. *The Essence of Talmudic Law and Thought*. Northvale, NJ: Aronson, 1993.
Jacobs, Louis. "The Uplifting of Sparks in Later Jewish Mysticism." In *Jewish Spirituality: From the Sixteenth Century Revival to the Present*, edited by Arthur Green, 99–126. New York: Crossroad, 1997.
Jenson, Robert. *Systematic Theology, vol. 1*. Oxford: Oxford University Press, 1997.
Jeremias, Joachim. *New Testament Theology*. New York: Charles Scribner's Sons, 1971.
Johnson, Elizabeth, and David M. Hay, editors. *Pauline Theology, vol. 4*. Atlanta: Scholars, 1997.
Josephus, Flavius. *Jewish Antiquities*. Translated by Ralph Marcus. Cambridge, MA: Harvard University Press, 1986; orig. pub. 1933.
Juster, Daniel C. *Jewish Roots*. Rockville, MD: Davar, 1986.
Kadushin, Max. *The Rabbinic Mind*. New York: Blaisdell, 1965.
Keck, Leander E. *Romans*. Nashville: Abingdon, 2005.
Keener, Craig S. *A Commentary on the Gospel of Matthew*. Grand Rapids: Eerdmans, 1999.
———. *The Gospel of John: A Commentary, vol. 1*. Peabody, MA: Hendrickson, 2003.
Kernaghan, Ronald J. *Mark*. Downers Grove, IL: InterVarsity, 2007.
Kinzer, Mark. "On the Nature of Messianic Judaism: Replying to My Respondents." *Kesher* 13 (Summer 2001) 36–67.
———. *Postmissionary Messianic Judaism*. Grand Rapids: Brazos, 2005.
———. *The Nature of Messianic Judaism*. West Hartford: Hashivenu Archives, 2000.
Lachs, Samuel Tobias. *A Rabbinic Commentary on the New Testament: The Gospels of Matthew, Mark and Luke*. Hoboken: Ktav, 1987.
Levenson, Jon D. *Sinai and Zion*. New York: Harper and Row, 1987.
———. *The Death and Resurrection of the Beloved Son*. New Haven: Yale University Press, 1993.
Levering, Matthew. *Christ's Fulfillment of Torah and Temple*. Notre Dame: University of Notre Dame Press, 2002.
———. *Jewish-Christian Dialogue and the Life of Wisdom*. New York: Continuum, 2010.
Lewis, C. S. *God in the Dock*. Grand Rapids: Eerdmans, 1970.
———. *The Problem of Pain*. New York: Macmillan, 1962.
Lieber, David L., editor. *Etz Hayim: Torah and Commentary*. Philadelphia: Jewish Publication Society, 2001.
Longenecker, Richard N. *The Christology of Early Jewish Christianity*. Grand Rapids: Baker, 1981.
Mason, Steve. "Chief Priests, Sadducees, Pharisees and Sanhedrin in Acts." In *The Book of Acts in Its First Century Setting, vol. 4: Palestinian Setting*, edited by Richard Bauckham, 133–57. Grand Rapids: Eerdmans, 1995.
McKnight, Scot. *A New Vision for Israel*. Grand Rapids: Eerdmans, 1999.
Milgrom, Jacob. *Leviticus 1–16*. Anchor Bible. New York: Doubleday, 1991.
Moore, George Foot. *Judaism, vol. 1*. Peabody, MA: Hendrickson, 1997; orig. pub. 1927.
Mosès, Stéphane. *System and Revelation*. Detroit: Wayne State University Press, 1992.
Mullen, E. Theodore. "Hosts, Host of Heaven." In *The Anchor Bible Dictionary, vol. 3.*, edited by David Noel Freedman, 301–4. New York: Doubleday, 1992.
Neuhaus, Richard John. "Salvation is From the Jews." *First Things* 117 (Nov 2001) 17–22.
Neusner, Jacob. *A Short History of Judaism*. Minneapolis: Fortress, 1992.

———. *An Introduction to Judaism: A Textbook and Reader*. Louisville: Westminster/John Knox, 1991.
———. *Genesis Rabbah*, vol. 1. Atlanta: Scholars, 1985.
Novak, David. "Beyond Supersessionism." *First Things* 81 (March 1998) 57–60.
———. *The Election of Israel*. Cambridge: Cambridge University Press, 1995.
Pannenberg, Wolfhart. *Systematic Theology*, 3 vols. Translated by Geoffrey Bromiley. Grand Rapids: Eerdmans, 1991, 1994, 1998.
Rosenzweig, Franz. *The Star of Redemption*. Notre Dame: University of Notre Dame Press, 1985.
Saldarini, Anthony J. *Matthew's Christian-Jewish Community*. Chicago: University of Chicago Press, 1994.
———. *Pharisees, Scribes and Sadducees in Palestinian Society*. Wilmington: Michael Glazier, 1988.
Sanders, E. P. *Jewish Law from Jesus to the Mishnah*. Philadelphia: Trinity, 1990.
Sarna, Nahum M. *The JPS Torah Commentary: Genesis*. Philadelphia: JPS, 1989.
Scherman, Rabbi Nosson, translator. *The Complete ArtScroll Siddur*. Brooklyn: Mesorah, 1984.
Schiffman, Lawrence H. *From Text to Tradition*. Hoboken, NJ: Ktav, 1991.
Schoeps, Hans J. *Paul*. Philadelphia: Westminster, 1961.
Scholem, Gershom G. *Major Trends in Jewish Mysticism*. New York: Schocken, 1941.
Schönborn, Christoph. "Judaism's Way to Salvation." *The Tablet* (29 March 2008) 8–9.
Sim, David. *The Gospel of Matthew and Christian Judaism*. Edinburgh: T. & T. Clark, 1998.
Simon, Maurice, translator. *Hebrew-English Edition of the Babylonian Talmud: Berakoth*. London: Soncino, 1984.
Soloveitchik, Joseph. *Halakhic Man*. New York: JPS, 1983.
Soulen, R. Kendall. *The God of Israel and Christian Theology*. Minneapolis: Fortress, 1996.
Spiegel, Shalom. *The Last Trial*. Woodstock, VT: Jewish Lights, 1993; orig. pub. 1967.
Stackhouse, John G., editor. *What Does It Mean To Be Saved?* Grand Rapids: Baker Academic, 2002.
Stern, David. *Messianic Jewish Manifesto*. Clarksville, MD: Jewish New Testament Publications, 1988.
Tendler, Moshe Dovid. "Harsh Words." *Moment* 23:4 (August 1998) 36–38.
Thoma, Clemens. *A Christian Theology of Judaism*. New York: Paulist, 1980.
Tiessen, Terrance L. *Who Can Be Saved?* Downers Grove, IL: InterVarsity, 2004.
Torrance, Thomas F. *The Mediation of Christ*. Colorado Springs, CO: Helmers & Howard, 1992.
———. "The Divine Vocation and Destiny of Israel in World History." In *The Witness of the Jews to God*, edited by David W. Torrance, 85–104. Edinburgh: Handsel, 1982.
Van Buren, Paul M. *According to the Scriptures*. Grand Rapids: Eerdmans, 1998.
———. *A Theology of the Jewish-Christian Reality, Part 2: A Christian Theology of the People Israel*. Lanham, MD: University Press of America, 1995.
Vanhoozer, Kevin J. *The Drama of Doctrine*. Louisville: Westminster John Knox, 2005.
VanLandingham, Chris. *Judgment & Justification in Early Judaism and the Apostle Paul*. Peabody, MA: Hendrickson, 2006.
Von Balthasar, Hans Urs. *Dare We Hope "That All Men Be Saved"?* San Francisco: Ignatius, 1988.

Wright, N. T. *The Climax of the Covenant*. Minneapolis: Fortress, 1992.
——. *The New Testament and the People of God*. Minneapolis: Fortress, 1992.
——. *What Saint Paul Really Said*. Grand Rapids: Eerdmans, 1997.
Wyschogrod, Michael. *Abraham's Promise: Judaism and Jewish-Christian Relations*. Grand Rapids: Eerdmans, 2004.
——. *The Body of Faith*. Northvale, NJ: Aronson, 1996.
——. "Incarnation." *Pro Ecclesia* 2 (Spring 1993) 208–15.
Yoder, John Howard. *The Jewish-Christian Schism Revisited*. Grand Rapids: Eerdmans, 2003.
Zemer, Moshe. *Evolving Halakhah*. Woodstock: Jewish Lights, 1999.

Chronological Bibliography of Material Related to *Postmissionary Messianic Judaism*

Sadan, Tsvi. "Mark Kinzer, Postmissionary Messianic Judaism." *Kivun* 47 (Sep–Oct 2005) 19.
Robinson, Rich. "Postmissionary Messianic Judaism." *Havurah* 8, no. 4 (November 11, 2005). Online: http://www.jewsforjesus.org/publications/havurah/08_04/kinzer.
Van Engen, Charles. "Response to Postmissionary Messianic Judaism." Delivered at the Hashivenu Forum in Pasadena, CA, January 2006. Online: http://www.hashivenu.org/papers/2006_Postmissionary_MJ_VanEngen.pdf
Stokes, H. Bruce. "Response to Postmissionary Messianic Judaism." Delivered at the Hashivenu Forum in Pasadena, CA, January 2006. Online: http://www.hashivenu.org/papers/2006_Postmissionary_MJ_Stokes.pdf
Rottenberg, Isaac. "Postmissionary Messianic Judaism? Observations on the Mark Kinzer Thesis." *Restore* 9, no. 3 (January 2006) 10–13.
Nerel, Gershon. "*Nostra Aetate*: Between Hebrew Catholics and Messianic Jews." *Mishkan* 46 (2006) 47–58.

KESHER 20 (WINTER/SPRING 2006)

Jonathan Kaplan, "A Synopsis of Mark Kinzer's Post-Missionary Messianic Judaism," 7–15.
David H. Stern, "A Response," 16–22.
Daniel C. Juster, "A Response," 23–29.
Mitch Glaser, "A Response," 30–36.
R. Kendall Soulen, "A Response," 37–42.
Douglas K. Harink, "A Response," 43–48.
Peter Hocken, "A Response," 49–55.
Mark S. Kinzer, "A Rejoinder to Responses," 56–64.

MISHKAN 48 (2006)

Kai Kjaer-Hansen, "Postmissionary in Three Senses," 3.
Kai Kjaer-Hansen, "Mark Kinzer and Joseph Rabinowitz," 4–7.
Rich Robinson, "Postmissinary Messianic Judaism: A Review Essay," 8–21.
Richard Harvey, "Shaping the Aims and Aspirations of Jewish Believers," 22–27.
Eckhard J. Schnable, "The Identity and the Mission of Believers in Jesus Messiah," 28–53.
Mark S. Kinzer, "Response to Mishkan Reviewers of My Book," 54–65.
Akiva Cohen, Derek Leman, Baruch Maoz, David Stern, "Four Comments on Postmissionary Messianic Judaism," 66–72.

Schebera, Richard L. "Postmissionary Messianic Judaism." *Dialogue & Alliance* 20, no. 1 (Spring/Summer 2006) 127–29.
Kellner, Mark A. "All in the Family: Unraveling the Church's Confusion about Messianic Jews." *Christianity Today* (March 2006) 75–76.
Daniels, David. "Avoiding Potholes on the Road to Jerusalem." *Christian Week* (March 3, 2006) 10.
Neuhaus, Richard John. "On the Square: Observations & Contentions." *First Things* (May 24, 2006). Online: http://www.firstthings.com/onthesquare/2006/05/rjn-52406-so-whats-your-church
Garner, Daniel. "Postmissionary Messianic Judaism." *Reviews in Religion and Theology* (January 2007) 36–38.
Soulen, R. Kendall. "Postmissionary Messianic Judaism." *Pro Ecclesia* XVI, no. 1. (Winter 2007) 105–7.
Brown, Michael L. "Is A Post-Missionary, Truly Messianic Judaism Possible?" Paper delivered at the North American Lausanne Consultation on Jewish Evangelism (April 18, 2007). Online: http://www.jewsforjesus.org/publications/bookreviews/Post-Missionary //www.ourrabbis.org.
Siegel, Jennifer. "Messianic Jews Find Fertile Ground in the Bible Belt." *Jewish Daily Forward* (June 13, 2007).
Sadan, Tsvi. "Hamision Hashlihut Vema Shebeinehem." Interview with Mark Kinzer (responding to Michael Brown), *Kivun* 56 (July-Aug 2007) 8–9.
Kinzer, Mark S. "Yeshua, The Glory of God and the Glory of Israel: Motives for Postmissionary Messianic Jewish Outreach." Teaching delivered at the annual conference of the Union of Messianic Jewish Congregations (July 2007, Chicago). Online: http://messianicjewishconversations.blogspot.com/
———. "Final Destinies: Qualifications for Receiving an Eschatological Inheritance." Paper delivered at the Borough Park Symposium (October 2007, NYC), now published in *Kesher* 22 (Spring/Summer 2008) 87–119. Online: http://messianicjewishconversations.blogspot.com/
Yeoman, Barry. "Messianics are Praying the 'Shema,' but Preaching Jesus as the Messiah." *Jewish Telegraphic Agency (JTA)* (November 15, 2007) Online: http://www.jta.org/news/article/2007/11/15/104640/evangtwo
Reagan, David R. "Messianic Judaism: Its Meaning and Significance." *Lamplighter* XXVIII, no. 6 (November-December 2007) 8–9.
Harvey, Richard. "The Hidden Messiah." Paper delivered at the International Lausanne Consultation on Jewish Evangelism (August 2007) (see *Lausanne Consultation on Jewish Evangelism Bulletin* 90, November 2007).
Marshall, Bruce D. "Elder Brothers: John Paul II's Teaching on the Jewish People as a Question to the Church." In David G. Dalin and Matthew Levering (editors), *John Paul II and the Jewish People*, 113–29. Lanham, MD: Rowman & Littlefield, 2008.
Yocum, John P. "On Mark S. Kinzer's *Postmissionary Messianic Judaism: Redifining Christian Engagement with the Jewish People.*" *Nova et Vetera* 5, no. 4 (2007) 895–906.
*Blomberg, Craig. "Freedom from the Law only for Gentiles? A Non-supersessionist Alternative to Mark Kinzer's 'Postmissionary Messianic Judaism.'" Paper delivered at the Biblical Studies Conference on Messianic Judaism (February 12–13, 2009 at Denver Seminary).

*Guretzki, David. "Karl Barth on Mark Kinzer's 'Non-supersessionist and Post-Missionary Ecclesiology': Yes! and No!" Paper delivered at the Canadian Evangelical Theological Association (May 23, 2009 at Carleton University, Ottawa).

*Colyer, Elmer M. "Post-Missionary Messianic Judaism," *Scottish Journal of Theology* 62:4 (November 2009) 516–519.

*Levering, Matthew. "Supersessionism and Messianic Judaism." In *Jewish-Christian Dialogue and the Life of Wisdom: Engagements with the Theology of David Novak*, 12-46. New York: Continuum, 2010.

Scripture Index

OLD TESTAMENT

Genesis

1	97
1—2	96
1:1—2:3	95
1:1—2:4	95n7
1:4	95
1:10	95
1:12	95
1:18	95
1:21	95
1:25	95
1:31	95
2	95n7
2:1	77n40
2:1–3	95
2:3	95
12	xviii
12:3	xviii
22	xix n. 28, 108
22:10	69
22:14	108

Exodus

3:5	96n8
4:22–23	67
12:1–13	32
12:5	33
12:9	33
12:16	96n8
13:2	96n8
15	85, 100
15:11	78n41
18	38, 55n91
18:5	34n16
18:13–27	34n16
19:6	95, 96n8, 103
19:10	96n8
19:14	96n8
19:23	96n8
20:10	32n6
21:7	32
24	103
24:9–11	38n35, 39n40
25:8	103
28	38
28:15–21	97
31:13	96
31:16–17	96
33:16	103–4

Leviticus

10:1–3	105
11:13–19	32n8
13—14	106
16:31	32n7
19	70n20
19:18	70
24:10–23	37n31

Numbers

9:6–14	37n31
10:33	96
11	38, 39, 40, 55n91

Numbers–continued

11:11–15	38n34
11:16	38n36, 39n39
11:16–17	38n34
11:17	38n37
11:24	38n36, 39n39
11:24–25	38n34
11:25–30	38n37
15	74, 74n32
15:32–36	37n31
15:37–41	68n9, 74
15:39–40	74n31
15:39b	74n33
15:41	74n34
16:1–11	105
16:16–22	105
16:35	105
18:21–32	32
27	37n31
36	37n31

Deuteronomy

1	38, 55n91
1:9–18	34n17, 35
1:15–16	34n17
4:19	77n40
5:14	32n6
6	74n32
6:4	68n13, 69, 75, 144n30
6:4–9	68, 68n9, 70, 72, 73, 73n29
6:5	71n24
6:6	74n31
6:6–9	71n24
6:7	68
10:1–8	96
11	72, 74, 74n32
11:13	71n24, 72n27, 74n31
11:13–17	71–72
11:13–21	68n9, 71, 73n29
11:16–17	74n33
11:17	72, 72n26, 73
11:18	73, 73n29
11:18–20	71n24
11:19	68
11:20	73
11:21	73–74
12:22–29	32
13:6	36n26
14:11–18	32n8
15:17	32
16:2	32–33
16:7	33
16:18	39
16:18–20	35n20
16:18–29	35
16:18—18:22	35n19, 39n41, 171
17	37, 38, 40, 43, 45, 51, 55
17:3	77n40
17:7	36n26
17:8	35n22, 36, 37, 45
17:8f.	36
17:8–13	35n21
17:10	35n23, 54, 55
17:11	35n24, 43, 44
17:11–13	36n25
17:14–15	39
19:19	36n26
21:21	36n26
22:21	36n26
24:7	36n26
30:14	143

1 Samuel

5	105

2 Samuel

6:6–7	105

2 Kings

2:9–10	38n38
2:15	38n38

Scripture Index

1 Chronicles
29:14	81n50

Esther
9:27	39n43

Psalms
22:29	100
44:23	68
92	98
104:24	79
113—118	12, 44
145—150	99
145:1	99
146	99
146:7	99
146:10—147n2	99
147	99

Proverbs
3:18	95n7

Isaiah
5:1–7	53n86
6	57n104
11:9	xx, 104
40:26	77n40
49:6	xviii
53	xvii n. 22, 13, 109, 109n47
59:21	119, 164
60:21	98

Jeremiah
31	162, 164
31:31–32	119, 164

Ezekiel
1:10	104

Daniel
12:1–3	110

Hosea
6:6	50n74

Obadiah
1:21	100

Zechariah
14	96, 101, 104
14:5	97
14:7	97
14:9	100
14:20–21	97, 97n12

NEW TESTAMENT

Matthew
1:23	xx, 104
2:2	170
3:1–12	137
3:7–10	130
3:13–15	73n30
5:7	134
5:20	133
6:12–15	134
7:1–2	134
7:12	57n102
7:14	147
7:21	132
7:21–23	131, 145
7:22–23	137
8:1–4	106

Matthew–continued

8:5–10	130
8:10	136
8:11	107
8:11–12	130
8:13	136
8:28–34	106
9:9–13	107
9:13	50n74, 57n102
9:15	107
9:20–22	105
10:32	138
10:33	137, 138
10:40	138
11:2–6	124
12:7	50n74, 57n102
12:28	124
12:31–32	132
12:36–37	132–33
13:51–52	57n101
15	49, 52
15:1–20	49n70
15:2	48n69
15:18–20	57n102
15:28	136
16:19	54n88, 57n102
16:27	132, 137
18:8–9	147, 147n34
18:18	54n88, 57n102
18:23–35	134
18:32–35	134–35
19:3	57n102
19:9	57n102
19:16–17	133, 147
19:16–21	137
19:21	137, 145
19:28	137
19:29	137, 145, 147
20:28	137
21:10–17	53n83
21:23–27	53n83
21:33–46	53n82
21:41	54n87
21:43	54n87
21:45	53n85
22:1–14	107
22:32	9
22:34–40	70n18
22:40	57n102
23	55
23:1–3	54, 55
23:2	55n91
23:23	57n105
23:23–24	50
23:25–26	51n77
23:34	57n101
25	138n22
25:1–13	107
25:14–30	135
25:21	135
25:23	135
25:31–33	131, 137
25:31–46	131
25:34	138
25:35–36	138
25:37	131
25:37–38	138
25:40	138
25:44	131, 138
25:46	147
26:28	137
26:29	107
26:69–75	138
27:11	170
27:29	170
27:37	170
27:52–53	137

Mark

1:23–26	106
1:40–45	106
2:5	136
2:13–17	107
5:1–20	106
5:25–34	105

Scripture Index

5:34	136	13:26	130n11
5:36	136	13:31–33	55n93
6:5–6	136	14:1–24	55n92
7	49, 52	15:25–32	56n94
7:1–23	49n70	16:9–13	134n16
7:2	49	16:19–31	134n16
8:35	137, 145	17:20	56n94
10:30	147n34	17:20–22	56n94
10:52	136	17:22	56n94
11:15–19	53n83	19:8–9	134n16
11:27–33	53n83	19:45–48	53n83
12:1–12	53n82	20:1–8	53n83
12:28–34	70n18	20:9–19	53n82
16:9–16	152–53	22:20	137
16:11	153	23:39–43	138
16:13	153		
16:14	153	**John**	
16:15	153		
16:15–16	152	1:1–3	79n42
16:16	136n20, 137n	1:4–5	151
		1:4–9	80n48
Luke		1:9	151
		1:13	151
2:32	168, 168n8	1:14	151
3:7–9	130	1:18	79
4:16	52n81	1:45	23
5:12–16	106	3:16–21	148–49
5:27–32	107	3:18	150
6:38	134n16	3:36	147, 150
7:11–17	106	5:21	148
7:36–50	55n92	5:24	147, 150
8:26–39	106	5:26	148
8:43–48	105	5:28–29	151
9:31	75n37	5:46	23
10:25–28	70n18, 133	6:35	147, 148
11:28	130n11	6:36	150
11:37–52	55n92	6:40	148, 150
11:38	49n72	6:47	147
11:42	50	6:53–58	148
12:10	132	6:54	148
12:47–48a	136	6:69	147
12:48b	136, 138	7:37–39	52n81
12:50	73n30	8:12	52n81, 80n48

John–continued

8:24	147, 150n37
8:51	147
8:58–59	147
10:11	70n21
10:15	70n21
10:17	70n21
10:18	70n21
10:26	148
10:38	147
11:25	148
11:25–26	148
11:27	146
12:41	79n46, 151–52
12:47–48	147, 150
13:19	147
13:34	70n20
14:6	147, 148
14:10–11	147
14:21	147
14:30–31	70
15:10	147
15:13	70n20
16:27	146, 147
17:2	148
17:3	148
17:8	146
17:11–12	147
17:21	146
18:5–6	147
20:31	146

Acts

3:16	136n19
4:1–6	53n84
4:9	136n19
4:12	136n19
5:17–18	53n84
5:21	53n84
5:27–28	53n84
5:33–39	53n85
5:34–40	56n95
15	xxi n. 38
15:5	56n96
21:20–24	10–11
23:6	56n97
23:6–10	53n85
23:9	56n98
26:4–8	56n97

Romans

1:2	23
1:5	144
1:16	142
1:45	143
1:48–49	143
2	140, 146
2:5–11	141
2:5–13	141
2:12–13	142
2:14–15	142
2:14–16	140
2:17–24	139
2:25–29	139
2:26–27	140
3:1–2	139
3:21	xxv
4	143
4:17	143
4:19	143
4:19–21	143
4:24	75n38, 143
6:5	144
6:8	144
8	xvi
8—11	184n
8:11	75n38, 144
8:18–23	139
8:23	99n18
9–11	xiv, xv, xvi
9:4–5	139
9:8	139
10	143, 144
10:1	12

10:8–13	143	**Galatians**	
10:14–17	140n24	1:14	48n69
11	169	2:11–14	189
11:6	113	3:13	xvi
11:14	xvi	3:25–27	144
11:17–22	140	3:28	xiv n. 12
11:25–36	113	5:6	144
11:28	12	5:14	142
11:28–29	163	5:19–21	145
13:8–10	142	6:2	142
14:10–12	141		
16:26	144	**Ephesians**	
		1	82
1 Corinthians		1:3–6	82
1:21	142	1:4	67
4:4–5	140	1:5–6	67
6:9–10	145	1:9–10	139
8:6	79n42	1:11–13	82
9:24–27	140	1:14	99n18
10:1–13	140	2:11–22	4, 188
10:16–17	189	4:1–3	142
10:18	162	4:5	144
11:17–32	189	4:31–32	142
12:3	144n30	5:1–2	142
13:8	142	5:5–6	145
13:13	142		
15:1–2	142	**Philippians**	
15:20	143	3:11–14	140
15:21–22	143		
15:28	139	**Colossians**	
		1:15	79n45
2 Corinthians		1:15–16	79n42
1:22	99n18	1:24	86
3:12—4:16	79n47	2:6	144n30
4:4	79n45	3:5–6	145
4:5	144n30	3:12–14	142
4:6	80n48		
5:5	99n18		
5:8–10	141		

Hebrews

1:1–4	79n42
2:1–3	131n12
6:5	124
10:26–31	131n12
11	71
11—12	71
11:39–40	71n23
12:1	71
12:2	71n23
12:18–24	71
12:25–26	131n12

James

1:12	133
2:5	133
2:8–12	134
2:13	134
2:14–26	145

1 Peter

1:17	133

2 Peter

2:21	131n12

1 John

2:7–11	70n20
3:16	70n21
5:1	146
5:5	146

Revelation

1:5	85n55, 136n20
2:10	136n20
2:13	136n20
3:14	137n
5:1–14	85n55
6:9–11	85
12:11	86
15:2–3	85
17:14	137n
19:11	137n
20:12–13	133
21	96, 104
21:2	97
21:3	xx, 97, 104
21:5	137n
21:6	137n
21:8	136n20
21:16	97
21:19	97
21:22	97
21:27	97
22:5	97

APOCRYPHA

2 Maccabees

7	109

4 Maccabees

16:20	108
17:21–22	108

JOSEPHUS

Jewish Antiquities

174–75	48n68

RABBINIC LITERATURE

BABYLONIAN TALMUD

Bava Kama

114b	44n57

Berachot

14a	44n55
15a	44n57
16b	44n57
17b	44n57
19b	44, 44n56
20b	44n57
21a	44n57
21b	44n57
45a	48
61b	69n15

Betsah

3b	44

Megillah

7a	39n44

Menahot

29b	42n48

Nidah

4b	44n57

Shabbat

23a	43n50

Sukkah

44a	44n57

MISHNAH

Berachot

1:5	74n35
2:2	68n12
9:5	68n14

Sanhedrin

10:1	98

Tamid

5:1	68n10
7:4	98n14

OTHER RABBINIC WORKS

Genesis Rabbah

17:5	98
56:3	108

Mechilta

Exodus 31:17	98

Sifre

Deuteronomy 6:5	69n15

Subject/Name Index

Akedah, xviii–xix, 69, 70
   Israel's suffering modeled on, 109
   significance of, 108
Albo, Joseph, 45–46
Allison, Dale, 105–7, 131
angelic powers, 77–78
apocalyptic eschatology, 121
apostolic writings, Oral Torah in, 48–58

Baeck, Leo, 114
Berkovits, Eliezer, 45, 46
Bible, eschatology of, shaping entire narrative, 92
Biblical Judaism, 20–24
bilateral ecclesiology, xx–xxii, xxv–xxvi, 178
   further discussion about, 189
   reaction to, 184–85
   in solidarity with Israel, 191
body of Christ. *See also* church
   concept of, as central to the church's identity, 157
   relationship of, to people of God, 169–74
Brawley, Robert, 56n99
Brit Hadashah, 21, 22–23
Brown, Michael, 195
Buber, Martin, 101–2, 107

canonical narrative, 91–92
   Christian, eschatological problems in, 113–18, 120
   Messianic Judaism, needing to lower the eschatological horizon, 113
   reshaping, 116–18
   three versions of, relating to eschatological horizon, 93–94

Cantalamessa, Raniero, 174
Catechism of the Catholic Church
   omitting discussion relating land of Israel and people of Israel, 168–69
   on the significance of the Jewish people, 165–66
Catholicism, incorporating different traditions, 189
charismata, 124–25
Chenoweth, Bob, 29n2
Chosen People Ministries, 185
Christianity
   in contradistinction with Judaism, x, xi
   dangers of, xxiv–xxv
   eschatological horizon of, 93
   extending Israel's covenant to the nations, 66
   mutual dependence of, with Judaism, xxiv–xxv
church. *See also* body of Christ; *ekklesia*
   functions of, 158
   as mystical reality and human community, 157
   as New Israel, 162–64
   as new reality in the world, 160–61
   relationship of, with the Jewish people, 158
Cohen, Arthur, 94
compound religious designations, 18–20
Cottier, Georges, 192–93
Crüsemann, Frank, 36–37

Dauermann, Stuart, 29n2
Davies, W. D., 105–7, 131

deeds, relation of, to salvation, 133–34, 154
Deuteronomic Code, 34–36
Dickson, Athol, 132n15
disbelief, linked with judgment, 149
divine perfection, obsession with, 42
divine presence, as element of Israel's vocation and identity, 103–4
Donin, Hayim, 65, 72–74
Dunn, James D. G., 106, 140n24, 144n30

Edersheim, Alfred, 23
ekklesia
    comprising two corporate subcommunities, xxi
    as extension of Israel, xiv
    founding of, 111
    restoring the Jewish branch of, xxii–xxiii
    rethinking eschatological nature of, 118–19
    twofold nature of, 123, 178, 188–89
eschatological horizon, 93–94
    lowering, for Christianity, 113, 120
    raising, for Jewish tradition, 121–22
eschatology
    martyrdom related to, 109–11
    place of, in Messianic Judaism's canonical narrative, 122–25
    proleptic, 94–102
    shaping entire biblical narrative, 92
eternal life, present possession of, 147–48
evangelicalism, conservative, 22
evangelicals
    approach of, to salvation, 153–54
    viewing salvation in negative terms, 127
exile, 72–73
exodus, remembering, through the Shema, 74–76
extensive eschatology, 121

faith
    implicit and explicit, 127n4
    linked with final condemnation, 149, 152–53
    role of, in salvation, 142–47
final destinies
    faith linked with, 149, 152–53
    John's tradition of, 146–52
    Paul's tradition of, 139–46, 149
    Peter's and James's traditions of, 129–39, 149
    question of, 128
Fishbane, Michael, 32, 33–34, 37n32
forgiveness, 137, 142
Freedman, David Noel, 188
Fuchs-Kreimer, Nancy, 94–95

Glaser, Mitch, 187
God. *See also* Hashem
    expressing love for, 68–69
    judging everyone's deeds on the final day, 140
    Name of, seen as distinct reality, 79
    personal relationship with, 9–10
God of Israel and Christian Theology, The (Soulen), 116–17
government, foundational law of, 39
Gruber, Daniel, 43–44
Guggenheimer, Heinrich, 100
Gunton, Colin, 171

halakhah, 29
    authority for, given to Yeshua's followers, 59–60
    importance to, of Oral Torah, 30–31
    process of, Jewish people's role in, 47–48
Halvini, David Weiss, 33, 34, 42, 44
Hammer, Reuven, 65, 74–75
hand washing, 49
Hartman, David, 68
Hashem. *See also* God
    as Creator and Redeemer, 76–78
    as God of Israel, 80–81
    as Israel's redeemer, 82–84
    self-revelation of, 84
Hashivenu Forum, 29n2, 62–63
Hasidic movement, extending sense of *kedushah*, 101–2

Subject/Name Index

Hays, Richard, xv–xvi
Hebrew Christianity, renaming of, 16
Hebrew language, 12
Hebrew Scriptures, 10
Hengel, Martin, xvii n. 22
Herberg, Will, 66, 103
Heschel, Abraham Joshua, 96nn10–11, 98–99
high court. *See* judiciary
Hocken, Peter, 189–90
humanity, God's corporate purpose for, 161

impurity, Yeshua's contact with, 105–6
incarnation, 103–4
Israel. *See also* Jews
    authority in, vested in people as a whole, 39–40
    central judicial institution in, 36–37
    Christians' "No" to, 181–82
    covenantal identity of, 103–4
    discontinuity in views of, 162, 163–64
    God's presence in, Yeshua as representation of, xix
    governmental institutions, authority for, 39
    holiness of, basis for, 100–101
    as incarnation of the Torah, 46
    land of, eschatological character of, 98–99
    life of, connected with Yeshua, xix–xx
    Mary's relationship to, 173
    as part of new covenant, 164–65
    praying in, 66–67, 87
    rejection of Yeshua, as sign of God's presence, xxiii
    suffering, xv–xvi, xvi–xvii, 109
    view of, in *Lumen Gentium*, 161–64

James, tradition of, on final destinies, 129–39, 149
Jenson, Robert, 75n38
Jesus, Jewish reaction to name of, 5–6
Jewish Christian. *See also* Messianic Jew
    distinct from Messianic Jew, 3n2
    perception of, 3–4

Jewish festivals, 12
Jewish mysticism, 25
Jewish practice, characteristics of, 181
Jewish prayer
    corporate and covenantal nature of, 66
    Siddur integral to, 65
Jewish worship, 11
Jews. *See also* Israel
    election of, 12
    as God's actual dwelling place, xviii
    obligated to follow Jewish practice, xii–xiii
    ontologically tied to their Messiah, xvi
    spiritual status of, 179–80
    unity of, with Gentiles, xiv n. 12
John, tradition on, on final destinies, 146–52
Josephus, 48
Judaism
    addressed in the *Catechism of the Catholic Church*, 165–67
    in contradistinction with Christianity, x, xi
    dangers of, xxiv–xxv
    eschatological horizons of, 93–94
    as genus, 16, 17–18
    movements within, 19
    mutual dependence of, with Christianity, xxiv–xxv
    proleptic eschatology and, 94–102
judgment
    linked with disbelief, 149
    occurring in the present, 148–49
judiciary
    central, 34–39
    subordinate courts, 38–39
Juster, Daniel, 103

Karaites, 21
kedushah (holiness)
    as eschatological concept, 95–97, 102, 103
    extending Israel's sense of, 101
    threatening and threatened by an impure world, 105

kedushah (holiness)–continued
  Yeshua's life displaying new type of, 107–8
Kesher, 176
Kierkegaard, Søren, 154
Kinzer, Mark, 29n2
  approach of, to Messianic Judaism, ix–xi
  background and family of, 4–6, 9, 12–13
  calling for church to reconsider its stance toward Jews, xiii–xiv
  Christology of, xvii–xix
  constant trajectory of his thought, xxvi
  cross-directional method of, xxvi–xxvii
  early years of, as a Jewish follower of Yeshua, 8–9
  ecclesiology of, xx–xxi
  faith of in Yeshua, deepening connection to Judaism, 9–13
  feeling a prophetic call, xi
  as Jew and Christian, 4
  religious reversal of, 6–8
  on significance of Yeshua as a name, ix n. 1
  theology of, core tenet of, xii
  theology as way of life for, xxvi
Lachs, Samuel, 53
laws, given in response to unforeseen legal problems, 37–38
Lewis, C. S., 155
Lord's Supper, centrality of, 189
Lumen Gentium
  appreciation of, 157–60
  concerns regarding, 160–67
  on the Jewish people, 160–63
  not developing relationship between people of God and body of Christ, 169–74
  omissions in, regarding Jewish people and Jewish faith, 168–69
  recognizing value of church's inner diversity, 158–59
Luria, Isaac, 25
Luther, Martin, xi

Maharal, 41
marriage, Jewish-Gentile union likened to, xiv n. 12
martyrdom
  Akedah as model for, 108
  related to eschatology, 109–11
  Shema linked with, 69–70, 73
Mary, as "type" of the church, 172–73
Matthew, Gospel of
  developing form of messianic faith, 57–58
  sharing features with later rabbinic literature, 57
McKnight, Scott, 107
measure for measure, principle of, 135
mercy
  dependence on, 134
  human need for, 135
Messianic, as species, 24–25
messianic community, *halakhic* authority of, 59–60, 61
Messianic Fulfillment of the Jewish Faith, The (Kinzer), xxvi
Messianic Jewish Manifesto (Stern), 113
Messianic Jewish Theological Institute (MJTI), xxvi
Messianic Jews
  distinct from Jewish Christians, 3n2
  encounter of, with Roman Catholics, 156–57
  as term, distinct from Messianic Judaism, 17–18
  viewing the canonical narrative, 92
Messianic Judaism
  becoming distinct from evangelical Protestantism, 191
  bridging role of, xxv–xxvi
  concerns in, about salvation, 127–28
  congregational movement of, 191–92
  covenant fidelity of, xii–xiii
  cross-generational Jewish life for converts to, 193
  defining, 14–15
  different expressions of, 19–20
  difficulties in association with, ix–x

distinctive feature of, 24–25
eschatology's place in canonical
  narrative of, 122–25
identifying, with Israel, xi, xiv–xv
importance to, of compound name,
  18–20
integrated approach of, 63–64
lacking continuous *halakhic*
  tradition, 60
making Yeshua the center of Jewish
  life, 64
postmissionary stance of, xi–xiv
recognition of, in Jewish world,
  194–95
renaming of, 16–18
respecting authority of rabbinic
  tradition, 61
solidarity of, with the larger Jewish
  world, xiv
theological study of, as term of self-
  designation, 15–17
as type of Judaism, 17–20
within Israel, 192–93
Messianic movement, 18, 59
messianic redemption, as an element of
  the Shema, 74–76
Milgrom, Jacob, 105, 106
Mishkan, 176
Moltmann, Jürgen, 118
Mosaic Law, observance of, for
  Messianic Jews, 10–11
Moses
  receiving all the words of the
    prophets and sages, 41–43
  relationship of, to future high court,
    38–39
Mosès, Stéphane, 102n27

Name of God, seen as distinct reality,
  79
Neuhaus, Richard John, 163n6
Neusner, Jacob, 98
New Covenant, rethinking of, 119–20,
  164–65
new Judaism, 186–87
newness, eschatological, 164

New Testament, Jewish practices in,
  xii–xiii, 178–79
nonbelievers, 151, 153
Novak, David, 39–40, 44, 47–48, 93,
  114–17, 121

Ochs, Peter, xxiii n. 47, 186
Oral Torah
  acting on people from the inside
    out, 46–47
  in apostolic writings, 48–58
  appearance of, in written form, 46
  denial and suspicion of, among
    Messianic Jews, 30, 31
  dependence of, on Written Torah,
    45
  distinguished from and identified
    with Written Torah, 40
  dynamic nature of, 46
  given to Moses but received anew
    by the prophets, 41–43
  Jewish people's role in, 47–48
  Messianic Jewish stance toward,
    xiii n. 8
  Messianic Jewish version of, 61
  minor influence of, in Tannaitic
    literature and among
    Babylonians, 42
  official custodians of, 60–61
  oral dimension of, 46
  in the Pentateuch, 31–40
  in rabbinic tradition, 40–48
  sages of, seeing authority as greater
    than Scripture, 43
  in theological-historical
    perspective, 58–61
Orthodox Judaism, 18, 19, 186, 187

Pannenberg, Wolfhart, 97n12, 118–20,
  137n21, 164–65
parables
  of the sheep and goats, 131–32
  of the talents, 135–36
  of the unforgiving servant, 134–35
  of the vineyard, 53–54, 59

Subject/Name Index   219

Paul
   remnant theology of, xiv–xv
   tradition of, on final destinies,
      139–46, 149
Pentateuch, distinguished from
   Talmud, 41
people of God
   concept of, as central to the church's
      identity, 157
   relationship of, to body of Christ,
      169–74
Peter, tradition of, on final destinies,
   129–39, 149
Pharisees
   different treatments of, by Matthew
      and Luke, 56
   halakhic tradition of, 48–50, 55
   as holiness movement, 105
   Matthew's close relationship to, 57
   positive portrayal of, 55–56, 58, 59
   Shammaite school of, 60
   Yeshua's attitude toward tradition
      of, 50–52
Postmissionary Messianic Judaism
   (Kinzer), ix n. 1
   Christology of, 189–90
   future discussion on issues of,
      191–95
   pneumatology of, 190
   reaction to, 175–77, 184–90
   role of Jewish covenantal obligation
      in argument of, 178–84
   soteriological and missiological
      implications of, 187
prayer
   daily liturgy, eschatological aspect
      of, 99
   problematic nature of, 64–65
   in Yeshua and in Israel, 66–67, 87
proleptic eschatology
   Judaism and, 94–102
   relation of, to Yeshua's mission,
      102–13
psalms, eschatological aspect of, 99–100
punishment, divine, 72–74

rabbinic decrees, setting aside, 44

rabbinic Judaism, xxiii–xxiv, 21, 186–87
rabbinic law
   based on oral instruction to Moses,
      question of, 45–46
   popular consent as element of,
      47–48
   subordinating, to biblical law, 44
rabbinic movement, *halakhic* authority
   of, 60–61
rabbinic tradition, 30
   building a doctrine of Oral Torah,
      58–59
   incorporated into Messianic Jewish
      canonical narrative, 112
Rashi, xvii, 72–73
Rav Avi'a, 43
redemption, prayer for, 81
remnant theology, xiv–xv, xxi
resurrection, eschatological nature of,
   110–12, 117
reward, divine, 72
ritual practice, Pharisaic preoccupation
   with, 50
Rosenzweig, Franz, xxiv–xxv, 102n27,
   115–16

Saal, Paul, 29n2
Sabbath
   eschatological character of, 97–98
   significance of, 95–96
salvation
   deeds related to, 133–34, 154
   evangelicals viewing in negative
      terms, 127
   faith's role in, 142–47
   faith in Yeshua not required for, in
      Peter's and James's traditions,
      136–37
   final destinies linked to, 149
   Messianic Jewish concerns about,
      127–28
   misunderstanding of, 126–27
   presumption of, 129–32, 154,
      139–41
   relating to an individual's
      circumstance, 142
Sanhedrin, 53–54, 59

Schiffman, Lawrence, 43–44
Schiffman, Michael, 29n2
Schönborn, Christoph, 168
Shammaite school, 60
Shema, 65
  blessings accompanying, 76–86
  as first and greatest commandment, 70
  interpretation and understanding of, 68–70
  messianic redemption as element of, 74–76
  origins of, 68
  praying, in light of Revelation, 85–86
  providing narrative framework for the good news, 86–87
  reward and punishment as themes in, 71–74
  significance of, for Messianic Jews, 71, 73, 76
Siddur Avodat Israel, 10, 65
Sim, David, 56
sola scriptura, 21, 22, 31
Soloveitchik, Joseph, xxvii
Soulen, R. Kendall, xix–xx, 91–92, 111, 116–18, 119, 124
Stackhouse, John, 126–27
Star of Redemption, The (Rosenzweig), xxiv
Stern, David, 103, 113
Suffering Servant passage (Isaiah 53), interpretation of, xvi–xvii, 13, 109
supersessionism, xxi–xxiii, 117, 163, 181–82

Talmud
  distinguished from Pentateuch, 41
  functional primacy given to, 43–44
  viewing two types of law, 43
Tanakh, 21, 22, 23
Taylor, John, 136n19
temple
  as eschatological signpost, 96
  implying distinction between levels of holiness, 96

Tendler, Moshe Dovid, 19
Thoma, Clemens, xvi
Torah, 10–11. *See also* Oral Torah; Written Torah
  inconsistencies and contradictions in, 32–33
  interpretation of, authority for, 52–54
  as Israel's national constitution, 31–32
  lacking detail in its legislation, 32
  messianic impulse in, 101–2
  new laws given in, responding to legal questions, 37–38
  observance of, 137–38, 142, 179
  requiring interpretive tradition, 32–34
  understanding, in the twenty-first century, 30–31
Torrance, Thomas, xvi, xxi–xxii
tradition, drawing on, 30

universal mediation, 79n43

van Buren, Paul, xv

Webster, John, 127
What Does It Mean to Be Saved? (Stackhouse), 126–27
wilderness period, judicial system in, 34–36
Wright, N. T., xix, 103, 110
Written Torah
  contradictions on, 45
  interpretation of, 30
  primacy of, 31
  requiring supplemental instruction, 34–35, 37–38
Wyschogrod, Michael, xiii, xviii, 45, 46, 60–61, 94, 109, 114, 121–22

Yachad, 105
Yeshua, attitude of, toward Pharisaic tradition, 50–52, 55–56, 58, 59
Yeshua, as center of Jewish life, 64
Yeshua, changing message about, in early generations, 182–83

Yeshua, connection of, to Israel's election, 82
Yeshua, covenant fidelity of, 70–71
Yeshua, creation through, 78–80
Yeshua, death and resurrection of, xix, 108–12, 117
Yeshua, divinity of, xvii–xviii, 104
Yeshua, family members of, 138n22
Yeshua, following of, as perfect Torah observance, 137–38
Yeshua, as fulfillment of Judaism, xviii–xix, 13
Yeshua, as God's first beloved, 81–82
Yeshua, healings of, indicating contact with sources of impurity, 105–6
Yeshua, identified with life, 147–49
Yeshua, importance of the name, ix n. 1
Yeshua, Israel's rejection of, as sign of God's presence in Israel, xxiii
Yeshua, Jewish "No" to, xv–xvi, 182, 184
Yeshua, life and mission, character of, 104–8
Yeshua, as link between Judaism and Christianity, x–xi, xiv
Yeshua, mediating the sacred, 105–7
Yeshua, message of, flawed when separated from Judaism, xxv
Yeshua, as one-man Israel, xvi, xix, 66–67, 103–4, 109, 111, 172
Yeshua, as part of Israel's narrative framework, xvii
Yeshua, placed within proleptic eschatological reality, 112, 118
Yeshua, pointing forward to consummation of Israel's history, xx
Yeshua, postmissionary witness to, 187–88
Yeshua, praying in, 66–67, 87
Yeshua, presence of, in traditional Jewish liturgy, 80
Yeshua, pronouncing judgment on the Sanhedrin, 54
Yeshua, redemption through, 85–86
Yeshua, redemptive work of, focused on Israel's final destiny, 137
Yeshua, remaining a Jew after resurrection, 170
Yeshua, response to, 149
Yeshua, resurrection of, 75–76, 108–12, 117
Yeshua, role of, in judgment, 137
Yeshua, threefold office of, 170–71
Yeshua, viewing Shema as first and greatest commandment, 70
Yeshua, warning against presumption of salvation, 130–31
Yeshua tradition, similarities of, to rabbinic tradition, 112
Yocum, John, 190
Yoder, John Howard, 163n6

Zionism, 192
Zohar, 25

www.ingramcontent.com/pod-product-compliance
Lightning Source LLC
Chambersburg PA
CBHW031809220426
43662CB00007B/577